Christ and History

Frederick E. Crowe, S.J.

Christ and History

The Christology of Bernard Lonergan from 1935 to 1982

NOVALIS

Cover design: Pascale Turmel
Layout: Renée Longtin

Business Office:
Novalis
49 Front Street East, 2nd Floor
Toronto, Ontario, Canada
M5E 1B3

Phone: 1-800-387-7164
Fax: 1-800-204-4140
E-mail: cservice@novalis-inc.com
www.novalis.ca

Library and Archives Canada Cataloguing in Publication

Crowe, Frederick E.
          Christ and history : the Christology of Bernard Lonergan from 1935 to 1982/
Frederick E. Crowe.

Includes bibliographical references.
ISBN 2-89507-630-8

          1. Lonergan, Bernard J. F. (Bernard Joseph Francis), 1904–1984. 2. Jesus Christ–
History of doctrines–20th century. I. Title.

BT203.C76 2005   232'.092   C2005-901533-0

Printed in Canada.

We acknowledge the financial support of the Government of Canada through the Book
Publishing Industry Development Program (BPIDP) for our publishing activities.

5 4 3 2 1   09 08 07 06 05

Table of Contents

Dedication

I dedicate this work to my cousin, Mrs M. Irene Haugen. Seventy-eight years ago she prepared me for High School Entrance Examinations and taught me to prize scholastic excellence. For many years she has most generously supported my ventures in theological publications. Now she is an inspiration for a host of friends and relatives as she looks forward, alert and serene, to August 17, 2005, and the completion of her first hundred years. I join with them to wish her well as she starts year one hundred and one.

Prologue

In Search of History

hristology is one of the great might-have-beens in the late Bernard Lonergan's unfinished business. For twenty-five years his work on this topic was in large part a function of his teaching assignments, first at the College of the Immaculate Conception in Montreal, then at Christ the King Seminary (now Regis College) in Toronto, and finally at the Gregorian University in Rome. At the end of that quarter of a century this treatise had emerged as the one on which he hoped to concentrate his future teaching at the Gregorian University. His assignments there had at first alternated between the Trinity and Christology in a two-year cycle. When the University needed to break the cycle, have each course taught annually, and thus divide the task between two professors, Lonergan had to choose which course to keep. He chose Christology, on which he had for some years been preparing a new approach.[1] His plan, however, was disrupted by an act of God that intervened soon after, in the form of surgery for lung cancer. This occurred in the summer of 1965 when he was back in Canada for the vacation months; it effectively put an end to his career at the Gregorian and also, as things turned out, to his exposition of Scholastic theology, which had been a major factor in his teaching.

His predilection for Christology remained, however, and some years later (1971–72), when he held the Stillman Chair at Harvard Divinity School, one of the courses he offered was Christology. The following year he began the same course at Regis College in the Toronto School of Theology, but health problems forced him to break it off. On resuming work with somewhat improved health a few months later he had to ponder his future. *Method in Theology* was now published[2] and he saw two options before him: to concentrate on Christology and rework it in the way his *Method* would suggest, or to return to his very early interest in economics. (There was no intention, even in his state of frail health, of quitting work; thinking and writing were his lifeblood.) He chose economics, working on it for the rest of his active career and producing material for two volumes, published posthumously.[3] This did not mean an end to his work on Christology, on which he continued to lecture from time to time, providing tantalizing indications of the treatise that might have been. That, however, is what it remained: a might-have-been.

This essay is not an ambitious attempt to turn that possible theology into full reality, but perhaps it does the spadework that will enable someone else to make such an attempt. In any case, as the time span in the title indicates, I will deal with Lonergan's Christology as a whole, in the sense at least that I gather together in chronological order, from his first article in 1935 to his last in 1982, his main writings and lectures pertaining directly or indirectly to Christology.

Such a work of compilation is a basic necessity, but it would not merit the name of theology. Is there, then, an idea that would carry us further? The compilation as such is defined extrinsically by the forty-seven years of Lonergan's active career, but is this artificial whole also an integrated whole? Can we discover also a conceptual unity intrinsic to his Christology, and if so, what might its unifying idea be? At least we start with the assumption, legitimate in a study of a thinker like Lonergan, that there is a unity in the temporal sequence, an intrinsic order to be discovered there; the pieces collected are not just pieces in a jigsaw puzzle that may be added to the puzzle at any time in any sequence.

To turn that assumption into verified fact I will apply the scissors action that Lonergan's *Insight* has made famous:[4] namely, the combination of a lower blade of painstaking attention to the data and an upper blade of very general considerations. It is in the meeting of the two that significant results are obtained. In my book as a whole the collection of Lonergan's various writings on Christology will form the lower blade of data, but it will join to that lower blade the upper blade of an overarching idea. The lower blade as a collection of data needs no explanation. To see the data in their unity, however, is another matter; it is the domain of the upper blade, of the very general view that governs the selection and interpretation of the data and gives them their unity.

I have to anticipate that unity somehow in this introduction, and the first step is to name it: the upper blade is history. History was a dominant theme in his whole life work; I see its role in Christology as creating from the various items of data an integral concept. So general a name, however, says everything and says nothing. Since I cannot reproduce my sixteen chapters in this introduction, I will try to indicate their unity through some exercises in picture-thinking. On the completion of my essay readers may expect an upper blade that is not just a picture but an explanation. Meanwhile I rely on images instead of ideas, metaphors that offer at best some distant analogy to the concept we seek. The plural 'metaphors' is deliberate: what one metaphor fails to offer, another may provide. So I turn to my prologue and its quasi-autobiographical search for an effective image.

1. A Few Metaphors

When it became fairly clear after *Method* was published that Lonergan was becoming immersed in economics and would never return to Christology as a major task in his life work, I said to myself: 'Christology will be his unfinished symphony.' It was a fleeting and merely casual thought; it did not assert any real similarity between Lonergan's Christology and a famous piece of music, much less envisage a book using the musical theme years later. Then I came across Butterfield's analogy between history and a Beethoven symphony, and noted his remark: 'History is not like a train, the sole purpose of which is to get to its destination ... each moment of it is its own self-justification.'[5] This suggested to me that 'unfinished symphony' might provoke insights that have explanatory possibilities. At the same time, however, I knew it was not a metaphor that I personally could exploit; although in a moment I will venture a limited application, I know too little of music to attempt an extended comparison.

Still, the more general possibilities in the use of metaphors intrigued me, and I began to collect other instances. One idea I toyed with is that of a trajectory: the course of Lonergan's thought on Christology through-out his life might be pictured as such a path. But there are questions about the use of this figure. For one thing, if we think in terms of a satellite of earth, there are three possible trajectories, depending on your combination of vectors. If the vertical vector is too big, our mini-planet goes shooting off into space and is lost; if it is too small, our projectile ends in a crash instead of a triumph. Only with the right combination will we have a satellite orbiting the earth. Would any of the three suit our purpose? I think even a nodding acquaintance with Lonergan's life work rules that out; a single trajectory is just inadequate. To take the obvious example, the gap between the Scholastic Christology of his *De Verbo incarnato* of 1964 and the new Christology of his Laval lecture of 1975 is just too large to be fitted into a single unbroken path.

A better figure is one Lonergan uses himself, apparently in reference to his own *Insight*: the spiral. Taking a new line, he says, and bringing it to success calls for years of thought 'in which one's understanding gradually works round and up a spiral of viewpoints with each complementing its predecessor and only the last embracing the whole field to be mastered.'[6] This notion offers real possibilities for understanding transitions from lower to higher viewpoints, but the transition is too smooth: arithmetic spirals readily enough into algebra, but the long struggle the Scholastic Lonergan had with the German Historical School implies a rougher path than that of a geometric spiral.

In still another possibility one might draw on Toynbee's withdrawal and return.[7] Then Lonergan's twenty-five years as a Scholastic theologian might be seen as a withdrawal from modernity while he works out an adequate method for dealing with it, and his breakthrough to functional specialties in 1965 would herald a return. This theme has the advantage of being a favourite of Lonergan himself, and we shall keep it in mind as possibly illuminating some particular points in his development, but it is a bit too neat for a general view of the manifold and somewhat disparate data in Lonergan's writings and lectures.

The best metaphor by far that I have found for present purposes is one that was applied by Lonergan to Thomas Aquinas, one that I will now apply in turn to Lonergan himself: namely, the shifting battle front of trench warfare. Remembering that Lonergan was a boy of nine when the First World War broke out gives point to his explanation of the way Aquinas thought: 'his thinking is on a moving front, and the front is not a single straight line but rather a jagged line with outposts and delayed sectors.' Thus Thomas 'went beyond Aristotle to acknowledge a real dis-tinction between essence and existence long before he drew the conclusion that what subsists in a material being is not just the compound of substantial matter and form.'[8]

To illustrate the way this might apply to Lonergan, I would say he was moving ahead in his graduate courses at the Gregorian University (outpost) while the theology in his basic courses lagged behind (delayed sector). Again, he recognized the principle of historicity in scholarship (outpost) before he put it into practice in his lectures (delayed sector). His tardy acceptance of the new biblical scholarship would be a delayed sector, while his work on schemata in the New Testament might be an example of a salient. In a more general way his earlier critique of Catholic studies (as in his 1935 letter to his Religious Superior) was a salient, while failure to apply it in certain areas of modernity was a delayed sector. (Information for references in this and adjacent paragraphs will be given in due course.)

More pertinent, however, for my purposes is the broken front of his thinking on the historical causality of Christ; it is a salient in 1935; it recedes to a backward sector in Lonergan's early Scholastic period (even while it strangely haunts his *De Verbo incarnato*); it is elaborated in an enigmatic work of 1958 that Lonergan never published (see Chapter 9 below); it is a strong influence in the Laval lecture of 1975 (see Chapter 11 below); and finally, in his declining years the historical causality of Christ is operative all along the line, though not always in a thematized way.

Is this image of trench warfare, in its disunity, in its discontinuous continuity, a candidate for the unifying image I seek? While acknowledging its imperfection, I believe it approximates to such an image, creating from the disparate data an integral concept. In any case, history was a dominant theme in Lonergan's whole life work and may, I believe, be equally dominant in his Christology. I will sketch that position in advance in the second part of this introduction.

To relate all our data on history to the image of trench warfare would risk the charge of overkill; nevertheless, in one way I would even extend the metaphor, for such a front is not static but is in continual motion as forces are concentrated at one point or another. This applies to theology too. Thus, while the force of an age-old tradition remains everywhere effective, the 'theological front' keeps adjusting its line of battle as history evolves, as new ideas come and go, as kerygmatic theology, biblical theology, death-of-God theology and a score of other movements one after another claim attention.

A disclaimer is in order here. In favouring the image of trench warfare I would not totally reject the other images I have mentioned, but would profit from a limited use of them. Is there in music, for example, a possible metaphor for the way method and Christology are joined in the Harvard lectures (see Chapter 11 below)? Are they a Christology guided by method, or are they a methodology illustrated by Christology? What of a third possibility: an analogy with the counterpoint form in music, with Christology carrying the main melody and method as a contrapuntal undercurrent? I venture only to ask the question, leaving the answer to those competent in the field.

For other images I grow bolder. There is a trajectory, I would say, for the limited path of Lonergan's Scholastic Christology from 1948 to 1964. There is one also, I believe, for the sequence from the graduate course *De intellectu et methodo* of 1959 through his summer institutes to the Dublin event of 1971. But in each case the metaphor has a limited application.

Further complexities may be introduced. *Verbum* and *Insight* have to be related, if only because Lonergan himself called *Verbum* a 'parallel historical investigation' – parallel, that is, to *Insight*.[9] The two great Thomist works, *Gratia operans* and *Verbum*, are certainly to be related to one another, and each to the *opera omnia*, but how? There is a clue in a remark Lonergan made late in life: 'I fear that my book did not emphasize enough the importance of research: my own work in that specialty was *Gratia operans* and *Verbum*, about eleven years of my life.'[10] Perhaps we could think of his Thomist work as spiralling into his modernity. Or should we try to develop a new image based on the move from positive history to a personal position? One expects his personal life to have an overall relation to his theology. *Insight* and *Method* have likewise to be related to each other, again on the basis of Lonergan's own statement on his early work: 'my intention was an exploration of methods generally in preparation for a study of the method of theology.'[11] Perhaps, then, we might see the pair as one great organon operative on all else in the *opera omnia*; I would see the organon as a withdrawal poised for a return. His work on economics at the end of his career might be seen as a salient, but on a new front.

It is time now to leave the pleasant domain of images, and to attempt a preliminary view of the book in explanatory concepts. My task, as I described it, is twofold: collecting the data and assigning them their unifying idea. I have further asserted that the data need no special word of introduction; they have simply to be collected – compiled, in Lonergan's term. Such a task is necessary, but did not rate high in his hierarchy of scholarly activities. The unification of the data, however, is another matter, so I leave metaphors in their multiplicity and variety in order to give, in this introduction, some advance notion of the way history affected Lonergan's Christology in the years from 1935 to 1982.

2. History as Architectonic Idea

Readers will perhaps agree by now that, if we have a reasonably active imagination, metaphors are available for the asking, that they may be a catalyst for insights, but may also tend to run wild. There has to be a control, and we cannot control the data, except in what we choose to select and interpret. There remains the control exercised by the upper blade. This function I have assigned to history. It will be the task in the sixteen chapters of this essay to verify that choice by reference to the data. Meanwhile I introduce, as well as I can in a few chosen cases, the place of history in Lonergan's Christology from 1935 to 1982. These cases will function not as a synopsis but as 'pegs' on which I hang the material to be considered. They are three: a beginning in 1935; a middle period ca. 1964; and an end in Lonergan's last years, ca. 1977 to 1982.

2.1. The Letter to the Ephesians

Lonergan's *pantôn* essay of 1935 (to be studied in Chapter 2 below) is heavily philosophical, but clearly derives its inspiration from the Letter to the Ephesians, and so the doctrine of that letter will be the first peg on which I will hang materials for my argument.

The letter describes the divine intention to bring all things into unity under Christ. Two points in the argument are to be noted. First, Chapter 1 (verses 3 to 10) declares the Father's purpose and plan: he 'has bestowed on us in Christ every spiritual blessing ... In Christ he chose us before the world was founded ... and he destined us – such was his will and pleasure – to be accepted as his sons through Jesus Christ ... For in Christ our release is secured and our sins are forgiven ... He has made known to us his hidden purpose ... to be put into effect when the time was ripe: namely, that the universe, all in heaven and on earth, might be brought into a unity in Christ.' *The New English Bible* turned verse 10 from an active clause into a passive, 'be brought into unity'; for my purpose it's better in the original active, 'bring into unity' – as it is in the Vulgate, 'instaurare omnia in Christo,' and in the Greek, 'anakephalaiôsasthai ta panta en toi Christo.'

Second, Chapter 4 (verses 9 to 13) announces more particularly the logistics of the divine plan: Christ descended to earth and ascended to heaven 'that he might fill the universe' (that is, earth and heaven). 'And these were his gifts: some to be apostles, some prophets, some evangelists, some pastors and teachers, to equip God's people for work in his service, to the building up of the body of Christ ... So shall we all at last attain to the unity inherent in our faith and our knowledge of the Son of God – to mature manhood, measured by nothing less than the full stature of Christ ... [S]o shall we fully grow up into Christ. He is the head, and in him the whole body depends.'

I could hardly ask for a more explicit endorsement of my thesis. The author talks of time and of what is going forward in time, in other words of history. He (Paul, presumably) talks of all time, time before the world was founded, the present time which is ripe for the divine purpose, future time in which we live and grow to full stature, built up into the body of Christ. And the author talks of what happens as happening in Christ, always in Christ, through Christ, to attain unity in Christ.

My final point: in choosing for his title, as he did, the restoration of all things in Christ, Lonergan makes the argument and message of Ephesians his own argument and message. All history is unified in Christ; Christ permeates all history. The two terms are co-extensive; are they not also, at the deepest level, interchangeable?

2.2. Historical Causality

Lonergan's position in 1935 is therefore clear enough, but we are still a long way from 1982. Did he maintain that position throughout his life? I answer yes, but I add that he did so from perspectives that detract a little from the clear focus of Ephesians. My answer remains yes, for history is still pervasive; but in my next two pegs it operates from new perspectives.

First, the perspective is that of the historical causality of Christ rather than the unification of all things in Christ. It seems as if Lonergan had experienced a strong influence directing him to the world and its needs, and so to the influence Christ had for the world's healing. This aspect is also pervasive, and must be studied in itself (see chapters 10 and 14, and passim below). For the present, historical causality will identify the middle stage and the second peg on which to hang the materials collected.

I say 'materials' in the plural, but it is remarkable that in announcing what I call the middle peg Lonergan offers no materials: only a two-line statement, occurring in all three editions of *De Verbo incarnato* and in the same context in all three. It is further remarkable that the announcement deplores the lack of studies of the question though Lonergan himself had made just such a study in manuscript a short time previously! To continue the anomaly, it is even more remarkable that at Boston College several years later (1974) he has forgotten that he ever wrote such a work, or perhaps does not count as a 'work' a manuscript he never published.

This complex history I will study more carefully in its proper place, but for the present let the following remarks suffice. The context at Boston College in 1974 is his apologetic confession that he had long wanted to study the historical causality of Christ but had never got around to it (see Chapter 11 below). The work that he forgot he had written (I shall refer to it as *de bono* — see Chapter 9 below) had actually treated that same historical causality in 1958, and indeed had done so at some length. For the moment I use it only to assign and identify historical causality as a middle peg in Lonergan's history.

2.3. Unity in Christ

Our third peg brings us back to the theme of 1935, the unity of all things in Christ. And yet it has its own perspective. The viewpoint is not exactly that of 1935; the stress now is rather on the Pauline 'being in Christ Jesus,' and it is in virtue of this being in Christ that we enjoy unity in Christ. This last phase cannot be precisely pinpointed in time and in Lonergan's history, but our study will lean heavily on a lecture of 1964 ('*Existenz* and *Aggiornamento*') and will gather data from the papers produced between 1964 and the end of Lonergan's active life.

3. The Plan of This Essay

The three 'pegs' mark certain phases in Lonergan's position on Christ and history. They are offered in advance to help readers keep their bearings through the various materials to be presented in the next sixteen chapters. To complete this introduction I sketch a kind of table of contents for the essay.

From a wide viewpoint I would say that chapters 1 to 6 bring us to the end of the Scholastic period of Lonergan's thought, chapters 7 to 9 deal with the transitional phase from Scholasticism to historicity, and chapters 10 to 16 study the new Lonergan. Descending to detail I will examine an early stage of history in two preliminary chapters, one on Lonergan's religious background (Chapter 1) and one on the student essay of 1935, the *pantôn* work just now mentioned (Chapter 2). Here, too, belong some of his popular publications and his writings of piety.

Scholasticism itself is so wide a topic that it must be divided. There is his early Scholasticism, covering the thirteen years of teaching in Canada (1940–53), and especially the two courses of 1948 and 1952 on Christology (chapters 3 and 4). Then (1953–65) there is the mature Scholasticism of his twelve years at the Gregorian University in Rome (chapters 5 and 6).

But the flowering of this phase is also its dying, and new thought patterns begin already to invade Lonergan's position. It is clear that the end of his Scholasticism is an event of great importance in his history, clear too that it is accompanied by the emergence of a new approach, but to categorize the new and determine the chronology of its takeover is difficult. One section, however, I devote to his critique of Scholasticism (Chapter 7), and one to his position on modernism, dogma, and the councils, and on the all-important role of the transcendence of truth (Chapter 8). Here, too, I believe, belongs what I may call the delaying action of that unpublished book-length manuscript, the curious, enigmatic work I am calling *de bono* (Chapter 9).

Positive preparation for the breakaway from Scholasticism had been initiated in his graduate courses at the Gregorian University and in various summer institutes. There was the Boston College institute in 1957 with its lectures on existentialism, there was his graduate course *De intellectu et methodo* at the Gregorian in 1959, and there was a succession of summer institutes from 1958 on. All this acquired new foundations with the 1972 publication of *Method in Theology* (Chapter 10).

The preceding paragraph did not mention Christology, but it is necessary background for the emergence of Lonergan's later doctrine on Christ. That background is studied *in fieri* in many of the essays of *A Second Collection*, covering the years 1966 to 1973. The new Christology itself, however, though sketched at the Boston College workshop of 1974, received its fullest actuation only in the Laval lecture of 1975 (Chapter 11). History, the architectonic idea, was by that time operative and in control (chapters 12 to 14).

I do not believe that in his few remaining years Lonergan's Christology went significantly beyond that of the 1975 lecture, but it is a legitimate question for this essay to ask how we, his students, might carry his thought forward. Two important areas challenge us here: that of faith and history (the context: controversies of the last two centuries) and that of Christianity and world religions (context: controversies of our own times), and these will be given some attention (chapters 15 and 16). A final task goes 'beyond history' to seek understanding of the divine counsels in their mystery.

With that much said by way of prologue and introduction we may now take up the task of collecting, ordering, and interpreting the data. At its base it is a work largely of compilation, what Lonergan called an 'opus compilatorium, at incompletum, nec vere historicum.'[12] In no way is it modelled on Lonergan's doctoral dissertation, which he called a study of speculative development in Thomas Aquinas. My essay does not aim so high, but perhaps it goes beyond a mere compiling of texts and finds its place at an intermediate level. In terms of Lonergan's functional specialties,[13] I would call its first contribution 'data researched and interpreted': the first two specialties, therefore.

Is the book also a work of history? That is, not only a work of research and interpretation on history in Lonergan but itself a historical work, moving Lonergan studies forward from research and interpretation to discussion on the level of the third specialty? I should be happy to think so, but to be recalled and noted is a point we easily lose sight of: the difference between history as a constituent in Lonergan's Christology and history as a constituent in my study of Lonergan. The latter is not pertinent to my study. The former is directly and in the highest degree pertinent, for I maintain that Lonergan's whole work is ordered in relation to Christ; not, then, a history *of* Christ, but rather Christ *and* history in a mutual relationship, perhaps one of identity.[14] But it is another question altogether, and altogether secondary, whether my essay as a study of Lonergan operates on that third level.

4. A Bias Confessed

I have been presenting what I hope is an objective view of Lonergan's work, but there is to my presentation also a subjective and personal side that I do not attempt to conceal: namely, I offer the book as a work of piety, in Wordsworth's sense of 'natural piety,' the Latin *pietas*, in this case the 'piety' of a student toward a revered teacher. In line with that admission it is a fair description of the work to say that *mutatis mutandis* it is the classroom transferred to print, a sort of running commentary on a moving text, retaining the alternation of question and answer, of inquiry and learning that characterizes a student–teacher relationship. (A reviewer of a book I wrote years ago saw the volume he was reviewing as a book of 'musings.' The word intrigued me, and I naturally tried to fit it into Lonergan's functional specialties. My verdict: musings belong in the specialty of interpretation, but are expressed in the mode and language of common sense.)

Readers will therefore detect a stance of advocacy in my work: I not only present Lonergan, I present him as a teacher. But they will miss an engagement with other theologians and, what is more regrettable, with other students of Lonergan. There are various reasons for this, but the simplest is an application of Lonergan's repeated slogan, 'You do what you can.' There is no way in which at my age I could do justice to the accumulating literature on my topic.

If dialogue is not a primary aim for me, it may still be asked, For whom, then, did I write the book? The question supposes a more specific readership than I envisaged, and the briefest answer is maybe the truest: I wrote it for myself, or under a kind of compulsion. Lonergan's account of his options after *Method* left Christology as an evident gap in the symphony of his life work. The objective gap and the subjective claims of *pietas* combined to exert a powerful tug, to whose influence I eventually succumbed. But whom do I expect to read the book? I suppose those who think as I do about Lonergan – a relatively small circle, which one hopes to widen and to that end takes such steps as lie open. But progress is slow. Meanwhile, 'You do what you can.'

Lonergan's Religion, and His Theology

The noticeable differences between the Lonergan, say, of his first Christology course in 1948 and the Lonergan of his final work in 1982 point to a rather radical development in his thought and raise the question of the unity of his life work, and consequently the question of the turning points in his story. In illustration one may adduce the shift from Scholasticism to a post-Scholasticism mindset, with its well-marked turning point in February 1965, when his thinking reached the breakthrough to the eight functional specialties.[1]

The clarity, however, of that breakthrough forces attention on the equally important continuity that underlay the change. A major carrier of the continuity, in my view, was his personal commitment to his own religion, inherited from his parents, nurtured by his Catholic schooling, strengthened by his community with other Catholic scholars, even those he disagreed with. There is a body of evidence to show his fidelity to his tradition: his insistence on the importance of Catholic schools; his respect for the community of Catholic scholars (cf. his use of the *Dictionnaire de théologie catholique*); his repeated claim that our present crisis is not a crisis of faith but one of culture – all this marks him as a believing theologian and testifies to his adherence to a religious tradition. That factor, so far as I know, has never been studied, but it operated as a force, sometimes latent, to maintain continuity through his pre-Scholastic, his Scholastic, and his post-Scholastic days. It is that religious undercurrent that I examine in this chapter, not directly to assess the man and his character but to illuminate his doctrine.

Of his boyhood and youth, little need be said. It followed a traditional path: altar boy at the local Roman Catholic church (St Gregory Nazianzen), attendance till he was thirteen at the local parish school under the Brothers of Christian Instruction, then a boarder at Loyola College in Montreal under the Jesuits till he was seventeen.

While at Loyola he received and with some struggle accepted a religious vocation to the Society of Jesus. The next eighteen years followed the standard Jesuit pattern of religious formation and study: novitiate and humanities at Guelph in Ontario, philosophy at Heythrop College in England, theology at the Gregorian University in Rome, with ordination to the priesthood there in 1936. The pattern included assignments particular to him: three years as a 'regent' teaching at Loyola, his *alma mater*; a year in France for 'tertianship' (often thought of as a third year of novitiate); and two years gaining a doctorate in Rome. In 1940, with these long years of formation behind him, he began, first in Montreal and then in Toronto and Rome, his twenty-five years of teaching theology 'under impossible conditions,' as he would say later (see Chapter 7 below).

It was during his Montreal-Toronto period (1940–53) that he wrote several of the shorter, more pastoral essays that we must notice next. Together with the pastoral activities that accompanied them they give us a quite new slant on Lonergan the theologian, showing along with his concern for academic standards his concern also for the people of God and their spiritual nourishment. To be sure, this surfaces also in his more theological writings, but it is most evident in what he wrote during those years for the pastoral journals of eastern Canada, especially for the two weeklies, *The Montreal Beacon* and *The Canadian Register* (Quebec edition), and for the monthly *Canadian Messenger of the Sacred Heart*. There is a rough correspondence at that time between the journals he wrote for and the city of his domicile: the *Beacon* and *Register* in Montreal, 1940 to December 1946; the *Messenger* in Toronto, January 1947 to September 1953.

In the interests of a rounded view of Lonergan's work, three remarks may be added. For one thing, concurrent with his pastoral involvement at both Montreal and Toronto, he was writing philosophy and theology of the highest order: for example, his *Gratia operans* articles and 'Finality, Love, Marriage' in Montreal, and the *Verbum* articles, followed soon by the monumental *Insight*, in Toronto. A second remark is that he was, throughout most of his life, carrying a teaching load; it is the teaching Lonergan, not the publishing Lonergan, whom many of us came to know first.

My third remark is of another character: it points to the influence of Pius X, who was Pope from 1903 to 1914 – like the World War, therefore, during the years of Lonergan's youth or boyhood. Relevant to Lonergan studies is the fact on one side that Pius took as his papal motto the Ephesians text on restoring all things to unity in Christ, the very theme of Lonergan's *pantôn* paper; on the other side is the fact that in 1907 Pius issued *Pascendi*, his famous encyclical against Modernism. It was a time of unquestioning obedience to Rome, an attitude certainly shared by Lonergan, as my next chapter will show, so both these acts of Pius would have had a profound resonance in his formation. In the light of these remarks we have now to examine the more popular writings of the Montreal and Toronto periods.

1. Montreal, 1940–46

The minor Montreal writings of this period are characterized by interest in current events, current literature, current questions being debated. It is remarkable that, long before the famous conference at Medellín, the concerns of the young Lonergan closely resembled those that would surface thirty years later in other lands and other contexts among the liberation theologians. Lonergan's context at the time was Canadian, and so we find him writing on such topics as Quebec's opportunity (some years before the Quiet Revolution!), on the Antigonish movement to help depressed fishermen, on the needed rebirth of rural living, and so on. His interests, however, are catholic, and take on added interest in view of his work on economics at the end of his career, so a few quotations on matters economic and political are in order.

Thus, the question is put, 'Why is the control of industry in the hands of fewer and fewer?' (*The Montreal Beacon*, May 2, 1941). We are told: 'Unless the masses achieve economic independence, then … [democracy] will be a noble experiment that failed' (ibid.). There is reference to the way in which 'governmental functions … have been multiplying and accumulating for a century under the evil influence of a mistaken economic system,' so that there is little use working out 'an elaborate palliative for a monstrous disease' (*The Canadian Register*, Quebec edition, April 10, 1943).

These quotations from diocesan journals of the 1940s have an obvious link with the *pantôn* paper of 1935, which we shall study in the next chapter.[2] The quotations themselves are but straws in an academic wind, the direction and force of which were still hidden from the public and appeared in full clarity only years later when Lonergan's economic manuscripts came to light. But they reveal a concern in the early 1940s that was pastoral par excellence.[3] We had just lived through a decade of economic depression and abject suffering for millions of people, and their cry for help came piteously to Lonergan's ears. Various bizarre theories on relief of the crisis had surfaced, but Lonergan realized that the real solution could come only from a valid economics. In other words, a moral theology in this area required a theory of economics as much as a systematic theology required a philosophy. So he wrote his manuscript on economics, but found little sympathy among the economists he consulted, and put his manuscript on the shelf for thirty-some years.

2. Toronto, 1947–53

In some contrast to the Montreal writings that went into political, social, and cultural questions, those of the Toronto period are characterized more by Catholic piety.[4] This difference did not just 'happen'; in Montreal Lonergan was prodded by students interested in higher journalism and so in current events, whereas in Toronto the prodding came from the editor of the *Messenger*, who was a good friend of Lonergan's, and who requested from him articles in accord with the religious character of his journal. But that is secondary to the two relevant points: that Lonergan wrote the *Messenger* articles at all, and that he wrote them the way he did, with no shying away from faith in our Lord and devotion to his Blessed Mother.

The simple piety of his beliefs appears in what he wrote of the love of the Sacred Heart of Jesus for us:

> … the love of a human will, motivated by a human mind, oper-
> ating through human senses, resonating through human emotions
> and feelings and sentiments, implemented by a human body with
> its structure of bones and muscles, flesh, its mobile features, its
> terrible capacities for pleasure and pain, for joy and sorrow, for
> rapture and agony.[5]

A useful exercise is to note the recurrence of phrases like 'our Lord' – for example, 'the mediation of God's grace through Jesus Christ our Lord'[6] – in which his faith and his theology go hand in hand. Thus there is revealed a personal side of Lonergan that also marks his theology. As he was fond of repeating, religion is one thing and theology another, and it is religion that is prior, with theology playing the secondary role of reflection on religion.

3. A Believing Theology

The question is currently debated whether theology is possible without faith; more concretely, whether an unbeliever can do Christian theology. Lonergan handles the question in the context of his eight functional specialties and the two phases of theology.[7] There is no need of faith to study the manuscripts of Mark's Gospel in order to determine the reading most likely to be correct; that can be a task of religiously uncommitted research, though without religious commitment one is less likely to undertake the research. The same is true for the other functions in the first phase of theology, especially for interpretation and history, though the higher one rises in the structure of consciousness the more likely it is that personal and subjective factors will influence one's judgment; indeed, the fourth level, dialectic, has the role of bringing us face to face with a decision on personal involvement.

The second phase of theology, however, propelled by the choice that dialectic forces upon us, can hardly be undertaken at all and certainly not with authentic engagement unless one believes. That points up the importance of the religious forces operative in the 'minor' writings of the Montreal–Toronto period. Minor they may be in size, but as an index to what in Lonergan's view theology is or ought to be, they have an important function. I have noted the theological significance of the simple phrase 'our Lord.' Even more revealing are Lonergan's references to Mary, showing the open piety in which she is not merely the 'mother of Jesus, wife of Joseph,' as the dictionaries describe her, but regularly 'our Lady.'[8] Lonergan speaks of 'our Lady' because he is a Catholic theologian and writes as such; his readers must accept that. It is true that he recommends a more neutral language for ecumenical dialogue but he is most at home in the theology that declares or supposes his faith.

If, as expected, we shall find Lonergan's Scholastic Christology dominated by the role of truth, and his post-Scholastic Christology offering more for the affections, we must also note his concern for combining these two aspects. For example, his 1943 article 'Finality, Love, Marriage' first establishes a theological base: 'as there is a human solidarity in sin ... so also there is a divine solidarity in grace which is the mystical body of Christ ... that body of Christ which takes over, transforms, and elevates every aspect of human life.' Application to married life, which is par excellence affective, readily follows: 'divine charity ... is to be effective as well as affective.' It is proved by deeds 'so that through their life in common husband and wife progress daily in virtue and most of all in charity towards God and their neighbor.' They have a model: 'Christ our Lord is not only the complete model of sanctity but also a model set before all by God himself ... this model is to be imitated by all.'[9]

4. The Spiritual Exercises of St Ignatius Loyola

It would be unthinkable to dwell on Lonergan's personal religion without reference to the Spiritual Exercises of St Ignatius, Exercises that Lonergan twice followed for thirty days (as a Novice in 1918 and as a Tertian in 1937) and probably followed for eight days fifty-some times in the other years of his active life. We are fortunate to have found in his effects a few pages of cryptic but precious autograph notes, headings for a talk perhaps never given, on grace and the Spiritual Exercises.[10] The Exercises, of course, have particular relevance to his Christology; and so he regarded the second, third, and fourth 'Weeks' as devoted to the following of Christ. But there is much more in these precious notes. There is not only a following of Christ; there is a becoming, asserted in language that anticipates the 'being in Christ Jesus' that we shall find so evident in the post-1965 period. An especially succinct passage defines grace as follows: 'Grace is that by which 1) we are 2) more and more we are 3) living members of [Christ] Jesus and 4) more and more fully and even ['ever'?] more consciously living members of [Christ] Jesus.'[11]

The autograph notes range widely. Besides their importance for Christology there is reason to believe they reveal aspects of Lonergan's personal prayer. In a section dealing with the effects of grace, where the series of headings is especially cryptic, the first manuscript (A164, p. 1) has 'vocation, times of retreat, 2nd conversion'; the other manuscript (A161, p. 2) has 'Discontent with one's mediocrity ... spirts made in times of retreat; 2nd conversion before ordination.'[12] I take these phrases to be autobiographical. A second conversion before ordination is not a general experience; it is Lonergan's personal memories, I believe, that prompted this heading.

Earlier in this chapter I mentioned Lonergan's extra-curricular ministry. I had in mind his apostolate of letters, spiritual guidance, sermons, retreat talks, sacramental ministry, and so on. This phase of his religion I cannot easily document. Nevertheless, sketchy though it be, the chapter describes a side of his life that is little known but important for an understanding of his life work. It is a feature that lies in the shadow of the great works: the two volumes on Aquinas (*gratia operans* and *verbum*), the two great theological treatises (*De Verbo incarnato* and *De Deo trino*), and the two self-standing masterpieces (*Insight* and *Method*). But brought out of the shade this feature adds a new dimension to Lonergan's Christology. In its personal piety and religion it links the early Christology to the 'being in Christ Jesus' of a later time (chapters 10 and 13 below) and reveals a continuity in Lonergan's thinking that survives some rather radical developments. At the very least it shows that a description limited to 'Bernard Lonergan, Scholastic thinker,' is quite deficient.

2

The Christology of 1935

remark in Lonergan's *De Verbo incarnato* of 1960, repeated in its two subsequent editions, has captured the interest of more than one reader: 'Furthermore, there is wanted a consideration of the historical causality that Christ as man clearly exercises' ('Ulterius desideratur consideratio de causalitate historica quam Christus homo manifeste exercet').[1] Curiosity asks: what would Lonergan himself say on this topic of historical causality, one that seemed to intrigue him? In 1960 we could only speculate on his possible answer. When later (1983) more of his papers became accessible, including the '*pantôn anakephalaiôsis*' and the complete text of the work I call *de bono*, some quite interesting facts came to light. For one thing the *de bono*, the substance of which could be dated 1956–58 and therefore prior to his three Christological manuals, took up quite explicitly the very question of the historical causality of Christ.[2] Another is that the *pantôn* paper, which can be dated very precisely April 28, 1935, and so twenty-five years before the first edition of *De Verbo incarnato*, is in effect and without using the term, a mini-treatise on the historical causality of Christ. Why would Lonergan affirm in 1960 and continue to affirm in 1964 the need for a treatise he had already written twice? We shall return in Chapter 9 to this question as it regards the *de bono*, but the *pantôn* paper is the subject of study in the present chapter.[3]

History, then, and historical causality belong to the context in which Lonergan worked out his Christology. That is a wide context, including the renewal of Catholic thought in its whole compass. As he reveals in a letter he wrote to his Religious Superior in January of the same year,[4] he was troubled by what he regarded as the decadent state of Catholic intellectual life and was committed to the task of its renewal. That renewal, too, is the task of historical causality and so belongs in a study of Christ and history. With that as background let us examine the *pantôn* paper.

On Whitsunday 1935 Lonergan finished a carefully dated essay (the manuscript has 'Dominica in Albis, 1935,' which was April 28 that year) to which he gave the title, taking the term and the topic from Ephesians 1:10, *Pantôn Anakephalaiôsis*. That is only one line of the seven-part title. It continues with the following six parts, allotted one line each: 'A Theory of Human Solidarity / A Metaphysic for the Interpretation of St Paul / A Theology for the Social Order, / Catholic Action, / And the Kingship of Christ, / *IN INCIPIENT OUTLINE*.' (Caps and italics as in the autograph.) The punctuation shows that the phrase 'A Theology for ...' governs grammatically the next three lines, so that the final subtitle is understood as 'A Theology for the Kingship of Christ'; this little point of grammar is of some importance for the drift of the whole essay.

The *pantôn* paper is a Christology and, as the phrase 'Kingship of Christ' indicates, historical causality enters the very title. The preface to the paper outlines the role of Christ in history, and the body of the paper, despite the interwoven metaphysics, is through and through a study of the historical causality of Christ. According to Lonergan's two-page introduction[5] he sees the essay as 'a synthetic view revealing the metaphysical convergence of all things on Christ Jesus, our Lord' (140). The metaphysical conception is of man as 'one in nature and operation, working through a material to an intelligible plurality in a transient dynamism in which no man is more than an instrumental cause and no causation fails to affect all men.' This squares 'with the conception of humanity as an organism: the purely instrumental causality of man and the way in which this causality affects all men is exactly parallel to the purely instrumental causality of the members of a body and the way in which the operation of the members affects the whole body' (141).

The link of a metaphysical conception with the world of history is clarified: 'the principle of premotion makes these instrumental causes into a solidary chain of causation in which each instrument transfers the motion received from those before, transmitting it to those that follow.' Then the link is extended to the world of religious history: 'thus, a place of singular responsibility falls to the first mover among men, to the first and second Adam. Adam corrupted the premotion and set up the reign of sin ... Christ set up a new motion to harmonize, readjust, reintegrate a humanity that had reached the peak of disintegration and death described in the first chapter of Romans. This is the *anakephalaiôsis*.'

The effects of the second Adam's chain of causation are outlined: '... the material unity of man in Adam is replaced by the intelligible unity of man in Christ, the blind course of nature by the voluntary course of faith, the sinful course of the reign of a premotion from the serpent by the current of charity that has its formal cause in Christ as Wisdom and its efficient cause in the indwelling of the Holy Ghost as Love' (141).

Lonergan concludes his introduction with 'an outline of the argument.' It has the six parts listed above: liberty as a disjunctive determination, and the rest. The sixth part takes as its subtitle the title of the whole essay: *Pantôn Anakephalaiôsis*. Further, though it is only one part in six, it fills half the pages of the essay; it is meant to carry the burden of the argument, with parts one to five as background.

For present purposes we need not dwell on section one, 'Liberty as a Disjunctive Determination,' where Lonergan gives his analysis of intellect and will, and his analysis of human freedom. Still, his mindset is more historical than metaphysical: his analysis of freedom has as consequent his analysis of the events of history, and he begins his final paragraph as follows: 'Hence human freedom is simply a choice between different determinate orders of events; if the will does not act, there is physical determination; if the will does act, then there is historical determination' (143).

The historical theme is named in the title of the second section, 'The Historical Interpretation of Intellect' (143–46) and is then set forth in the body of the text: 'every act of intellect will be specified and so determined by a phantasm and ... the phantasm has to be drawn from some historical situation.' Every act of intellect is a universal – an important point for a philosophy of history, for it means that one universal act of intellect controls an indefinite number of acts of will. The role of matter as the principle of individuation leads Lonergan to political and social consequences, for the isolation effected by matter exists only for the sake of a higher intellectual unity. Thus the 'exploitation of natural resources calls for a higher organization of men than the natural unit of the family or tribe,' and so there arise the political and juridical forms of society. Advance in the satisfaction of physical needs 'gives the leisure necessary for the pursuit of culture' (144–45).

In statements that introduce a lifelong interest of his, he describes 'a threefold dialectic in the historic progress of intellect': that of fact, that of sin, and that of thought. In the dialectic of *fact* an incomplete idea is put into execution as though it were complete; when its incompleteness is revealed there is the emergence of a compensating idea. In the dialectic of *sin* false situations lead to the phenomena of depraved polytheism, liberalism and religious wars, and communism. In the dialectic of *thought* there is a pure dialectic in the development of the perennial philosophy, but as contaminated with the dialectic of sin it gives the actual course of abstract thought since Socrates. Exposition of this section closes with an account of concupiscence (145–46), a notion that returns in section six.

All this we may call an anthropology and understand as an ingredient in a philosophy of history; but further study of it would be out of proportion to our specific topic. The same may be said of the third section, 'The Unity of Human Operation' (146–48), of the fourth, 'The Synthesis of Human Operation' (148–50), and of the fifth, 'The Unity of Man in the Ontological Ground of His Being' (150–53); they simply continue Lonergan's general anthropology.

Section six requires more study. Lonergan paraphrases its title, *Pantôn Anakephalaiôsis*, as 'the Pauline conception of the role of Christ in creation.' He restates his argument: 'since man's operation is necessarily an instrumental operation, then there is a particular significance to leadership, to being the first agent in human history.' He goes on to 'set forth the fundamental antitheses of the first and second Adam' (153).

Adam, premoved by Eve and the serpent, set up the reign of sin; Christ conceived by the Blessed Virgin Mary set up the kingdom of God. Omitting pro tem the role of the angels, Lonergan continues with a second antithesis: Adam communicates fallen human nature; Christ communicates the divine adoption. The third antithesis follows: Adam and his progeny die in penalty for sin; Christ transmutes death into the rite of sacrifice and makes of death the seed of resurrection (154). A fourth antithesis is allotted more space (154–60): Adam reversed the course of history and set up the tradition of ignorance and difficulty called 'concupiscence'; Christ restored the harmony of man by the grace of dogma (154).

I pause here to note two special usages of Lonergan.

1. Excursus on the Terms 'Dogma' and '*Geist*'

Lonergan does not formally define these two important terms, but some instances of his usage will convey their meaning. First, there is his reverence for dogma; it is a 'grace' (154). The data on its development are complex. On one side it is stated that development *through* dogma cannot be a development *of* dogma, 'for the pure dogma is above reason' (155).

On the other side we have a remark which Lonergan wrote by hand (with a *nota bene*) on the margin of his text: 'NB. The development of dogma is the developed absolute *Geist* turning back upon the content of revelation and seeing more there than was seen before.'[6] This accords with the 'expansion from the primitive tradition of dogma': we read of 'the development of the mind of the mystical body and its expansion from the primitive tradition of dogma so as eventually to include a conscious body of social science illuminated by supernatural light' (157). In that special sense, therefore, there is development of dogma. In a general way 'dogma' seems to mean 'truth' in the sense that term has in John's Gospel, except that there is false dogma, too: 'the dogma of communism unites by terrorism to destroy; the dogma of race unites to protect, but it is meaningless as a principle of advance and it is impotent as a principle of human unity ... There remains only the dogma of Christ' (156).

Second, there is Lonergan's usage of *Geist*. The 'objective *Geist*' is 'the common mind of man' (147), but this, though it can advance (147) and develop (148) and expand (156), is nevertheless inclined to wander and needs correction from 'the absolute *Geist*' (154). Though varying continually with differentiations in time and place (152) it has a determinate order (149) and practical aims (147); it is perhaps Lonergan's notion of the *Zeitgeist* (155). Development through dogma is 'by the selection of what is true in the incomplete acts of intellect of the objective *Geist* ...' (155).

The absolute *Geist*, on the other hand, seems to rise above the vicissitudes of the objective *Geist*. The absolute *Geist* of humanity is found in 'the grace of dogma' with its focus on truth (154). It contributes an intellectual benefit (155) that can make issue with the expanding objective *Geist* of humanity (156). It is the 'natural means' to cope with low *energeia* (157). 'Christ as the new head of humanity ... is the originator of the absolute *Geist* of dogma ... that progresses without ever falling back ... that selects the pure element of truth in the incomplete acts of the objective *Geist*' (158). It seems rather like the charism of infallibility.

2. The Role of History

After that excursus on two terms that keep cropping up, we return to the main point: the role of history in all this. 'First, the coming of Christ coincides with the breakdown of philosophy and its recognized impotence to solve the problem of intellectual unity' (154). 'Second, the supernatural revelation to which Christ was a witness is not only a content but premoves a living and developing mind ...' (155). 'Third, the development of the absolute *Geist* through dogma cannot be a development of the dogma ... for the pure dogma is above reason' (155). 'Fourth, the intellectual benefit of the absolute *Geist* is something that ... fallen man ... easily overlooks' (155).

There follows a historical reference of great interest, though it is presented rather bluntly (Lonergan was decidedly not at his ecumenical best in 1935); the reference is to 'the breakup of Protestantism ... the insolvency of the Orientals' (156). His critique, however, does not delay on these two historical developments but goes on to take a wider sweep, drawing attention to the 'Crisis in the West' and 'the necessity of a *Summa Sociologica*' (156). He pinpoints the danger:

> A metaphysic of history is not only imperative for the church to meet the attack of the Marxian materialist conception of history ... it is imperative if man is to solve the modern politico-economic entanglement, if political and economic forces are to be subjected to the rule of reason, if cultural values and all the achievement of the past are to be saved both from the onslaughts of purblind statesmen and from the perfidious diplomacy of ... communism.(156)

As noted earlier (in the excursus on 'dogma'), reason is impotent here: 'The only possible unity of men is dogma': not, however, the dogma of communism or the dogma of race (recall the date: April 1935). 'There remains only the dogma of Christ' (156). So we come to the significance of the moves made by Pope Pius XI (156): his proclamation of Christ the King,[7] his proclamation of Catholic Action,[8] his command that 'all candidates for the sacred priesthood must be adequately prepared ... by intense study of social matters.'[9]

'So much for the brief expansion we have permitted ourselves on the development of the mind of the mystical body and its expansion from the primitive tradition of dogma so as to include a conscious body of social science illuminated by supernatural light' (157). 'It is in this sphere of the role of the absolute *Geist* that Christ most luminously appears as *pantôn anakephalaiôsis*' (157). This, too, is spelled out: 'Christ as the new head of humanity, as the reunification and reintegration of what is torn asunder by sin, is the originator of the absolute *Geist* of dogma, is the absolute of intellect' and 'intellect is the principle of human operation in unity; it is the principle of peace …' (158). There follows a multitude of references to scripture (158–60). And not only to scripture: 'Christ is Plato's philosopher king … But what Plato dreamt of, Christ would realize' (158).

The essay continues. 'We now come to the final antithesis between the first and second Adam; this is at the same time the final synthesis of history, Christ as the formal cause and through the Holy Spirit the efficient cause of the end of all creation, the manifestation of divine wisdom in heaven as well as on earth' (160).

Here, surely, is a Christology that makes a good fit with the one Lonergan almost wistfully referred to in 1960 as lacking ('desideratur'). Yet it does not seem to have entered deeply into that 1960 volume or into its later editions, though that of 1964 was revised on other points. It has, however, a closer kinship with *de bono*, a treatise he was writing in the late 1950s even while he was regretting the lack of such a treatise. More on that later. For now his 'desideratur' has to be interpreted as a silent pre-publication announcement of a book on the way.

Still, questions abound. The *de bono*, though giving a key role to the historical influence of Christ, will do so in categories rather different from those of 1935. Will we find him then repudiating in *de bono* the *pantón* of years earlier? Not likely, given his preservation of the latter till his death.[10] But did he not realize in 1960 that he had already drafted, twenty-five years before he expressed a wish for it, a Christology in which the historical causality of Christ was not only acknowledged but was a central element? Had he forgotten about the 1935 essay? Or did he think his theology of the 1960s made his 1935 essay obsolete, or perhaps look like a youthful indiscretion? Against all such doubts and objections, like a Thomist *Sed contra*, stands the hard fact that all his life he kept this essay in his papers, in the same file with those of 1937–38, which in 1973 he referred too with approval.[11]

In any case we have the document itself and its content and, if we are not repelled either by his somewhat triumphal Catholic position, or by his unfamiliar philosophic terms, we might find here in *pantón* a Christology of the kind solicited in 1960 and 1964. Moreover, as we shall see in Chapter 9, the *de bono* was meant to complement the Christology he was then teaching at the Gregorian University.[12] Despite some rather notable revisions, then, he saw a continuity in his Christology extending from *pantón* and the early years throughout the Roman period of 1953 to 1965.

Continuity by itself, like the constant velocity of a moving body, requires no explanation; Lonergan's personal religious life, which I have argued was the carrier of all his theology, is sufficient explanation and guarantee of continuity. Yet, as we shall see, this continuity in his Christology exists side by side with great developments in his summer institutes and graduate courses. How do we explain that? Perhaps for this particular point I may invoke the notion I have found inadequate for the total history of his thought: Toynbee's withdrawal and return. The idea fits. Lonergan in 1935 was deep into matters of empirical history: Marxism, racism, continental Liberalism, the role of philosophy in human affairs, and so on, matters from which more mature reflection may have led him to withdraw, leaving the field to historians. Further, it was just in the early 1940s that he read the first six volumes of Toynbee.[13] They made a deep impression on him and ever after he continued to refer favourably to Toynbee.[14] He did pay heed to the criticisms voiced by the empirical historians, and concede that Toynbee's study 'can be viewed, not as an exercise in empirical method, but as ... a formulation of ideal types.'[15] Nevertheless, late in life he remarked: 'With *Reconsiderations* available, the critics are far less impressive.'[16]

It is quite possible, then, and even likely that to some extent he saw his own life in Toynbean terms, and realized that the *pantôn* essay, which was so concerned with world politics and current issues – so 'engaged,' a modern theologian might say – was premature, that there was an enormous work to be done, and done in withdrawal, before he could return and make his own specific contribution to the question of Christ and history. What specifically would that enormous work involve? I would include the construction of his great two-volume organon: *Insight* and *Method*.[17] And equally important was his engagement with the German Historical School; this was 'a long struggle,' as he called it in '*Insight* Revisited.'[18] But those are questions of general biography to be studied more fully in their own right.

One final point on this topic: I have not forgotten the favourite metaphor of my prologue. I return then to the image of a broken battle-front and ask what light it might throw on the present question. The essay of 1935 appears now, I would say, as a strong outpost on our Christological battle line, and provides material for a sharp critique of the tardy front of Scholasticism. I call the latter a front because it involved a whole campaign and could hardly be described as a pocket; I see it now, continuing our metaphor, as a persistent concentration on a front that was no longer the key to victory; the crucial campaign was being fought elsewhere, on another front and about other causes.

Causality in Sacraments and Sacrifice

The twenty-five years from 1940 to 1965 form a distinct period in Lonergan's life: in 1940 he completed his doctoral dissertation, and in 1965 he made his breakthrough to a new concept of theology. The distinct period has its distinct content: it was dominated, at least in his basic theology courses, by Scholasticism. This positive content can, however, be seen from a negative perspective as a long delaying action against the forces of modernity.

Today, with *aggiornamento* reigning in theology, it seems a strangely unattractive period and I find it difficult to recapture the enthusiasm with which I began to follow Lonergan's courses in the spring of 1947. But the enthusiasm was genuine enough, and on reflection I realize the benefit of having encountered Lonergan's Scholasticism first before following his *aggiornamento*. In itself, and without the competition of modernity, Scholasticism could be, and was in the 1940s and 1950s, an engrossing study; it is only now in competition with the research, hermeneutics, critical history, dialectic, and foundations of Lonergan's functional specialties that it loses much of its appeal. But its contribution to a Christology cannot be denied, and I shall give it more space than most readers would perhaps desire.

1. Some Contextual Data

I will single out two of Lonergan's courses as a focus for the present chapter, setting them, however, in a wider context, which I summarize as follows. The period we are studying is the first decade of his career in teaching and writing theology. It is a period when the new courses he had to prepare must have put a steady pressure on any leisure he had. Nevertheless, it was also a period of important published work. I will simply mention the well-known major publications: his work on *gratia operans* and on *verbum* and of course on his monumental *Insight*, but I will pause a bit on some articles that too easily escape the researcher's attention.

There is, for example, the article 'Finality, Love, Marriage,'[1] published in 1943 while Lonergan was teaching sacramental theology in Montreal. I have cited this article as witness to the union of truth and affectivity in Lonergan. I examine it now from another viewpoint. The article was preceded by his review of Dietrich von Hildebrand's book *Marriage*; this review provoked some correspondence in the local diocesan weekly newspaper,[2] and may have been the proximate stimulus for writing the article. It is important, not for any explicit reference it makes to historical causality, but rather for its treatment of certain related and fundamental issues. I quote the introduction to the Collected Works edition.

> This article is, in fact, a mini-*Summa* of theology: a theology of creation in its outline of nature, civilization, and grace; a theology of history in its analysis of human process; a theology of culture and religion in its study of life, the good life, and eternal life; and, finally, in the context of all this, a theology of marriage.[3]

Now, fifteen years later, I would add the importance for that mini-*Summa* of the doctrine on the mystical body of Christ, which certainly bears on Christology, and I would quote the introduction to the first edition of *Collection*, which remarks that the article shows 'a remarkable ability to respect traditional views while remaining open to development and, indeed, carrying forward development to incorporate personalist thinking into the older doctrine on marriage.'[4]

Less interesting but more directly pertinent to our topic is the next essay in that volume, a review of Eduardo Iglesias's book, *De Deo in operatione naturae vel voluntatis operante*. Unusually long for a book review, it was given the title 'On God and Secondary Causes' by its editor and inserted as a chapter in the 1967 *Collection*.[5] It illustrates the way Lonergan was forming a new conceptuality in this period. I quote the editorial introduction: 'Lonergan's doctoral dissertation [written 1938–40] studied *gratia operans* in St. Thomas. It germinated a flock of very basic ideas, but he did not find opportunity for their systematic elaboration till the academic year of 1946–47, when he wrote for his students in Montreal the little work, *De ente supernaturali* (On Supernatural Being).' Here is what the editor of the 1967 *Collection* says about *De ente*:

It set out the notion of grace in what he would later call the *via synthetica*, beginning with the idea of the natural–supernatural relationship and the communication of the divine nature to men in habitual grace, going on to the resulting virtues and operations, to come finally to the great debate on grace and free will. In this last section he discussed instrumentality, immediacy of divine operation, etc., questions that figure largely in his criticism of Fr. Iglesias … in fact, some pages of the review are found again without any disguise except that of language in the Latin work.[6]

For this mini-survey I mention a third article: 'The Assumption and Theology.' Later it will figure largely in my short section on Mariology (Chapter 4 below), but for the present I simply quote once more the Collected Works edition of *Collection* where our article is introduced as follows:

The theological importance of the paper is found not so much in its position on Marian privilege as in its position on the development of doctrine. Lonergan has already moved far beyond logical deduction, and into the area of understanding … [T]he theory takes on meaning through this concrete application to development in our understanding of Mary's role.[7]

With that said on the general context in which Lonergan did his first work in Christology, we can turn to the Christology itself, and specifically to the role of causality that seemed so important to him. Since his plea in 1960 for a study of the historical causality of Christ supposes that topic to be missing from the explicit Christology of the time, including his own, we have to look elsewhere for light, and I find some help in his work on the sacraments and sacrifice, which were among the very first treatises he taught.

There was a pecking order in the seminary teaching assignments of sixty years ago and a kind of hierarchy of kudos in the professors who taught them. Sacramental theology was rather lower in the list than, say, the Trinity, which was handled by big-name theologians. Fr Lonergan, as a junior professor at his college in 1940, was assigned sacramental theology. There is no evidence that this disturbed him; all theology deals with God and the mysteries God has revealed to us, and there is always new and rigorous thinking to be done about both areas – witness Lonergan's rethinking of the sacrament of marriage. In any case, we are grateful for an assignment that helps fill a gap in his Christology.

As announced earlier our focus is on two of his courses: one on sacraments in general, and the other on the Eucharist. For documentation there are a few rather ordinary notes Lonergan issued for his students, there is probably the equivalent of a *reportatio* of some of his lectures, and there is the manuscript of his essay, only recently published, on 'The Notion of Sacrifice.' Altogether they provide a slim but useful documentary basis for some ideas on the missing Christology.

When Lonergan came in his *De Verbo incarnato* to the potency of Christ, he simply wrote: 'more can be found on this question in the treatise on the sacraments in general, where the causality of the sacraments is studied' ('plenius ubi de causalitate sacramentorum in tract. de sacr. in genere').[8] This is a good clue to the logistics of seminary assignments: what courses Lonergan taught or did not teach and what he included in them or did not include was not always a matter of his choice. The notion of sacrifice is, of course, an integral part of Christology, but at L'Immaculée it was taught with the sacraments, and so fell to Lonergan under that heading. We shall research the question under both headings: sacraments and sacrifice.

2. Causality in the Sacraments

We have possibly two sources for Lonergan's doctrine on causality in the sacraments. One certain source is the small sheaf of mimeo notes he issued for his course in 1940–41. The other, with high probability, derives indirectly from his position when he taught the same course three years later.

2.1. The Mimeo Notes of 1940–41

In Lonergan's first year at the College of the Immaculate Conception in Montreal he taught courses 'De sacramentis in genere,' as well as 'De baptismo' and 'De confirmatione.' From these courses a few pages of mimeographed notes survive.[9] The notes are largely just positive theology: lists of theologians with their various doctrines. It is a minor puzzle that he bothered to write them. But he was after all just beginning, and the subject matter was not especially his forte. Further, he had other irons in the fire: for one thing, he was preparing his dissertation for publication, and this work soon appeared in four articles, beginning in September 1941.[10] But, puzzle or not, the notes have his name entered by the typist at the top of the pages and are certainly his composition. Their relevance to Christology appears in the 'Thomistic Synthesis' Lonergan formulates on the causality of the sacraments.

> The foundation and first principle is that Christ the Lord as man stood forth in such a way as an efficient instrumental cause joined to the divinity that he could do all that pertained to reaching the goal of the incarnation ... And so the passion of Christ accomplished our redemption in the manner of an efficient cause ['efficienter' – underlined by Lonergan] ... And this redemption and justification is communicated to human beings by the sacraments.[11]

What precisely is this instrumental efficiency? Lonergan answers: 'spiritual beings do not act in a blind spontaneity but by commanding.'[12] He continues: 'thus the sacraments themselves operate.' In this context he makes a point that is central for us: 'Therefore the sacraments operate by signifying.'[13] All this is attributed to Thomas, but there is no doubt that Lonergan accepts it and makes it his own.

Signs of Lonergan's personal input appear more clearly in his 'Critique of Opinions' ('Crisis Sententiarum').[14] Here is a key passage:

> There are two kinds of agent: an agent acting through intellect (this kind can choose from opposites, and puts forth its effect by commanding), and an agent acting by nature (this kind produces its effects in blind spontaneity, when the conditions for acting have been fulfilled). Now since the being of a sacrament is the being of a sign, and since action follows being, the conclusion is immediate that sacraments act by signifying. But only the one who commands the effect acts by signifying; therefore sacraments are the instruments of God who commands grace.[15]

In taking issue with those who see God as intermediate cause between sacrament and grace, Lonergan refuses to think of God as mediating, and accounts rather for divine causality in a phrase that is typical of him, 'The cause of a cause is the cause of what has been caused.'[16] Note that, though this is the argument of adversaries, Lonergan accepts the principle. In trying to avoid 'causa Dei' (which is involved in making God an intermediary) the adversaries in effect deny causality to the sacraments. Lonergan's position is that both God and the sacraments are causes of grace, but God causes it by causing the cause.[17]

That is all we have of Lonergan's views on causality as they appear in the mimeo notes of 1940–41, but in treating Christ as an instrumental cause, analogous to the causality of a sign and a sacrament, they make a useful contribution to our account of his early Christology.

2.2. The Course of 1943–44

In the revolving cycle of the seminary curriculum, Lonergan taught the same course a second time three years later, in 1943–44. We have no documentation bearing directly on that course, but we have notes on the same course as taught by Fr John Hochban in 1947–48 at Christ the King Seminary in Toronto.[18] Having attended the Hochban course and kept careful notes of a very speculative part in it, I have good reason to believe that he followed closely the Lonergan course of 1943–44. My reason runs as follows.

The possibility of Hochban's dependence on Lonergan is clear enough from the association of the two in 1943–44 and 1947–48. In 1943–44, the second time Lonergan taught these courses at Montreal, Hochban was a student there, and belonged to the same theological community as Lonergan. It is quite possible, even likely, that he followed Lonergan's 1943–44 course, and took notes on it in his own careful way. It is also possible that, four years later, when he himself began to teach sacramental theology in Toronto, he took the opportunity for further study of any notes Lonergan had kept from 1943–44, perhaps even to the extent of borrowing Lonergan's own class notes for that period. The probability heightens when we realize that he and Lonergan were again living in the same religious community and were now fellow professors on the same faculty.

There was, then, opportunity for Hochban to use Lonergan, and a priori likelihood that he did so. There is also empirical evidence pointing the same way. Certainly Hochban's treatment of the speculative questions of the course reflects Lonergan's style, and I would say with equal certainty that it does not reflect Hochban's own favourite style of theology. A remotely relevant point: I have my personal copy of the mimeo notes of 1940–41, with several corrections made in my hand (including the one already mentioned), corrections that seem, from the manner of their insertion, to have been dictated by my professor using those notes in his lectures; the professor could only have been Fr Hochban, for he taught me this course, and Lonergan did not. Where then did he get those corrections if not from Lonergan?

Further, there are phrases and attitudes throughout the notes that sometimes singly, sometimes as part of a pattern, have a Lonerganian ring. For example, the manner of distinguishing 'to id' and 'to quo,' and 'essentia logica' and 'essentia metaphysica' (15). Even more suggestive are the examples of 'sign,' which show a Lonerganian imagination and sense of humor: Spadina (a street near the college where Lonergan and Hochban taught), RSVP, a dollar bill, the footprints Robinson Crusoe saw on the sands, and so on (16). Doctrinal phrases and statements reinforce the point: the reference to Aquinas on 'instrumental power' ('virtus instrumentalis,' 16); the example from mechanics of two colliding bodies (18); the phrase 'on causes ordered of themselves' ('de causis per se ordinatis,' 18); the distinction of 'in regard to themselves – in regard to us' ('quoad se – quoad nos') and the reverse order of their application; most of all the principle, 'the cause of a cause is the cause of what is caused' ('causa causae est causa causati,' 20). One has the sense that one is reading Lonergan, not Hochban.

I therefore consider it probable that Hochban used Lonergan's ideas in the course on the sacraments that he taught me in 1947–48. At any rate, Hochban seems to teach a Lonerganian view of sacramental causality. In an area where hard data are lacking we take what we can get; I turn then to the content of the Hochban course as a possible source for Lonergan's views.

My notes begin with a tableau of the divisions of the term 'sign' (p. 14 of notes on the whole course). From the viewpoint of one purpose it can be speculative, and this in four ways: indicative (Spadina Avenue), suasive (RSVP), preceptive (No smoking), or minatory (Trespassers will be prosecuted). For another purpose it can be practical: not only to make something known, a cognitive purpose, but also to make something be; for example not merely to let us know that this dollar bill is money, but to effect its 'moneyness,' to make it 'be' money (14).

Another division is based on the foundation of the sign (14), for a sign has a relative character and everything relative has to have a foundation. From the viewpoint then of the foundation, we distinguish the formal and the material. Formally we find signs that are natural (the footprints Robinson Crusoe saw) and signs that are conventional (languages). Materially we find signs that are homogeneous (for example, a sign using words only: This way out) and signs that are heterogeneous (for example, → This way out →) where two types of sign, words and arrow, are joined (14).

Now a sign is in the genus of instruments, where an instrument is that by which something is effected, and a sign is that by which something is signified (15). We must then examine the essence of an instrument. First, there is the point already made: an instrument is that by which something is effected. Now we add that it is an agent that moves something through being itself moved. It produces an effect beyond the proportion of its nature. It has an aptitude, which is in the instrument as moved, to produce what Aquinas called 'virtus artis.'[19] Further, the character of 'instrument' may accrue to the subject, as a rod becomes a fulcrum only when it is used as a fulcrum. And so on, and so on, in detail that need not be discussed here (16).

There follows, however, a section of special relevance (17): the question of juridical entities ('entia'). First, some of these are enumerated: societies, values ('dignitates'), powers, laws, rights ('iura'), offices, and so on. Then they are described: they are not mere 'beings of the mind' ('entia rationis') and they are not 'physical beings' ('entia physica'). They are directed toward an end, the common good; they are caused by God, the author of nature and grace, or by human society. This 'direction' is juridical as coming from legitimate authority; it is moral as effected by the free will of persons; it is an instrumental force. These juridical beings have their 'real being' ('esse realia') just as any other motion has, but their intrinsic reality is 'incomplete being' ('ens incompletum,' 17).

Their causality partly resembles, partly differs from mere material causality (18). There is similarity: their use may be for an instant, but their effect remains even when they cease to be. For example, a meteor striking the earth, or a sentence passed by a judge. As with the meteor, the effect remains after the cause has ceased to be, but a higher cause remains in effect: for example, authority. Besides similarity there is difference: as causing by signifying, a moral cause is in the intentional, not the material, order. In the material world, the cause and effect are always simultaneous; in spiritual matters and moral causality (as with the judge's sentence), that is not the case.

Causes that are 'ordered per se' ('per se ordinatis,' 18) are considered next. For example, in communication by writing: cause A is the intellect and will of the writer, cause B is the art of writing learned at school, cause C is the pen. The total effect is the scriptum, which is totally from each cause, totally from the pen as well as totally from the author (18).

To illustrate this in practical signs, there is the case of a dollar bill (19). Its first cause is the civil government which authorizes this practical sign. The next cause is the body of artificers, who prepare the paper, the printing press, and so on; they give the sign its aptitude to signify. The third cause is the citizens who use the sign, who accept it in financial matters. We may illustrate the matter in speculative signs as well as in practical; take the example of a word we use in communication. The first cause is common agreement, in which such-and-such a word is specified as a sign of such-and-such an entity. The second cause, operating in virtue of the first, is the users: those who accept and use this sign to express their mind.

At this point finally the Hochban course applies these ideas to the sacraments (19–20), a method of approach that is typically Lonerganian: a massive campaign of clarifying ideas, then application to the case at hand – one thinks of the battle plan attributed to Montgomery. So we come to the present application: first, in the order of things 'in regard to us' ('quoad nos'); then, in the order of things 'in regard to themselves' ('quoad se').

'Quoad nos' (19–20) the first cause is the sacrament considered according to its name: water, oil, and so on. The second cause is the minister of the sacrament, but we distinguish what the minister does in exercise of his or her own competence and what the minister does as instrument of a higher cause. For the minister becomes an instrument as intending to do what the church does, and an instrument is a 'movement moving something to an effect beyond its proper power' ('motus movens ad effectum ultra propriam virtutem'). The minister, then, is moved by the church; ministers are the instruments of Christ and the church insofar as they intend to do what the church does. The third cause is the church (20), which conserves and gives back in return ('rependit') the doctrine and institutions of Christ. The church teaches and ordains the ministers of the sacraments; it is the vicar of Christ, the instrument of Christ, moved by Christ, and in turn moving to what Christ wishes. The fourth cause is the sacred humanity of Christ: the instrument who instituted the sacraments, the instrument of God, and indeed an instrument joined to God in unity of person ('hypostatice'). The fifth cause is God. In the divine universal salvific will there came the incarnation, the redemption, and the fruits of redemption applied through the sacraments.

'Quoad se' (20) the first cause is God, who gave all power to our Lord and effected the obediential potency of all creation to obey God, and not only to obey God but also to obey Christ; hence the miracles, prophecies, and so on. Second, Christ delegated some of his power to the church, as his vicar, his minister. Third, the church acts in the power of Christ, teaching, dispensing, instituting ministers. Fourthly, the minister intends to do what the church does. Fifthly, words and things are put to sacramental use; the power of the minister passes into these things and words; there is such and such a motion in such and such an aptitude ('motus talis in tali aptitudine'). Mainly the cause is God, who is cause of the subordinate causes, and so cause of their effects ('causa causae est causa causati,' 20). On the created side, aptitude for effecting and signifying grace is in the order of relations, with something relative operating directly on the correlative, which in the realm of signs is the mind. The aptitude so described is in obediential potency to obey the divine commands (20).

This account of causality in the sacraments is in effect Lonergan's own partial reply to his appeal for a study of the historical causality of Christ. It might be made longer still by a general account of the causality of Christ in the diversity and fullness of his human activity; such an account would have to include the causality of his preaching, his healing, his prayer, his social life, his carpentry, and every phase of his human life. We shall touch briefly on this wide area when we consider the human historical life of Jesus (Chapter 10 below), but I do not know of any place in Lonergan's works where he attempts such a sweeping study, though there is precedent and ample material for it in the *Tertia pars* of Thomas Aquinas.

3. Causality in Christ's Sacrifice

Most students of Lonergan will have seen his treatise *De Verbo incarnato* before they knew of the little essay written nearly twenty years earlier but only recently published, 'The Notion of Sacrifice' ('De notione sacrificii').[20] They may wonder that the theme of the essay is not taken up more explicitly in *De Verbo incarnato*, but the explanation is probably simple enough: a matter perhaps of what I have called seminary logistics, assigning different topics to different locations in the curriculum. When Lonergan wrote the earlier work his teaching assignment was not Christology but the sacraments, and so 'De notione sacrificii' was a 'Scholion' in sacramental theology, specifically the Eucharist, not in Christology. And in fact, the prevailing theme is Eucharistic. One surmises, therefore, that at the Gregorian University (and earlier at the Montreal and Toronto seminaries) the question of sacrifice was handled in another treatise by another professor. We are fortunate, then, to have this document from his sacramental theology in the 1940s to fill a gap he left in his Christology of the 1960s.

Both the theme of the essay on sacrifice and the link with Christology appear in its opening lines. First, sacrifice is defined as 'A proper symbol of a sacrificial attitude' ('proprium symbolum affectus sacrificalis,' 3). The definition is enlarged. 'Sacrificial attitude' denotes that state of mind and heart that human beings should have toward God: first, to God as God (worship), then to God as offended by sin (propitiatory), then to God as the source of all benefits we have received (eucharistic in the wide sense) or hope to receive (impetratory).

In Lonergan's usage here a symbol is simply 'an objective manifestation that is perceptible and is social in itself.' It has a double ground in human nature which, as sensible and corporeal, needs a sensible and corporeal expression of internal sentiments, and as social requires that what we experience internally we should express together and in community (3–4).

What is the meaning of 'proper' in the definition of symbol? Lonergan has located 'symbol' in the genus of objective manifestation, but the purpose of manifestation is to reproduce or express in a lower order a perfection that is higher. Thus, God manifests infinite perfection in a finite order by creating. Similarly, human beings represent spiritual perfection in the sensible and social order by symbolizing, and so in a religious culture poetic arts, paintings, and so on are filled with symbols (5, with a reference to Sorokin). A proper symbol is a proper manifestation, one that has the required degree of perfection, and this is realized only when there is an analogy of proportion ('analogia proportionis') between the lower element that manifests and the higher element that is manifested (5–6).

'Analogy of proportion' is one of Lonergan's favourite thought patterns. A simple example from arithmetic gives the pattern: as four is to two, so eight is to four. A theological example could be constructed from his own argument here: as God is to the manifestation of his infinity by creation, so human beings are to the manifestation of their spiritual perfection by symbols. Better still, there is his example later in the essay: 'The eucharistic sacrifice is to the sacrifice of the cross as the sacrifice of the cross is to the sacrificial attitude of Christ at his death' (27).

To this rather abstract consideration Lonergan adds three specific headings. There may be in the materials or actions used a natural aptitude for signifying or representing; thus rites of animal sacrifice had a natural aptitude to express realities on the religious level (6). What else but a symbol of religious spirit could such actions intend? Still, even a natural aptitude could be only an obscure signifying of a determinate spiritual perfection: a holocaust could be part of the cult of God or the cult of demons. So next there may be convention, law or institution to give certitude, clarity, distinctiveness. A third heading for the propriety of a symbol is the real connection between the symbol that manifests and the spiritual perfection that is manifested. The connection may be moral, as when in the Old Law an animal was substituted in moral estimate and offered to God in place of a human being. Or the connection may be physical, as when our Lord in his own body expressed the symbol of his sacrificial spirit on the altar of the cross (7).

Lonergan's first application of his definition is to the perfect sacrifice of the cross (7), where a singular and most perfect sacrificial spirit is represented with the highest propriety. For there is a natural aptitude to signify a sacrificial spirit when a violent death and shedding of blood takes the most precious life. Again there is the greatest certitude, clarity, and distinctiveness when the law and the prophets and the leader himself of lawmakers and prophets declare by divine authority what this natural symbol signifies. Finally there is the closest connection of the spiritual and sensible orders in the union of body and soul in one and the same person. In sum, it is not by some equivocal similarity but by analogical proportion that the sacrifice of the cross represents or symbolizes the sacrificial spirit of Christ. And so the sacrifice of the cross is the proper symbol of the sacrificial spirit of the dying Christ (8).

A second application of the definition is to the eucharistic sacrifice where the sacrificial spirit of the mystical body of Christ is properly symbolized. The argument for this is long (8–16), running through parts (a) to (f), and taking up nearly half the work. As concerned with the sacramental aspect of the Eucharist it is less pertinent here, but as concerned with Christ the head of the mystical body, it is very directly pertinent.

Nevertheless, it will suffice to give an overview of the six steps in the argument. First, 'the eucharistic sacrifice is a proper symbol of the sacrificial attitude of Christ himself, the Head of the Mystical Body' (8). Then, 'the eucharistic sacrifice … is also a proper symbol of the sacrificial attitude of the members of the Mystical Body, that is, of the church.' But the 'sacrificial attitude of the church can be considered in two ways, namely, in its origin and in its term' (10); steps three and four take up the question under those headings. Third, then, by reason of analogical proportion, 'the sacrificial attitude of the church, considered in its origin, is properly symbolized in the eucharistic sacrifice' (11). Fourth, what we have demonstrated in regard to the origin we must also demonstrate in regard to the term, but this time by reason of the outward appearances of the sacrifice, by reason of its institution, and by reason of its real connection (13–14), that is, the connection between the symbol that manifests and the spiritual perfection that is manifested. The fifth step turns from causes to effects. 'So far we have been considering the sacrificial attitude of the members as existing in its causes: first, in the mind and heart of Christ, next, in the sacrifice of the cross, and third in the eucharistic sacrifice. Now we must turn our attention to the sacrificial attitude of the church as it is in its effect ... in the minds and hearts of Christians' (15). The sixth step recapitulates the previous five.

From essence Lonergan turns to causes (17–22). 'So far we have been dealing only with the essence of sacrifice ... Now we broaden our consideration to determine its various causes'; these he lists in the normal way: exemplary, final, efficient, material, and formal, with subdivisions and explanations. In the course of that discussion, however, he had occasion to quote the Council of Trent on the Cross and the Mass, affirming the identity of Cross and Mass in what is offered but also their difference in the manner of offering (21). The last general heading is 'Differences between the Sacrifice of the Cross and the Mass' (22); on this point Lonergan resorts again to his favourite analogy of proportion: 'The eucharistic sacrifice is to the sacrifice of the cross as the sacrifice of the cross is to the sacrificial attitude of Christ at his death' (27). Further, 'Just as Christ's sacrificial attitude was not superadded as something different from the sacrifice of the cross, since it is the invisible sacrifice of that visible sacrifice, so also the eucharistic sacrifice is not superadded as something different from the sacrifice of the cross; for it is the perpetual sacrifice of that unique and unrepeated sacrifice' (27). A final quote from 'Conclusions': 'The sacrifice of the cross and the eucharistic sacrifice are numerically the same' (27).

4

First Courses in Christology: 1948, 1952

E ight years of various teaching assignments brought Lonergan to the academic year 1948–49 and to his first treatise on Christology proper. In that year he began to teach seminary courses under the title *De Verbo incarnato*, and would continue to do so till 1965, producing a number of published and unpublished works for his students.

His general thinking at this time was dominated by the results of his *verbum* study (1946–49) and his intellectualist understanding of Thomas, as opposed to the prevailing conceptualist view. As to particular questions we shall find him bringing new understanding to the old question of the hypostatic union and breaking new ground on the question of the consciousness of Christ. His full Scholastic position on those two questions will, however, await his courses from 1953 on at the Gregorian University, and even then he would still be far from the final recognition of modernity that we find, say, in his 1975 paper on 'Christology Today.'

1. The Course of 1948

Lonergan's first course in Christology was taught in the fall semester of 1948–49 at Christ the King Seminary, Toronto, and repeated there with the return of the cycle in 1952–53. He followed traditional paths in his course structure, and was still strongly Scholastic in his method and his doctrine. He used a manual, as was the universal custom at the time, but naturally there was personal input: it was not in his nature simply to repeat tradition as a catechism might. The manual he used was not of his own composition, but one that happened to be available, written by an author he respected: Adhémar d'Alès.[1] D'Alès was a scholar, strong on erudition, and Lonergan would rely on the manual to convey the substance of Catholic tradition, while he made his own contribution on selected questions.

Naturally his selections were in the areas of deepest speculative understanding. He had said of Anselm, 'Only what is difficult seems to his taste.'[2] We may say the same of Lonergan; his understanding had to be challenged or he was not interested. And in fact I can say, as a student of his through four years of basic theology, that not every lecture was equally thrilling. If the matter was simply bread-and-butter theology, he might say, 'You can read; consult the manual.'[3] If particular points of erudition needed his input, he would make his point briefly and move on. But on difficult questions like that of the hypostatic union he would happily spend days, to the bewilderment of those students who didn't want to understand the hypostatic union, and to the joy of those who did. Further, in order to put his theology across, he had to teach us his own philosophy, notably his cognitional theory, his epistemology, and his metaphysics. The fact that his writings, especially the *verbum* articles, were just then getting into print, with offprints available for some of them, added to the impact of his lectures.

My handwritten notes on the 1948–49 course[4] show Lonergan to have followed for the most part the order of the d'Alès manual. He began with lectures on the messianic doctrine of the scriptures, especially of the Old Testament, giving space to the position of liberal Protestantism and to the Catholic doctrine on prophecy. He then took up the first theses in d'Alès: the doctrine of the Old Testament on Christ, the divinity of Christ adumbrated in the Old Testament, the declaration of Jesus on his identity as the Christ promised by the prophets.

At this point Lonergan interrupted the sequence to give several lectures on modernism, taking as source the encyclical *Pascendi* and following the numbered paragraphs in the Denzinger *Enchiridion*.[5] This procedure rather conflicts with his position that students could read for themselves, but it indicates the importance he attached to modernism: first, for understanding the mind of non-Catholics, and second, for understanding the works of Catholic apologists. He concluded this set of lectures with a straightforward account of the Catholic position: truth is one and absolute, but there are two orders, the natural and the supernatural, not parallel but one subordinate to the other. There is no real conflict between the two; apparent conflicts are reconciled in the long run; heresy is a matter of impatience in the short run at the delay. This fairly standard position would become more complicated some years later (see Chapter 8 below).

Lonergan resumed the order of the d'Alès manual at thesis 4 on Jesus of Nazareth as the Christ promised by the prophets. He acknowledged the difficulty of proving the thesis: it arises partly from the huge amount of relevant material, but partly also from the form of the argument. On the latter he describes the general form of any argument: If *A*, then *B*; but *A*; therefore *B*. As for the major premise, he demolishes the mechanical way of arguing without understanding. Positively, he distinguishes the perception of a nexus from the positing of the nexus; the first is a matter of direct understanding, the second a matter of reflective understanding. We apprehend a series of texts in Old and New Testaments, we perceive a nexus between the texts (*A*) and the thesis (*B*); we posit our assent. Further points are made: prophecies are related to Christ as potency is related to act (his analogy of proportion again!) but the potency is only gradually brought to act as text is added to text; and clarity is found mainly in the whole rather than in the parts, and in Christ himself rather than in single texts (21–22).

Beginning thesis 5 on the divinity of Christ, Lonergan maintained that the radical philosophical difficulty on the question of the God-man is the notion of reality itself. This is vintage Lonergan, and he devoted a section (24–25) to various views on realism: naive realism, idealism, and critical realism. He sketched the rationalism of Kant, Lessing, Reimarus, Herder, Schleiermacher, Strauss, Ritschl, and Harnack (26–28), not omitting the conservative Protestants and Anglicans (29).

Prior to his own proof he put the question in all honesty: why do thinkers of such stature, erudite, intelligent, possessing goodwill, find difficulty in admitting the divinity of Christ? It is a necessary question if we are to remove the appearance of arrogance, to eliminate doubts on our side, to avoid the facile claim of demonstrating a truth that others cannot accept, and to be clear on the 'status quaestionis' (30).

In answer to that prior question Lonergan made three points. First, there is the difference between experience and truth. If we make judgment a mere symbol of experience, since we do not experience the divinity of Christ, we are unable to make the judgment that he is divine. The second is the analogy between truth and the evolution of dogma. The creeds came slowly to the affirmation 'God from God, Light from Light, true God from true God.'[6] Our opponents see this evolution as occurring under the influence of Hellenic philosophy, where we instead distinguish imperfect knowledge of the truth from error. The familiar principle says 'whatever is received is received in the way proper to the receiver' ('quidquid recipitur ad modum recipientis recipitur'), and Lonergan describes the way the principle applies to truth as held by youths and as held by adults; accordingly he asserted the possibility of knowing a particular fact without requiring a comprehensive knowledge of the universe. The third point simply collects several more particular points: we are dealing with understanding a high mystery, an understanding not fully achieved at Chalcedon. Also, the Lord's manner of speaking was oral and pedagogic; again, on the side of motives, the Lord wished his message to be received in faith, not in logical demonstration; and finally, there is the need of grace and goodwill to receive the message (31–32).

These prolegomena were followed in the traditional manner by proof of the thesis from the New Testament and the faith of the early church. Lonergan's personal contribution to the proof laid two fallacies to rest. First, the process is not a mere dialectic ('processus mere dialecticus') in which we take texts as premises for the deduction of the thesis; the question is not one of deduction from a text but of understanding texts inductively. The other fallacy holds that the process is to have no presuppositions. Lonergan exploded that view: no one ever investigates a question without presuppositions. What is required is that we be aware of our presuppositions and hold them critically. Present presuppositions are that the criterion of reality is truth, that truth can be apprehended first imperfectly and then more perfectly, that we may build on the theses already established (32).

Skipping over several traditional theses[7] we arrive at thesis 15, on the one person and the hypostatic union – the kind of question that was a delight to Lonergan ('only what is difficult seems to his taste'). His position is sketched in my notes from page 48 to page 56. I have also in my files seven typed pages which marginal notes show I copied from Lonergan's own lecture notes, but they are undated, seem to omit chunks of material, and in part mix up the order of the actual lectures. I will therefore, for Lonergan's doctrine in 1948, use the notes I made as he lectured, where the order is, first, a critique of the various views of the theologians, then a statement of the thesis, and third, a proof of the opinion Lonergan himself holds. I depart from that order, however, to begin with the thesis itself.

It reads as follows (52): 'In the one who is God and man, the correspondence required by truth between reality and understanding is saved insofar as a certain human and individual nature is finitely actuated by the infinite act of being of the Word' ('In eo qui est Deus et homo, adaequatio veritatis inter rem et intellectum salvatur, inquantum humana quaedam et individua natura per infinitum Verbi actum essendi finite actuatur'). Lonergan posits the thesis after several pages of discussion, but it helps to have it up front, for it shows the key factor in the argument: we start with truth and proceed to reality, for reality and truth must correspond. The whole argument is based on that rock of Gibraltar.

Let us turn, then, to Lonergan's discussion of opinions. There are six main views on the hypostatic union. All agree that the divine Word is in no way changed, either in his existence or in his nature. They disagree on what is added ('accedit') to the Word, and on the way this added element is united to the Word. On what is added there are two groups. Scotus, Tiphanus, and Suarez hold that what is added to the unchanged Word is an individual human nature with its proper existence. Opposed to this, Capreolus, Cajetan, de la Taille, and others (including d'Alès) hold that what is added to the unchanged Word is an individual human nature without its existence (48–49).

The causes of this diversity are the real distinction between essence and existence; the modalism of Suarez and Cajetan; the question of the correspondence required by truth between reality and understanding ('adaequatio veritatis'). On that last point Scotus, Tiphanus, Capreolus, and Cajetan all fail. Those who require an 'adaequatio veritatis' follow Suarez or de la Taille.

At this time Lonergan believes the view of de la Taille to be demonstrable (49). He argues for it as follows. First, there is a real distinction between essence and existence. Next, the constitutive elements of a finite being (act and potency, form and matter) are united of themselves (no glue is needed!). Then, to have a 'being which' (an 'ens quod'), it is required and sufficient that there be an act of existence. Now Christ is an individual, an 'ens quod,' and has a single act of existence. This single act of existence is the Pure Act ('Actus Purus') of God, and so of the divine Word who has existed eternally. This single act of existence is communicated to the human and individual nature of Christ; otherwise Christ would not be a man. The communication implies ('dicit') an entity that is contingent, supernatural, received in a human nature, and indeed received in the existential line; that is, instead of an entity received as existence, there is an entity received in the line of existence or the mode of existence ('in linea existentiali; i.e., loco existentiae, ad modum existentiae' – 52, and see 55).

The thesis rests on two principles (53): on the dogma of Ephesus and Chalcedon, and on the fact that dogma is not just an utterance of the voicebox ('flatus vocis'), is not just a rule of speaking, is rather and much more a rule of believing. For dogma to be true there must be a corresponding reality, an 'adaequatio veritatis.' On the side of intellect this is found in the judgment and only in the judgment, which is an assent of faith; on the side of the real, it is found in 'beings–which and beings–by–which' ('entia quae et entia quibus'), not in 'modes' that are neither 'entia quae' nor 'entia quibus.' As for the 'adaequatio' itself, it is found in the correspondence of the logical and the real, between judgment and the field of reality.

To have 'adaequatio veritatis' in a contingent truth about God there is a special requirement: there must be a contingent reality. But there is no contingent reality in God; there must therefore be an extrinsic denominator. Now what applies in general to contingent truth about God applies like-wise to the truth that God became man: to have 'adaequatio veritatis' there must be an extrinsic denominator. For the truth that 'Peter understands' there is an intrinsic denominator; but for the truth that 'God became man' the denominator is extrinsic. The Word becomes man then through 'a finite actuation by an infinite act' ('actuatio finita per actum infinitum'). It is an actuation for it confers a perfection. It is finite for it confers a contingent perfection. It is an actuation by Infinite Act for what is communicated is not just the entity received but God himself. On the side of Christ's hu-manity the entity received cannot be an accident; that would result in a Nestorian unity. It cannot be in the line of essence, for then the nature of Christ would be altered and he would not remain human. There is left only the third possibility that it is in the existential line (52–55).

What is to be said about this thesis? For one thing, Lonergan seems to be repeating his argument for the position he and de la Taille hold. True, in a way he is doing just that, but this is because in the course of his critique of others he is led to give his own contrasting position which then recurs in its proper place in his proof of the thesis. (I may add that repetition of such difficult matter was quite acceptable to his students.) A second and more serious criticism is the obscurity of the phrase, 'instead of an entity received as existence, there is an entity received in the line of existence or the mode of existence.' This is left unexplained.

A third point touches on the approaching change in Lonergan's way of doing theology. In the 1972 lecture 'Revolution in Catholic Theology,' he remarked that in the theology of the future 'there is going to be a lot less metaphysics.'[8] The reason why may be surmised from this thesis on the hypostatic union: it is not theology for the masses! And the same may be said of Lonergan's later abandonment of de la Taille in favour of his own position, simpler though the latter be. It is another question, however, whether we can drop metaphysics. A position more likely to be acceptable, one that Lonergan himself will adopt, would retain metaphysics but reduce it to third rank after cognitional theory and epistemology.[9]

Let us therefore leave the metaphysics of the hypostatic union and continue, along easier paths, our survey of Lonergan's 1948 Christology. We may notice, in thesis 17 on the grace of Christ, the attention he gave to the mystical body. The topic came up naturally under 'gratia capitis' and was treated by d'Alès in that context, but Lonergan gave it special attention in his argument (63–64), pausing on a theme that was dear to him from the 1930s and so introduced his theology of sacrifice. The encyclical *Mystici corporis* that Pius XII wrote in 1943 would resonate very well in Lonergan's thinking.

More elaborated in 1948 is the question of the knowledge Christ had. It is thesis 18 in both d'Alès and Lonergan, and the last thesis in Lonergan's course. (The d'Alès volume continues with several theses on Christ as Mediator and Redeemer, but at Christ the King Seminary that question was handled in a separate course by another professor.) The knowledge Christ had takes up pages 65 to 73 in my notes and contains a number of intriguing observations, from which I will choose a few samples.

The first regards the beatific knowledge ('scientia beata') that Christ had – the main question here, according to Lonergan (66). There is the question of fact, which is not to be settled by quoting scripture, since scripture speaks without distinguishing the divine and the human in Christ. Lonergan has therefore to institute an argument, for which he takes as premise the undoubted fact that Christ knew himself as Son of God (66). This is an absolutely supernatural item of knowledge; how then did Christ know it? Lonergan answers: either by vision ('scientia beata') or by faith (he appeals here to Paul: 2 Corinthians 5:6 and 1 Corinthians 13:9–12). But not by faith, for faith does not give that plenitude of knowledge which scripture attributes to Christ. Nor is faith compatible with the way Christ teaches in John's gospel: 'we know what we speak' (John 3:11, 'quod scimus loquimur,' and various texts in John). Therefore he knew it by vision (67).

That raises an interesting question for Lonergan: how could Christ as man act, suffer, and think if he had the vision of the blessed? We are dealing with the analysis of mental states, and such analysis, Lonergan says, is very difficult. When we are hungry for dinner we can easily isolate that movement in our consciousness, but generally life is not so simple and so we rely on psychoanalysis. Analysis on the intellectual level is even more difficult. The intellect gives connection and order to the flow of sensitive life within us, but is itself a barely conscious element. Similarly, we know very little about the consent of the will.

But the classic illustration of the difficulty regards the mystical life, where Lonergan seems to rely on Mager's book, *Mystik als seelische Wirklichkeit* (Graz, 1945). In the dark night of the soul the mystic is without any sensible consolation. There is basic love of God that rules his life effectively, but of affection there is none. The basic ruling act (love of God) is so fleeting, so intangible, so un–get–at–able, that the mystic looks on himself or herself as a mere pagan. Lonergan asks the question of the unity of consciousness: in what does it consist? There is a radical unity in that the potencies are all radicated in the soul, and there is a further formal unity in the communication of the potencies with one another. Health and prayer have a mutual effect, each on the other.

How does this apply to the beatific knowledge Christ had (70)? The different levels of consciousness do not conflict with one another, and neither does the beatific vision conflict with ordinary consciousness. It enlarges the field, and adds a new dimension, as three-dimensional geometry adds a new dimension to two-dimensional, but does not cut out the lower (70). In a similar way the mystics have a new dimension, the experience of a new order, an awful enlargement of consciousness which they cannot express in terms of the lower level.

The last heading for this thesis regards the extent of the knowledge Christ had (70). Lonergan tends to amplify this rather than restrict it. His principle is that Christ knows all that pertains to his mission, but everything pertains to his mission, for he is head of all that is, all that has been, all that will be (70). He knows even as man the day of the last judgment. Lonergan explains the text that has provoked so much comment among theologians (Mark 13:32; 'about that day or that hour no one knows ... not even the Son') as meaning that Christ as man had a mandate from the Father on what he should reveal (John 7:16, 8:26, 28; 12:49-50) and he had no mandate to reveal the time of the last judgment. Still, despite the plenitude of his knowledge, Christ learned, acquiring experiential knowledge, as many texts in scripture testify.

My notes on the last lectures of the course suggest that Lonergan was hurrying to include matter integral to the question of Christ's knowledge. At any rate my scribbling could not keep up with his lecture, and we have no other documentation than my 'reportatio' on this early Christology. (Notes on Lonergan's courses were also taken with care by Fr W.A. Stewart. He turned them over to the Lonergan Archives, but on the Christology course there remain only pages 19–26 and 37–38 – all on the early part of the course.)

2. The Course of 1952

We have no student reports of Lonergan's lectures the second time Christology came around at the Toronto seminary (the fall term of the academic year 1952–53); we may presume that, fully occupied with the writing of *Insight*, which filled the years 1949 to 1953, he was not likely to revise in any radical way the course he had taught four years earlier. We do, however, have a little essay that Lonergan allowed to be mimeographed for his students, on the new question *On the consciousness of Christ*.[10] Later this would be greatly expanded and become an important theme in his Christology.

There is little in the way of early history of the theme, but a longish footnote in the fourth *verbum* article, published in 1949, shows Lonergan in touch with the question: '… consciousness is either concomitant, reflective, or rational. Concomitant consciousness is awareness of one's act and oneself in knowing something else …'[11] Just around this time, or soon after, Lonergan was writing Chapter 11 of *Insight*, where we find a full account of consciousness.[12] Further, in 1952–53 Lonergan actually lectured at Christ the King Seminary on the book he was writing, and there are student notes on those lectures.[13] So we have the interesting conjunction of four sources for Lonergan's thinking on consciousness in the period 1949–53: the footnote in *Theological Studies* (volume 10) in 1949, the notes *De conscientia Christi* in 1952, the lectures on *Insight*-in-preparation in 1952–53, and Chapter 11 of *Insight* itself, certainly ready in manuscript by 1953 and probably a couple of years earlier; to determine the precise relationship of the four to one another is an interesting little task for some future researcher.

The topic of consciousness was therefore coming to the fore, in itself and to some extent in its application to Christology. The d'Alès textbook, *De Verbo incarnato* (1930), has nothing on our topic (two pages on the Messianic consciousness of Christ are not relevant). Nor was the topic studied by Lonergan during his 1948 lectures though, as we saw above, he did touch on the related problem of Christ having consciousness of his everyday experiences along with the immediate knowledge of God.

By the time the seminary cycle brought the same course round again in 1952–53, Lonergan had become aware of this new problem, probably through Galtier's book on the subject.[14] Presumably wartime and post-war conditions had prevented arrival of the work in Toronto in time for the 1948 course. In any case the book presented Lonergan with the kind of problem he loved, though only in 1956 would he be able to deal with it thoroughly (see *De constitutione Christi* in Chapter 5 below); meanwhile, however, he was able to produce for his 1952 class the notes *De conscientia Christi*.

No student report has yet been found on the lectures that presumably accompanied these notes. Lonergan's own table of contents (page 1, # 4) lists the divisions: 1. objectivity; 2. objective self-knowledge; 3. experience; 4. consciousness; 5. the experience and consciousness of Christ as man. A major difference from *De constitutione Christi*, written four years later, is the distinction between experience and consciousness. In 1952 experience is the passive aspect and consciousness the active. 'If the operation is considered as a change in the subject, a "passion," the reception of an operation, then the presence of the operation is called "experience"; but if the operation is considered as referring to the attention or effort or action of the subject, its presence is called "consciousness."'[15] (Notice the recurrence of 'presence'; later a particular type of presence will be a key notion in the explanation of consciousness.) The distinction between experience and consciousness is maintained throughout the work, but was dropped from *De constitutione Christi*; and indeed the 'effort or action of the subject' is ambiguous, compared to the simplicity of the later definition: 'consciousness is interior experience of oneself and of one's acts.'[16]

After this buildup comes the application: the consciousness of Christ. Lonergan focuses on the consciousness Christ had of the beatific vision and asks how on the basis of that consciousness he could know himself as Son of God. 'He who is God is conscious of his own vision of God in such a way that he could affirm with certainty and did affirm with certainty that the one knowing himself is the same one that is known in the beatific vision.'[17] The essay concludes with a paragraph on the consciousness Christ has of his other operations; these are seen by Christ to be beyond the proportion of human nature but not beyond the proportion of the person; they therefore allow Christ to affirm that he has another nature than the human and that this other nature is divine.

3. Mariology

Catholic theologians often add to their Christology a short discourse on Mariology. That is doubly fitting in a book on Lonergan. There is the element of his Marian piety that we examined in Chapter 1, but there is also the link between Marian doctrine and the development of dogma: in the years preceding the definition in 1950 of Mary's assumption into heaven, development of dogma was a live topic for bishops and theologians. Lonergan made his contribution in the paper 'The Assumption and Theology,' on which the editor's 'Introduction' to the *Collection* of 1967 has this to say.

> Its chief interest for the theologian now is certainly its reflections on the development of dogma. As Lonergan saw with dispassionate clarity, the doctrine under discussion is obviously of faith, but it is evasive to appeal to some unwritten and unknown tradition to justify it, and simply faulty thinking to deduce it by formal implication from some other particular prerogative of Mary. The premises are far more general: the role of suffering and death and resurrection in the total scheme, and the place of Jesus and Mary in the total salvific plan.[18]

Let us turn to Lonergan himself and his argument from scripture for the assumption of Mary: 'sources for the doctrine … lie in the account of man's fall through Adam and his redemption through Christ. There are two solidarities: a first in Adam through sin to death; a second in Christ through death to resurrection.'[19] Lonergan describes these solidarities, and continues.

> But where in this picture stands Mary, the virgin blessed amongst women, the Mother of God? … was she too assumed, soul and body, into heaven? Or does she still await, with sinners, the trumpet of an angel to be summoned from death to life? If there have been Christians who felt they had not the grounds to affirm the first alternative with certitude, there have been none to venture to affirm the second. Too clearly, Mary's position is a position of privilege.[20]

Lonergan proceeds to enumerate her privileges: full of grace, without sin, ever a virgin yet a mother without the pangs of motherhood, blessed among women for all generations, the woman spoken of in Genesis ('I will put enmities between thee and the woman'). Then he enumerates the implications of the opposite position: Mary anticipating the fruits of redemption as regards original sin but not as regards entrance into heaven; freed from Satan's empire of sin but not from his empire of death; adoring the body to which she gave birth, yet without the body that gave it birth; coming under some law that overrules the best of sons' love for the best of mothers; that permits the Sacred Heart to be a living heart but forces the Immaculate Heart to be a dead heart. 'The more one thinks about it, the more numerous the aspects one considers, the fuller becomes the evidence and the greater its cogency.'[21] The process is far less syllogistic than logic would wish, but it is remarkably like the process by which Newman would justify his judgment that Great Britain is an island. Single items do not make a premise, but together they are seen to be moving to an understanding and a judgment that could become a premise.

Yet along with this forward-looking attitude, there is Lonergan's conservative position on the knowledge had by the Apostles. Speaking from the viewpoint of apologetics he says: 'No theologian would deny that the assistance of the Holy Spirit enabled the Apostles to understand the full implications of divine revelation. But it is quite another matter to affirm an explicit, oral, apostolic tradition when there is not sufficient evidence to justify such an affirmation.'[22]

The context of that remark was, in his own word, apologetics, but a quarter of a century later the apologetics will be somewhat different. 'Perhaps I might suggest that human psychology and specifically the refinement of human feelings is the area to be explored in coming to understand the development of Marian doctrines.'[23] The meaning of 'implications' will also develop:'... the shift from a predominantly logical to a basically methodical viewpoint may involve a revision of the view that doctrinal developments were "implicitly" revealed.'[24] I remember from his seminary lectures of April–May 1947, On the Theological Loci ('De locis theologicis'), that he was already keen on the development of doctrine, with Newman as his authority. But development in Newman's sense would not be a matter of deduction in strict logic from propositions in scripture; it would be a matter rather of understanding in the very strong sense Lonergan had given that word.

Understanding of truth, however, is one thing and understanding of data is another, and as much as Lonergan understood this in a general way, he had not in 1952 realized how drastically it would affect his concept of theology. In consequence, despite use of the word 'historicity,' he had not yet fully assimilated the reality of historicity as a feature of the human race, had not accepted the exegesis of scripture that assumed this historicity, did not look on research, interpretation, and history as integral parts of theology, much less give dialectic and foundations the role they would have in 1972. Theology for him began not with data but with given truth; its business was to understand the truth that was given it.[25]

First Courses at the Gregorian University

Back in 1938 Lonergan had been slated by his Religious Superiors for a professorship at the Gregorian University in Rome. In the summer of that year he was doing priestly ministry in Great Britain and Ireland, and pondering the line he might follow for his doctoral work in philosophy, which was meant to be his field of study. Meanwhile, however, a flurry of letters between his Canadian Superior and the American Rector of the Gregorian (excellent postal service in those primitive times!) resulted in his transfer from philosophy to theology, on the grounds that he was destined to teach at the Gregorian and the English-speaking students in theology there greatly outnumbered those in philosophy. One gathers from Lonergan's account that he was not consulted on the matter, but probably he was not displeased with the new status.[1]

In any case he spent the next two years in Rome doing doctoral studies in theology, just finishing them in 1940 when the war became real and Italy intervened. He returned, therefore, to his own country, teaching theology first in Montreal and then in Toronto. When the war was over, the authorities in Rome made overtures to have him transferred there, but from 1949 he had been occupied with his book *Insight* and was in no hurry to move across the Atlantic, fearing that Rome would not allow him any leisure for writing. He seems to have received two deferments of the transfer, but finally, being a religious and not his own master, he sailed for Europe in September 1953 and began to teach at the Gregorian in what was meant to be a lifelong assignment.

But God disposes! After twelve years in Rome, when he was back in Canada for the summer, Lonergan was discovered to have lung cancer. Serious surgery, a long, slow convalescence, and weakened health intervened to rule out Rome as a base for the work of his remaining years, and Lonergan never returned there.

During his Roman period he taught Christology seven times – first in alternate years: 1953–54, 1955–56, 1957–58, 1959–60, 1961–62, 1963–64; then again in 1964–65 in what was intended from that time on to be an annual course. For the first three of these recurring courses he was able to use the manual of Charles Boyer.[2] Boyer may not have matched d'Alès in erudition but his book was available and Lonergan, not yet ready to provide his own manual, simply used Boyer's.

From the start, however, it must have been an awkward situation, with Lonergan not entirely free to plot his own course, and soon he felt the need to write supplements on certain questions. So in the spring of 1954 he provided mimeo notes, *De ratione convenientiae*. Then, in the spring of 1956 he published *De constitutione Christi ontologica et psychologica*, a work that enjoyed considerable success, being reprinted several times till its final edition in 1964. We shall examine these two works presently, but neither was suitable to serve as a manual, and meanwhile the university bookstore ran out of stock of Boyer's work, so Lonergan faced the options of finding another manual or writing his own. He chose the latter, and in 1959–60 issued the first edition of his own *De Verbo incarnato*, which was reissued first in 1961–62, and then again in 1964, considerably revised.

It is not easy to get full clarity on Lonergan's Christology during his first years at the Gregorian. There is some control of it in his use of or departure from Boyer; this can be measured in the set of theses printed for the course's final examination; for example, Boyer speaks of Christ offering his own satisfaction ('propria satisfactio'), but Lonergan's examination sheet has him offering vicarious satisfaction ('satisfactio vicaria'). More helpful is a report on the whole course of 1953–54, done by an un-known student auditor, discovered in a bookstore by John Brezovec and donated by him to the Lonergan Archives. Other sources are Lonergan's letters and the reminiscences of his students. Altogether they give some indication of Lonergan's lectures, suggesting that in this, his first course at the Gregorian, he did not depart greatly from current manuals.

1. 'De ratione convenientiae' (1954)

Lonergan's first writing in Christology at the Gregorian appeared in 1953–54. The work has been known, from the three words that begin the title, as *De ratione convenientiae*. The two key words there are notoriously difficult to translate – 'ratio' because of the wealth of its multiple meanings; 'convenientia' for the opposite reason: the vernacular lacks a suitable word for it. Literally, we have to say 'On the Meaning of Fittingness.' Perhaps to overcome these handicaps the full title reads more like a table of contents than a title: *Schematic Supplement: On the Meaning of Fittingness and on Its Root; On the Excellence of Order; On the Steps in the Systematic and Universal Ordering of Our Concepts of God; Finally on Fittingness, Contingency, and the End of the Incarnation.*[3]

A few notes on the title are in order. The notion of what is *fitting* is a favourite theme of Lonergan's: theology deals with the possible, not with the necessary, and so is satisfied to show that the incarnation was fitting, that it has its intelligibility without being necessitated. 'Intelligibility' does not mean simply the absence of internal contradiction; more positively, it means what divine wisdom, coextensive with divine power, sees as good and possible. *Order* is another favourite theme; it takes us into the good of order, the relation this good has to individual persons and to the community, and the highest good which is the order of the universe. Third, there are the *signa rationis*, a term which we have to paraphrase in translation as 'steps in ordering our concepts of God, especially our concepts of divine understanding and divine willing.' These steps are the following: (a) God's self-knowledge; (b) God's love of the divine goodness; (c) God's understanding simply as understanding of all that could be; (d) God's knowledge before choosing what order to create of all that would be in any world order God might choose to bring into being, knowledge therefore based on divine infallibility, efficacy, irresistibility; (e) God's choice of the actually existing order of the world, on which basis (f) divine understanding, which was simply understanding, becomes now the knowledge of vision of the order actually chosen.

Three terms in the title pertain specifically to Christology: the fittingness, the contingency, the end of the incarnation. The relatively long exposition of the fittingness of the incarnation might be called a theology of history in the style of Chapter 20 of *Insight*.[4] It has the well-known structure: first, what human history would be if everyone followed the dictates of reason; then, the reign of sin which human history actually becomes when we act against the dictates of reason; and third, the restoration when the reign of sin is destroyed and the human race recalled to a life in conformity with reason.

We are now led naturally to the topic of redemption, for as sin is not just an act against reason but also an offence against God, so the remedy will involve more than right human reason. That in turn brings Lonergan to another favourite theme: the role of the theological virtues of faith, hope, and charity in making human life human. Thus, faith is an act of obedience to divine truth but is also a guide to right reason; hope calls us to immortal life but also corrects our excessive love of sensible things; charity, besides giving us what is most basic, love of God above all things, also converts us from love of our private good to love of neighbour (for extended discussion, see Chapter 14 below).

In an unexpected addition to this threefold help from the virtues, Lonergan finds a fourth element: mystery. This is mystery in the wide sense: not just the mystery to human understanding that God is, but the mystery we intend in speaking about the mysteries of the Rosary or the mysteries we contemplate in the life of Christ. These mysteries become known to us in sensible representations. They are signs of what we know by intellect; they invite us to more profound understanding and move us to affection. What gives them special importance is the fact that our knowledge begins from the senses and our choices are carried out more promptly and easily when our sensitive part can call up appropriate images and affections.[5]

This has now to be applied to the fittingness of the incarnation. There is a two-point argument. First, the incarnation is the principle of the restoration of the actual world order; as sinners are reconciled, the reign of sin is overthrown, nature is raised to its highest perfection, and God is communicated to creatures. Next, in regard to the manifestation *ad extra* of divine goodness, the restored order achieves this in the highest degree; as the infinite goodness of God is communicated to creatures, nature is perfected beyond the level proper to nature, and this communication of divine goodness is made to unworthy sinners.

Part 6 is headed 'On the Necessity of the Incarnation' ('De necessitate incarnationis'), though the title of the whole work had said 'contingency' ('contingentia') rather than 'necessity.' In their application, however, the two terms come to the same thing, for 'necessity' is discussed in order to deny it, and the denial of necessity is the affirmation of contingency. Lonergan's only concession to necessity is to grant the necessity arising from its own supposition ('ex suppositione sui'); this, of course, he got from Aquinas.[6]

Part 7, 'On the End of the Incarnation' ('Circa finem incarnationis'), is more complex, but the following four points offer a synopsis. The incarnation is for the sake of the order of the universe. Then, the incarnation is the principal part within the order of the universe. Third, the incarnation is the supreme benefit for single members of the human race, but in such a way that the race is subordinated to Christ and not Christ to the race. The fourth conclusion is that, given God's present decree, there would have been no incarnation had Adam not sinned. This says nothing about what would have been decreed in some hypothetical order in which Adam did not sin. It does not make sin a cause or a true condition or a true occasion of the incarnation, for those three all suppose an intelligibility, and sin has no intelligibility. It does not suppose sin to be willed by God or Christ or the just or the blessed. It supposes only that God permits sin. And it affirms only the order between end and means: take away the end and you remove the means. But given the present decree, the end of the incarnation is the restoration of the order of the universe; there is no restoration unless first there is loss; and there was no loss except through the sin of Adam.

This *opusculum* has some importance for the mediating role it might play in Lonergan's thought, namely, between 1935 and the unfinished work on historical causality in the work I am calling *de bono* (Chapter 9 below). The mediation found in chronology matches that found in thought. The dialectic of history and the restoration of world order through Christ are in continuity with the themes of the *pantón* paper on one side (1935) and with the more systematic treatment of *de bono* on the other (1958 – as I shall argue). In between we have *de ratione convenientiae* (1954) with its three-tiered structure of history: what human history would be if all followed the dictates of reason; what history actually becomes in the reign of sin; and the restoration when the reign of sin is destroyed and the human race recalled to a life in conformity with reason.

2. The Ontological and Psychological Constitution of Christ[7]

Like the 'De ratione convenientiae,' this slim volume (150 pp.) on *The Ontological and Psychological Constitution of Christ* has an importance out of proportion to its size. That is due in an obvious way to Lonergan's personal analogy for understanding the hypostatic union (quite different now from that of de la Taille), and especially to his ground-breaking treatment of the consciousness of Christ, but it is due in a less obvious way to his engagement with existentialist thought, a forecast of his 1957 lectures at Boston College on existentialism. Part 1 deals with the notion of a person, part 2 with the constitution of a finite person, part 3 with theological understanding, part 4 with the ontological constitution of Christ, parts 5 and 6 with human consciousness and the consciousness of Christ. Some of these questions are familiar to Scholasticism, but some of them are new, a presage of the radical move, now looming, beyond Scholasticism.

The order Lonergan assigns to the two main parts of the book might be challenged by his own reasoning: since 'conscious' or 'psychological' does not add to being, he says (otherwise it would be simply nothing), he will deal first (parts 1 to 4) with the ontological constitution of Christ and then (parts 5 to 6) with the psychological constitution.[8] This is strangely in conflict with his order in the *verbum* articles where he tried to start with the metaphysical but found the materials unmanageable in that order, so dealt first with the psychological.[9] Is this another irregularity in the battle line of our trench warfare? Quite possibly it is, and the same may be said of *De Verbo incarnato* (Chapter 6 below). 'Order,' however, is a gem of many facets, and different interests demand different orders; for example, the synthetic order of thinking is the reverse of the analytic order. I will give some attention to this later but the whole question calls for a more thorough study than I can give it in this essay.

In parts 1 to 4, therefore, we have two main questions: why the human nature assumed by Christ is not a human person, and why Christ-God and Christ-man are one and the same. He prefaces this with a discussion (part 3) dealing with the relation of theology as science to metaphysics as science: 'On Theological Understanding' ('De intelligentia theologica'). Turning in parts 5 and 6 to the psychological question he proposes the neglected view that consciousness is not perception of an object but experience of the subject (part 5, 'De conscientia humana': 'On Human Consciousness') and so concludes that Christ is not only the ontological subject of two natures but also the psychological subject of two consciousnesses. At the same time he sets forth the dialectical necessity of the many diverse views on this question (part 6, 'De conscientia Christi': 'On the Consciousness of Christ').[10]

There is no need for us to study all these questions. Therefore, setting aside the rest of Lonergan's book, I will consider the two topics on which his personal input is most significant: the hypostatic union, and the consciousness of Christ.

2.1. Metaphysics of the Hypostatic Union

The metaphysics of the hypostatic union had been studied in Lonergan's Christology courses of 1948 and 1952. He now both revises considerably his own doctrine of those years and deals more fully with opposed positions – from Tiphanus through de la Taille to Rahner. The difficulty of the question regards the unity of the God-man. There are those who see the hypostatic union constituted by relations: thus, Scotus, Tiphanus, and Suarez (117). There are those (not named) who appeal to an analogy in created things (117, 119, 121). More recent opinions are those of H. Diepen (121, 123, 125) and B. Xiberta (125, 127, 129, 131).

Lonergan himself, no longer a disciple of de la Taille, presents a very personal opinion. He appeals, as all theologians must eventually do, to an analogy. His analogy, however, is not an analogy of what we naturally know about the composition of a finite being; rather, it is an analogy of what we naturally know about the very Godhead. He takes his stand on the accepted doctrine that God, by one infinite act of knowing, *knows* both the necessary and the contingent and argues that in the same way by the one infinite act of being God *is* both the necessary and the contingent: the necessary, for God *is* the divine essence; and the contingent, for God *is* man.

Let us make the point in slightly different words: as an infinite knower by one and the same act of knowledge knows both what is contingent and what is necessary, and by one and the same act of willing wills both what is contingent and what is necessary, so by one and the same act of being, the infinite being is what God necessarily is, namely God, and is what God contingently is, namely man (131, 133, 135). If it did not do violence to the English language we could think of God as know-er, as will-er, and as be-er; in all three God is infinite act, of knowing, of willing, of being, whether the act regards the necessary or the contingent.

2.2. The Consciousness of Christ

The consciousness of Christ was a topic in the Christology of 1952 and will be again in that of 1960; *De constitutione Christi*, however, gives the fullest treatment. In all three Lonergan is conscious of entering new territory. As he said in defending his position against an attacker:

> The notion of the subject [that is, of a conscious person] is difficult, recent, and primitive … It is difficult … Everyone knows

he is a subject ... Not everyone knows the nature of the subject. ... The notion is also recent. If one wishes to find out what a soul is, one has only to read St Thomas. If one wishes to find out what a subject is, it is not enough to read ancient or medieval writers ... In the third place, the notion is primitive. It cannot be reached merely by combining other, better known concepts.[11]

Lonergan's position is that consciousness is not perception of an object, but inner experience of a subject. He defines consciousness as interior experience, in the strict sense, of oneself and one's acts. It is experience in the strict sense, that is, as understood in the compound of experience, understanding, and judgment. It is not, therefore, a perception, and Lonergan devotes a good part of his book to refuting the view that it is perception. Still less is it knowledge; consciousness of self and knowledge of self are two quite different things. Further, it is interior experience – not, therefore, the experience of seeing colours or hearing sounds or tasting flavours or any similar act of perception. All these have to do with an object. True, all of them are conscious acts and there is consciousness; but the consciousness is consciousness of oneself, not consciousness of an object, just as consciousness of one's acts is not consciousness of them as objects.[12]

The difficulty is the consequence of an ambiguity in that innocent little word 'of,' which we use for both perception and internal experience. I perceive a sound and so may say I have perception 'of' the sound. I experience an internal act and so may say I have experience 'of' that act. We then fall naturally into the supposition that we are dealing with the same 'of' in each case. But they are not the same; the first 'of' is of an object; the second is not of an object but of the subject and the subject's acts. Later Lonergan will rely more on the notion of consciousness as presence to oneself[13] (a notion already a theme in *De constitutione Christi*), and the difficulty is not so pressing. He does not, however, abandon his first definition, and the notion of human consciousness as experience instead of perception is one of his main contributions to the history of ideas.

But what of the consciousness of Christ? The problem arises because consciousness includes consciousness of self, and the self in Christ is divine: how can there be human consciousness of a divine self? Lonergan's resolution of this is quite simple: he merely applies the notions he had worked out so carefully in the preceding chapter. In the consciousness of Christ we are not dealing with knowledge of the divine but with

71

experience of the divine; we do not attain the divinity under the formality of being but under the formality of the experienced. I would put the matter in all simplicity as follows: Did the contemporaries of Christ see God in human form? Yes, but not God as affirmed or understood; they saw God under the formality of the experienced. More simply still: Did the birds and beasts of Palestine see the men and women of the time? Did they see God? Of course they did, but only as experienced by eye and ear. That God can be so experienced is simply part of the divine *kenosis*, in which God became man and hence able to be experienced.

I referred a moment ago to an attack on Lonergan's view of consciousness. It had appeared as an article in the journal *Divinitas* in 1958, attributing to Lonergan opinions that seemed to him little short of heresy. Lonergan's reply[14] is unusually vehement; he did not relish criticism that associated him with heresy. It belongs to his personal history, then, but it belongs also and especially to his Christology, going into greater detail on several points than the book had done. In terminology, too, it adds to the book. For example, the second part of the article, 'The Notion of the Subject' (162–79), and the third part, 'Christ as Subject' (179– 82), transpose into the terminology of the 'subject' what the book had put in the terminology of 'consciousness.'

3. Appendix to Chapter 5: The Boyer–Lonergan Relationship

As we begin our study of Lonergan's own independent treatise *De Verbo incarnato*, it is proper to add a note on the Boyer manual he is leaving behind. I have mentioned Boyer's 'satisfactio propria' and Lonergan's 'satisfactio vicaria,' but have not undertaken a detailed comparison of the two authors. Neither will I do so now. An overview of the Boyer manual may, however, be useful. My reference will be to the 1948 edition of his book, for almost certainly Lonergan used this, or a re-issue of it, in 1953, 1955, and 1957.

There are two parts: on the mystery of the incarnation ('De Incarnationis mysterio,' pp. 7–314) and on the passion of the Saviour ('De passione Salvatoris,' pp. 315–357). The three sections of the first part are on the existence of the mystery of the incarnation ('De exsistentia mysterii Incarnationis'), on the mode of union of the incarnate Word as regards the union itself, ('De modo unionis Verbi incarnati quantum ad ipsam unionem'), and on the consequences of the union ('De consequentibus unionem'). The second part has a single section with four theses, answering these questions: whether Christ ought to die for man's salvation, whether Christ immolated himself on the cross, whether in dying Christ made satisfaction for us, and whether we are reconciled to God by the passion of Christ. A comparison of Boyer's theses with the Brezovec 'reportatio' of Lonergan's course shows Lonergan following the theses of the book, but generally simplifying them.

6

De Verbo incarnato

Lonergan's *De Verbo incarnato* of 1960 is a manual of 741 pages, which became 546 pages in the more neatly printed (but otherwise almost unchanged) edition of 1961, and 598 pages in the revised third edition of 1964.[1] It covered the matter that a manual was expected to cover in that period, and most of it need not detain us, but there are more interesting points that reveal his personal input. Some of them deal with prolegomena: the structure of the book, its use of scripture, and the nature of the proof from scripture. Others are theological in the usual sense: the metaphysics of the hypostatic union, Christ's consciousness, his grace, the knowledge he had, his freedom, his role of mediation. Lonergan's short bibliography on the first page of each of the three editions is mildly interesting for its division titles: 'Biblica ... Patristica ... Theologica ... Manualia.' Manuals win a hearing!

1. Structure of *De Verbo incarnato*

The structure of the book has some peculiarities, due maybe to the fascicles being written and issued piecemeal as the course advanced, without a later tidying up of the order and the transitions. Parts 4 and 5, beginning at p. 313 and p. 445 respectively, are the only ones called 'parts' in 1964; so the first 312 pages somehow contain parts 1 to 3. How to divide those 312 pages into three parts is a neat but minor question. The first edition (1960) had three parts: part 2 ('On the things that belong to Christ': 'De iis quae Christi sunt') began on p. 419, and part 3 ('De Redemptione') began on p. 521. The 1961 edition anticipates that of 1964, with part 4 ('De iis quae Christi sunt') beginning on p. 314 and part 5 ('De Redemptione') on p. 391.

Skirting the problem of division into parts, I divide the whole book according to the numbering of the theses. The first ten of sixteen, or about half the book, deal specifically with the unity of the God-man, the hypostatic union. A summary as we begin part 4 (1964, 313) states that so far we have dealt with the hypostatic union according to the scriptures (thesis 1), according to the councils (theses 2 to 5), according to its ontological foundation (theses 6 to 9), and according to its psychological manifestation (thesis 10). The 1960 Index (p. 737) puts theses 6 to 9 under the heading 'Scholastics,' but the corresponding index is lacking in 1961 and 1964; similar bits of scattered data (see my next paragraph) give the impression of a work in progress.

Part 4 itself, on the things that belong to Christ ('de iis quae Christi sunt'), is put in sequence with the previous parts as follows. We have been dealing, Lonergan says (1964, 313), with the God-man, but God became man to share with us what is proper to himself, so we turn now to those properties: his grace, his knowledge, his impeccability, and his liberty. With these matters behind us, so Lonergan continues, part 5 will deal with the redemption ('Quibus peractis in quinta parte de redemptione nostra tractandum erit'). The 1961 edition has the same announcement (314) but the first edition (1960, 419) puts it differently: After the properties of Christ, in a third part we will deal with our redemption ('Quibus peractis in tertia quadam parte de redemptione nostra tractandum erit'). Thus part 3 of 1960 becomes part 5 in 1964!

When a third part comes to be a fifth it is clear that we are dealing with a work in progress. Adding to the puzzle is the difference in the number of fascicles: there were four in 1964, but five in 1961 (data for 1960 on this point are lacking). The last two sections preceding part 4 (ontological foundation and psychological manifestation) I will provisionally call part 3. I underline the point just made: what we are calling parts 1 to 3 (theses 1 to 10) are all, even thesis 1 on the New Testament, put under the heading of the hypostatic union.[2] If my surmise is right that Lonergan was providing fascicles for the printer one by one as he taught and wrote, we should attend to the architectural whole rather than to the scaffolding for the parts. Further study has the appeal of a detective story, but would create imbalance in the present volume.

2. Scripture and *De Verbo incarnato*

We shall see more in Chapter 11 of the rather radical change that Lonergan underwent some years later in his method of using scripture. In principle, however, the change occurred in 1955 when he decided to abandon a 'proof from scripture' that relied on what Jesus said as reported by the Evangelists and especially by John. Lonergan would now appeal rather to what John said as witness to the faith of the church in John's time and place.[3] But twenty years intervened between the change of mind recorded in 1955 and its implementation in 1975. Lonergan had to come to terms with the German Historical School and with human historicity in general and, as he repeatedly declared, this was a hard struggle and a long, drawn-out process (see Chapter 7 below).[4] Finally, there was full acceptance of the historicity of scripture.[5]

In his Gregorian period, however, Lonergan's Christology coalesces around the theme of truth, and indeed the truth of Catholic dogma. His *De Verbo incarnato* is constructed of seventeen theses, each of which affirms a truth. The pattern starts in thesis 1 with a statement and its authority: 'It is clear from the doctrine of the New Testament that ...' ('Ex doctrina Novi Testamenti constat ...'). His approach at the Gregorian is similar to his 1948 course, where he showed his concern to understand the process of truth (Chapter 4 above), though now a survey of various philosophies of truth, and of the repercussions of those views on theology, gives a more historical cast to his approach.[6]

One aspect, however, of his cognitional theory has a more specific application to scripture: the notion of 'schema' and the role in understanding of the schematic image or symbol or diagram. In *Verbum*, though the main cause of an act of direct insight is agent intellect, still the instrumental cause is 'a schematic image or phantasm.'[7] In *Insight* Lonergan distinguishes representative images from the symbolic image we have, say, in mathematical notations.[8] The reader might take the example of an infinity of numbers; we can conceive it – the very fact of talking about it supposes some kind of concept – but how can one imagine infinity? There is no way we can do that, but mathematicians have a symbol for it that comes to the aid of a helpless imagination, enabling us to talk about it, to use it in discussion, and to combine it with other symbols.

Lonergan's *De Verbo incarnato,* in its use of 'schematic' in the New Testament doctrine on the God–man, starts with the general notion of a schema (23–29) and Paul's synthetic schema (29–36). A schema, we are told, is a determinate conjunction of four elements: a name; a sensible presentation or imaginative representation; an act of understanding and its consequent formulation; and the act of faith in assent. If any component element is essentially altered, so too is the schema (23). In studying schemata we attend especially to what is easiest to know: that is, the name, and the image linked with the name. Of course, since revelation and tradition progress historically, so too do the schemata (24).

In the New Testament doctrine on Christ three schemata are note-worthy. The 'prospective' scheme is most characteristic of the synoptic gospels (24). The corresponding name here is 'Son of Man.' The image itself is complex. We have on one side the Lord in his earthly life, in converse with those around him. To this are linked two elements of the future: his passion and death, and the coming of the judge. So texts on the Son of Man tend to be divided into three classes: his life on earth; his passion, death, and resurrection; and his future coming. Lonergan gives multiple references to all three.

There is also a 'retrospective' schema (24), often found in Paul. The corresponding name here is Lord, or Christ, or Son of God in power. The image is again complex: we have the risen Jesus represented as sitting at the right hand of the Father; but linked with this in retrospect is an image going back through the earthly life to his pre-existence in the beginning and his role in creation.

Third, there is an 'inverse retrospective' schema; for example: Philippians 2:6-11. It begins with the pre-existent one who came into the world, died, and was glorified to reign now in heaven (25).

All three types have a temporal succession, but that is not necessary to a schema (26). Paul's schema consists originally in the nexus of similars, in the nexus of dissimilars, and in the transition from dissimilarity to similarity (29, and see 29–36). John has a general schema in which Jesus begins from a sensible fact or a dispute to bring his hearers to a more profound understanding, and so lead them to mystery (26). Later gen-erations had their own schemata, such as the Logos-sarx of the Arians and others, and the Logos-anthropos of various church Fathers. But when in the course of time theologians begin to speak of 'Christ as God' or 'Christ as man,' they have gone beyond the field of schemata and are in the field of concepts (26).

What is the value of schemata? In Lonergan's view (27) they confirm the historicity of the New Testament (I take this to mean historicity in the apologetic sense) showing the complex process in which the apostles and early Christians learned from concrete events. Next, they contain the doctrine of one person in two natures, for we use schemata to bring several elements into unity; thus our three schemata either start from the human to arrive at the divine or proceed from a pre-existent one to the humanity. Third, they are a remedy for both anachronism and archaism, both of which fail to see that the same doctrine in the course of time is expressed in diverse schemata as well as in evolving concepts. Fourth, they are a help to accurate understanding of a text, for they introduce distinctions and determine differences; then, in what is distinct and de-terminate they show similarities, additions, interconnections – a great advantage when we are dealing with a process of teaching and learning, one in which we proceed by slow increments, adding new elements to what has gone before.

Lonergan sees his schemata as relating in particular to proving the divinity of Christ (28–29). Just to start with, they show exactly what is contained in the sources of doctrine. More directly to the present purpose, it is one thing to say 'Jesus is true God' and to find this proved in the correct understanding of a text; it is another to achieve that correct understanding, in which the schemata can be a considerable help. Third, the New Testament proof of Christ's divinity consists especially in seeing two movements coalesce. In the first movement the one who as a general rule is called God begins to be called God the Father and finally is often called simply the Father *tout court*. In the other movement the one who is a man and is known to all as a man is also one who participates in many ways in the divine, doing miracles, correcting the law of Moses, taking away sin, and so on; further, he is one who is pre-existent in divine glory as the image of God and as the Son who, though from the Father, is the equal of the Father. The two movements coalesce in this way: the beginning is from the concepts of the one God and a particular man; the end is the concept of two, Father and Son, who share the divine name.

3. 'De argumento theologico ex sacra scriptura'

This short document (only four pages) is the set of notes Lonergan wrote in 1962, in preparation for a seminar with professors from the Gregorian University and the Biblical Institute in Rome.[9] A book by E. Gutwenger (*Bewusstsein und Wissen Christi*, Innsbruck, 1960), discussing the use of 'I' by Jesus, gave Lonergan the theme, and he takes up the question of 'proving' from scripture such an interpretation as Gutwenger proposes.

After setting forth Gutwenger's position (1–2), and giving a logical, methodological, and critical analysis of his argument (2–3), Lonergan asks whether it is a typical example. This question divides into three:

first, did the Fathers, the Scholastics, the dogmatic theologians after Melchior Cano draw questions from a post-biblical context? Second, did they define these questions through that post-biblical context? And third, did they solve these questions through loci selected here and there from the scriptures (3)?

Lonergan's own positive contribution to the discussion begins by offering a list of the various aspects under which the scriptures are invoked, either in practice or thematically ('exercite vel signate'). Scripture, he says, can be considered in many ways: for example, as a use of language, and then we engage in philology; or as expression, and so we have romantic hermeneutics; or as encounter ('occursus') and then there is an existential change in the readers, a conversion; or as the source of multiple encounters (tradition, doctrine, system); or as concerned with events, whence we have biblical history and biblical studies; or as obscure, as badly understood, where exegetical labour is required; finally, it can be considered as the word of God, which we may not contradict, and so we have dogma (3).

Lonergan then sets up the various contexts in which discussion occurs: first, the dogmatico-theological context systematically explained since the Middle Ages and today historically derived by modern writers (3); second, the context of human life understood in living ('existenziell') but explained by the phenomenological philosopher ('existenzial'); third, the Pauline context understood by Paul as the one providing the context ('pensée pensante') but not explained by him (4); and fourth, the Pauline context understood by an exegete as to be given a context ('pensée pensée'), where, however, it is disputed how far the context admits explanation. There is a reference here to the use of Heidegger's categories in Bultmann, and of Aristotle's in the Thomists (4).

Lonergan offered the foregoing ideas on theme and context as possibly useful for discussion in the seminar, but for his own position we must go back in the document to the remarks he made from a logical, from a methodological, and from a critical viewpoint. The third of these is characteristic. He asks, namely, what the possibility is for a transition from context to context, and what the foundation might be for such a transition; the answer, he says, seems to be the transcendence of truth. Truth has a public character: it transcends the context in which it may be uttered, it can be transposed into other contexts, it can be communicated. For example, a doctor questions the patient and transposes the answers into medical categories; for another example, a judge questions the witnesses, not in order to take part in some human tragedy, but to transpose the words of the witnesses into juridical categories (3).

We have no report on the proceedings of this 1962 seminar – a pity, for it is packed with challenges, and the notes provided in advance are in large part just headings for discussion. Notice that when I spoke of presenting Lonergan's own position my concern was not his position on the 'I' of Christ (that will engage us presently as we explore the consciousness of Christ, below), but the light *De argumento* throws on Lonergan's use of scripture. Nor is it the point of this short section to exegete particular passages in scripture – Lonergan kept insisting (not always following his own advice) that exegesis of scripture is the task of specialists. His concern here is not the content of scripture but the way we use scripture, and beyond that, the broader concern that applies to all questions: namely, putting Christology in a modern context and arguing from the ancient documents of tradition.

4. Consciousness of Christ

From the 598 pages of Lonergan's *De Verbo incarnato* (1964), I select four topics of greater interest for Lonergan studies: the consciousness of Christ, the knowledge had by Christ, the liberty of Christ, and redemption. I omit the metaphysics of the hypostatic union, which was sufficiently studied in *De constitutione Christi* (the consciousness of Christ was also studied there, but *De Verbo incarnato* adds some revisions).

First, then, the view of consciousness in the *De Verbo incarnato* of 1964. The basic position remains: human consciousness is interior experience, in the strict sense, of oneself and of one's acts. The 'adversary' remains the same: consciousness as 'perception' (playing a role in Christology analogous to that of conceptualism in epistemology). But there is a change: the concept of presence comes to the fore and in the *De Verbo incarnato* from 1960 to 1964 consciousness is primarily seen as presence to oneself. True, the concept of presence to self was already explicit in the 1956 work,[10] but it was not a key concept there. In the trinitarian work of 1957, however, Lonergan begins a new approach to the question.

Now he proposes three steps toward a concept of presence. One can think of merely local propinquity, as one stone is next to another, but we do not say it is present to the other. We move to presence when there is a certain psychic adaptation, and thus one animal is present to another. A third step belongs to intellectual beings in whom the one known is in the one knowing and the one loved is in the one loving. As the poet said, A friend is the very half of his soul.[11] The theme, then, is not presence to self, but rather the presence in us of the divine inhabiting persons: the presence therefore of person to person. Still, the varieties of presence listed there widen the context for presence to self.

Thus, *De Verbo incarnato* in both 1960 and 1964 tells of another triad of presence. There are three senses in which we say something is present (1964, 267). One way is locally, physically, ontologically present – presence without knowledge (Lonergan has extended the notion to make local propinquity a sort of presence). In the second way something is present as an object – as colours are present to those who see them. In the third way one is present as a subject – by the very fact that someone sees colours, that person is present to self as seeing. This last, defined as 'that by which a subject is present to oneself and the acts of a subject are present to the subject,'[12] is consciousness.

A few pages later (1964, 272) the concept is set forth once more: there is local presence, as everyone has his face present; there is the presence of an object as everyone may have his face present in a mirror; and there is a third presence, namely, presence to oneself. This last is not had in deep sleep; it begins if one dreams; it is greatly heightened when one wakes; it gains an intellectual quality if one inquires, understands, and so on; it gains a rational quality when one reflects on one's ideas and makes a judgment; finally, it acquires its full perfection when one goes beyond truth to good and to responsible action.

As light is seen by light, so consciousness is known by consciousness (273, 'innotescit'). There is not some other presence by which this third presence is known ('cognoscatur') but it is in itself a kind of knowledge ('notitia').[13]

5. Knowledge Had by Christ

The grace of Christ is the first topic Lonergan treats in part 4 of his manual ('de iis quae Christi sunt'), but his traditional approach adds little to our history and may be omitted. It is true that one question (326), 'Whether every grace is a grace of Christ' ('Utrum omnis gratia sit gratia Christi'), is eyecatching in the context of the present sharp debate about the grace given to non-Christians, but Lonergan's question turns out to be the stock one on the grace the angels receive: is it the grace of Christ? Lonergan opts for the affirmative!

I turn, then, to the question of the knowledge Christ had (avoiding the ambiguous phrase 'knowledge of Christ' – is 'of' objective or subjective?). This had been discussed in *De constitutione Christi*, but mainly in the context of consciousness and its distinction from knowledge. In *De Verbo incarnato* it gets full coverage in its own right. Moreover, Lonergan did further work on the question between 1960 and 1964: in 1960 the thesis on the knowledge Christ had ran from page 446 to page 485; in 1964 it runs from page 332 to page 416. Some forty pages have become more than eighty.

The knowledge Christ had was an old question in Scholastic Christology, one on which the tradition, based largely on the Gospel of John, attributed almost boundless knowledge to the human mind of Christ, including the beatific vision. While Lonergan held with the tradition that Christ had immediate knowledge of God, from the start he had his own explanation of this doctrine (1960, 464–80). He took his time, however, in formulating his own doctrine; the formulation of 1960 (and 1961) was brevity itself: 'Besides divine knowledge Christ had human knowledge: blessed, infused, and acquired' ('Praeter scientiam divinam Christus habuit scientiam humanam et beatam et infusam et acquisitam')[14] – two lines to Boyer's ten, and adding nothing to Aquinas! Quite different is the edition of 1964. Not only is there a new formulation of the doctrine, but there is a very thorough examination of the tradition, from the Gnostics and Arians through the Fathers up to the Middle Ages.[15] It is that new formulation that we have to study. Thesis 12 in Lonergan's 1964 manual reads as follows in translation:

> Besides divine knowledge Christ living here on earth had human knowledge, both effable and ineffable; for as comprehensor he both knew God immediately by ineffable knowledge, also called beatific knowledge, and by the same act but mediately knew everything else that pertained to his mission ('munus'); as pilgrim, however, he elicited by effable knowledge those cognitive acts, natural and supernatural, which constituted his human and historical life.[16]

This is a remarkable body of doctrines and spread of ideas. The 'human and historical life' of Jesus comes up for study below in Chapter 10. My present interest is in the concepts of 'effable' (a neologism in both English and Latin) and 'ineffable' as applied to the created and finite knowledge Christ had. His ineffable knowledge is the traditional 'immediate knowledge of

God,' but the new term directs attention to the difficulty of formulating in 'effable' terms what is beyond formulation and so is 'ineffable.' Both terms point to the interior life of Christ and its expression; the latter, however, is declared impossible by the term 'ineffable' itself – we are reminded of what the mystics tell us of their life of prayer.

If beatific knowledge is ineffable we can approach it only by way of analogy, and the analogy that Lonergan favours has two aspects: the light of intellect, and the notion of being. On the knowledge given by the light of intellect he quotes Thomas: 'in this light all knowledge is in some way originally given us.'[17] The notion of being is our intending intention of being which is not restricted to any genus but proceeds beyond every genus even to ask whether God is and what God is.

What we, therefore, by the natural light of intellect intend and desire but do not as yet know is what Christ the man saw in immediate knowledge. What intending does in us, immediate knowledge did in him. For just as we proceed from the intention of being to the acquisition of our effable knowledge, so also the man Christ proceeded from his ineffable knowledge to the formation of his effable knowledge.[18]

Such is Lonergan's basic analogy for Christ's knowledge of God, but I believe that, with the help of a hint from him, we can find another analogy for this ineffable knowledge: namely, the experience of the mystics. For we may suppose that what the mystics have, once we get below the superstructure of their accounts, Christ too had in even greater measure. Further, despite its being ineffable – one might say *because* it is ineffable – the mystics speak about it at length, but we have no similar account from Christ of his experience, and it would be the height of anachronism to think of him speaking as the mystics do. May we not, however, use analogously the wealth of mystical accounts to give us some idea of the experience Christ had?

Though Lonergan does not seem to have used this analogy here, he does hint at it.[19] Further still, elsewhere he compares the experience of Thomas Aquinas with that of Teresa of Avila. On Thomas he writes: 'At the end of his life his prayer became so intense that it interfered with his theological activity.' In contrast, 'Teresa of Avila combined prayer and business.' Lonergan suggests that Thomas, had he lived, might have reached a later stage in which, like Teresa, he would combine prayer with the 'business' of theology.[20]

There are, then, different degrees of mystical experience, but for present purposes it is enough to postulate a close parallel between Jesus and Teresa – the former having immediate knowledge of God but perhaps keeping silent about it, the latter having knowledge analogous to that of Jesus and speaking as articulately about it as she can. It is true that we understand neither the experience of Teresa nor that of Jesus, but at least Teresa by her own analogies tries to communicate with us. Thus, if mystical experience is analogous to that of Christ, by an analogy of an analogy she tries to give us some dim understanding of Christ's experience.

What about all that John says on the knowledge the Son had of the Father? I have mentioned the rather important shift by which Lonergan came to see John's Gospel, not as direct witness to what Jesus said but as witness rather to the faith of Christians in John's time and place. So it is worth repeating that in 1964 he had still not put into practice the new exegesis; it remains, in our metaphor of trench warfare, a delayed sector. Further, it is also worth noting that in *De Verbo incarnato* (384–89) he remains adamant on continuity between what Christ knew in immediate knowledge of God and what John reports Christ as saying.

6. The Liberty of Christ

I have remarked that Lonergan's thesis on grace, as stated in *De Verbo incarnato*, was quite traditional. In contrast, his doctrine on the liberty Christ had shows Lonergan at his deepest and most original, and this from early on. The problem arises in a number of ways. Christ's human will follows his divine will and does so without resistance. Further, Christ had the beatific vision through which he knew all his acts, even his future acts, and this does not seem compatible with his freedom. Further still, Christ had a mandate from his Father to lay down his life, and disobedience was impossible for him (427). What does all this say about the liberty of Christ?

The two key concepts are divine transcendence and the 'extrinsic term' ('terminus ad extra') of divine contingent willing. The latter is simple: when God knows and wills and effects our free act, the extrinsic term is our free act itself.[21] Divine transcendence is not so simple. Lonergan gives a full definition here (433–34), but since his position remained constant from 1940 to the end, we may use the shorter form in his doctoral dissertation: 'God knows with equal infallibility, he wills with equal irresistibility, he effects with equal efficacy, both the necessary and the contingent.'[22] The 'contingent' in question is the free act of a human being (the 'terminus ad extra'). Christ enjoyed freedom as much as, and even more than, the rest of the human race.

Lonergan has his own list of difficulties against the freedom of Christ. I will focus on the fourth, which in my view is the real difficulty. It states that Christ not only knew his future acts, he also knew he ought to choose according to the least will of the Father; his knowledge of his future acts obliged an obedient Son and so removed liberty (436–39).

Lonergan has both a halfway answer to this and a basic answer. The halfway answer is that the Father's mandate was to some extent indeterminate; the mandate to die left open various options for dying, and so gave Christ freedom to choose. But that is not the basic answer; for if we suppose a mandate fully determined, it would remove freedom if it is prior to Christ's choice. The basic answer therefore is that the Father's mandate is not prior in time to Christ's free choice. The case is rather that the two acts (God's determinate mandate and Christ's obedience) are involved simultaneously in the same truth ('in eodem signo veritatis'), so that it is not a prior truth that the Father gives the precept and a subsequent truth that the Son obeys.'[23] The Father's precept is not prior, then, to the Son's obedience (438); the two are inseparably simultaneous.

The same difficulty had been presented in 1954, in the two pages attached to the notes *De ratione convenientiae* (see Chapter 5 above), and was given substantially the same answer. On one level of thought the Father's mandate was not fully determinate till the Agony in the Garden (Christ could have had twelve legions of angels come to his aid; Matthew 26:52). But in this work, too, the basic answer applies even when the mandate is fully determinate: namely, the Father does not issue a precept prior to his knowing and willing; but his knowing and willing as true are simultaneous ('in signo simultaneo') with Christ's free choice. Therefore, the Father's precept is 'in signo simultaneo veritatis' with the choice made by Christ.'[24]

The phrase 'in eodem signo veritatis' and its alternate form 'in signo simultaneo veritatis' are very hard to translate, but the meaning is clear enough. Two truths are inextricably involved with one another, and involved simultaneously, so that on the level of true statement neither one has priority: namely, the truth that God wills the occurrence of x and the truth that x is occurring.

7. Redemption

This fourth note (see p. 76, above) deals with Lonergan's three theses on redemption, the last three in the volume *De Verbo incarnato*. Those acquainted with the book will spontaneously, and rightly, expect me to stress the Law of the Cross, and I will indeed come to that. But first I call attention to another and somewhat neglected doctrine: the manner in which the Father is active in our redemption. It is his hatred of sin, a hatred shared by the Son, that is a prime mover in the redeeming process. We naturally think first of the Son: in accepting the cross he is expressing his hatred of sin and his sorrow for the offence sin is against his Father. As part 8 of thesis 16 puts it: 'The satisfaction of Christ adds to his vicarious passion and death an expression of the most profound hatred of all sins and the most profound sorrow for every offence against God.'[25] But for Lonergan, the Son's sorrow for our sins has its original expression in the Father's hatred for sin; the Father, too, and primarily the Father, is speaking to us from the cross, is expressing in the sufferings of the Son the hatred that he, the Father, has for sin: 'That hatred of sin which Christ expressed through the passion and death that he accepted, that same hatred God too expresses.'[26]

Illuminated here is another aspect of the redemption needing more attention: the redemption as revelation. Notice the references to 'expression' in the quoted passages: 'The satisfaction of Christ adds to his vicarious passion and death an expression of the most profound hatred of all sins ...' And, 'That hatred of sin which Christ expressed through the passion and death that he accepted, that same hatred God too expresses ...' There is an utterance, someone has spoken, a statement has been made. God is not only saving the world but is also revealing the divine hatred of sin in a way that was never done before, that never could be done before; and in that revelation, as everywhere in the divine saving work, the primacy belongs to the Father as he speaks to us from the cross. The flow of thought is not from us to God, but from God to us.

Of course, there remains the direction from us to God, and par excellence from the Son as one of us to God the Father; the Son fully accepts the Father's utterance, fully accepts the judgment on sin that his passion and death will express, and desires with the full weight of his love and reverence for the Father to make reparation by his passion and death for the offence we have committed. The Son's 'statement,' made on the cross, is both his agreement with the Father's judgment and his obedient acceptance of the Father's sentence of death. But always the initiative belongs to the Father, as obedience does to the Son.

This doctrine is in line with Lonergan's general approach to the incarnation as a work of God, undertaken on the initiative of God, giving primacy always to God. Even the doctrine of Christ's mediation of grace centres on the Father: Christ is the mediator of all grace because the love of the Father for the eternal Son is extended to the Son as man, and through the Son to the sons by adoption (325). There is perhaps a debt here to the Ignatian Spiritual Exercises on the incarnation. In any case, Lonergan elsewhere takes issue with those who accept only a Christology from below; he holds for both a Christology from below and a Christology from above, but the primacy in systematic theology must be given to the God above.[27]

Having said all that, I turn more readily to the Law of the Cross, which has captured the interest of so many and is regarded by them as Lonergan's main contribution to the theology of the redemption. It is stated as follows in thesis 17: 'The Son of God was for this reason made man, suffered, died, and was raised again, because divine wisdom ordained and divine goodness decided not to remove the evils of the human race by an exercise of power but according to the just and mysterious law of the cross to convert those evils into a highest good.'[28]

As stated in the explanation of terms, this Law comprises three steps (1964, 556): first, from the evil of guilt to the evil of punishment; next, the voluntary transformation of punishment into good; and third, the blessing of this transformation by God the Father (note again the role of God the Father). The law is found in Christ as an individual man, in Christ as the new Adam, and in us as his members. But there is a difference. The law is found in Christ as in the principle of our redemption, as in him who was made for those obeying him the cause of eternal life (Hebrews 5:9). It is found in us as in the 'material' to be redeemed; it is rational material, to be sure, which ought to learn and believe, which freely consents to Christ in love, which lives in Christ, operates through Christ, is united with Christ, to be assimilated and conformed to Christ dying and rising from the dead (556–57; and see 558).

The process of the Law of the Cross is clarified in the scriptural proof. The first element is the fact of sin and of death as its punishment (568). Then there is the transformation of death, not as a leap to new realities but a transformation of death itself: the exaltation of Christ was due to his obedience unto death, and the same transformation is found in us, for Christ was handed over because of our sins and rose for our justification (569). This transformation of death is accomplished in Christ not only as an individual but also in Christ as head of the body. In Christ and in us it involves two things: voluntary acceptance of evil or punishment, and the subsequent blessing of God the Father (570; 'subsequent' here is relative to a part in a series, but the whole series is subsequent to the Father's mandate; that remains primary). It is prescribed for us as love of our enemies, as the wisdom of losing one's life in order to gain it, according to the example of the seed dying in order to bear fruit and according to the blessedness promised to the patient (571). And we are reminded that the resurrection, no less than death, is proposed for our example (573).

Critique of Scholasticism

W e are at the end of an era. This trite old phrase does in fact describe the situation. If the metaphor of a trajectory were to apply, we might say that the high Scholasticism of the two 1964 volumes (*De Deo trino* and *De Verbo incarnato*) had reached the end of its flight path, and the projectile needed new impetus to continue its journey. But that metaphor does not apply. There is indeed a new impetus, not to renew the old trajectory but rather to restructure theology in the radical new situation established by the insight of February 1965 on the eight functional specialties. I began this book with an insistence on continuity (Chapter 1 above) and I am not reneging on that commitment, but I found in the metaphor of trench warfare a way of conceiving a discontinuous continuity, and that is my guide as we enter the new era.

So now more than ever that metaphor applies: a battle front that is a jagged line with outposts and delayed sectors. But I would modify the application in a significant way: it is not so much a matter of outposts and delayed sectors on one front, as it is a matter of different battle fronts and different campaigns seeking an integrating idea. Not that we any longer expect an objectively integral theology like that of St Thomas, but perhaps an integrated view of *doing theology* is possible. In any case the old front had become a stalemate, but elsewhere salients of varying character had been forming, notably in Lonergan's graduate courses at the Gregorian, with their counterpart in summer institutes in the United States, Ireland, and Canada. I think of the 1957 lectures on existentialism at Boston College and of the 1959 course *De intellectu et methodo* at the Gregorian University. Besides these more ambitious campaigns, there are the sallies of half a hundred lectures, articles, reviews, and interviews that echo the *parola nuova* his Roman students found in his courses.

1. Point of Arrival

It will help to understand the transition if we look ahead to the point of arrival: not, perhaps, the arrival of the new Christology but of the new theology that will generate new Christologies, and not so much the arrival of a new theology *in facto esse* but the arrival of a new theology or theologies *in fieri*. The *De Verbo incarnato* of 1964 was written in the triple context of Scholasticism, Thomism, and a theological method of proving theses that derives from Melchior Cano.[1] Lonergan was affected, positively or negatively and in different degrees, by all three. But great changes were on the way, and they would greatly affect Christology as they would all other branches of theology.

Under the five headings Lonergan used in 1968 to characterize the time, the new theology was a move from logic to method, from an Aristotelian view of science to a modern conception, from soul to subject, from human nature to human history, and from first principles to transcendental method.[2] In greatest brevity what we seek to define is the arrival of historical consciousness: 'By historical consciousness I shall mean what I believe to be the nucleus, the core, the key to what is meant by "modernity," "modern man," "the modern world." No less than modern science, the modern world cannot be overlooked by contemporary theology; if modernism was condemned by Pius X, "aggiornamento" was demanded by John XXIII.'[3]

2. German Historical School

A strong agent in introducing Lonergan to modernity in the field of history was the German Historical School. Asked later about the change in his thinking after *Insight*, he replied: 'It was being sent to Rome and having to deal with students … who were totally immersed in continental philosophy … it involved getting a hold of the whole movement of the *Geisteswissenschaften*.'[4] It was not easy, this initiation into historical thinking. On the contrary, 'It was a long struggle that can be documented from my Latin and English writing during this period and from the doctoral courses I conducted.'[5]

The last spike in nailing down the transition seems to have come from his reading a book by Peter Hünermann, but there is an ambiguity to be noted here, for the concepts of historical consciousness and historicity had been worked out several years before his encounter with

Hünermann. What he learned from the latter, then, must have been new light not on historicity as a human trait but on history as a science, history as set forth in chapters 8 and 9 of *Method*, history that up to then the German Historical School had not fully clarified for him.[6] It is clear, in any case, that in the second half of the 1960s his work on *Method* was held up till he had mastered the position and work of the German Historical School, clear too that the Hünermann book gave him the last step toward that mastery.[7] In a long-range view, his sojourn in Rome, 1953–65, put him in contact with European thought on the *Geisteswissenschaften*. There had indeed been a great breakthrough to the functional specialties of *Method* in February 1965.[8] This gave him the structure of history, Hünermann gave him the role of history as a science, and with that his critique of the twenty-five years of Scholasticism had what it needed.

3. '... twenty-five years under impossible conditions'

I have described, as I see it, the transition in Lonergan's thinking in the 1960s. But, of course, he did not know all this in 1960 or 1964. The term of a transition is hidden from its inception. This has its importance for understanding his critique of Scholasticism and its timing. Starting around the year 1970, in one situation after another, he became extremely critical of the theological method that during a quarter of a century he had endured and some extent followed in his own work. Of course he had been critical of Catholic thought far back in his student days, but there was a new edge in his critique from 1970 on.

Here are some of his criticisms: '... the situation I was in was hopelessly antiquated, but had not yet been demolished – it has since been demolished.'[9] '... acceptance of the new, highly specialized methods made it evidently ridiculous to suppose that a single mind could master not only all the Scriptures, but also all the Fathers, councils, and theologians, not to mention the *sensus fidelium*.'[10] 'I taught theology for twenty-five years under circumstances that I considered absurd. And the reason why they were absurd was for lack of a method, or because of the survival of a method that should have been buried two hundred years ago.'[11] 'The result of these innovations has been to eliminate the old style dogmatic theologian ... [They] reveal [his] performance ... to be simply out of date.'[12] 'I taught theology for twenty-five years under impossible conditions.'[13]

Note that these statements are not directed against Scholasticism alone or against particular details, but against the whole system of seminary education. Note further that all these critiques are dated 1970 or later. Something new seems to have entered Lonergan's thought around that time to focus his critical aim; the 'new' was not historicity, which was lucidly set forth in what seems to be the 1964 Georgetown file; it was not historical consciousness, which was part of his mental furniture in *Topics in Education* back in 1959. The new, in my opinion, was what he learned from Hünermann's book. Once history found its place, the rest fell into line: historicity as an objective fact and part of human nature, historical consciousness as subjective awareness of historicity, history as the concrete determination of historicity, and the Hünermann book as the science of critical history.

Prior to the realization of all this in the early 1970s, was Lonergan's criticism muted? Had he been slow to realize the historical deficiency in what he had, perhaps tacitly, accepted, and was his sharp critique now directed as much against his own early work as it was against the backward spirit of the times? I do not think there is a simple yes or no answer to these questions. Of course, his criticism of the state of Catholic thought goes far back; it is found in his letter of January 1935 to his then Religious Superior. True enough, the article of 1954 on 'Theology and Understanding' already shows an openness to new ways of thinking; on the other hand, it gives good marks to the theological education of the past as preparation for priestly ministry.[14] True also, he was quite critical early on of particular features of the church's program for studies and would remark that it was framed for a time before we had electric lights and printing presses to make reading a rival to listening ('Nostri auditores possunt legere!'), but that did not touch the intrinsic merits of seminary education. Add to the puzzle the fact that in his own Scholastic period Lonergan made some use of Cano's method of proving theses. He may have taught theology for twenty-five years under impossible conditions, but he understood this much better at the end of the twenty-five years than at their beginning.

There was, then, a learning period in which he came to a firmer grasp of the new situation of theology. The 1967 paper 'Theology in Its New Context' goes deeper and does speak more explicitly of theology as having fallen behind the times, even giving that event a fairly precise date.[15] In that paper Lonergan was building momentum for his critiques, so they do not come out of the blue. Still, they show a new severity, and if I am right in my surmise about the influence of Hünermann, it may be that only around 1969 did Lonergan come to realize with full clarity what the fundamental defect in Catholic thought was, and so how it might be remedied.[16] But again we must beware of oversimplification, for his doctoral dissertation (1940) shows a keen interest in scientific history, and as we have seen, at that time he had wanted already to make history the focus of his life work. It may be a case again of the jagged front in the battle line!

Nevertheless, in a time of widespread chaos one had to find a centre between a solid, immovable right and a scattered left.[17] As always for Lonergan it was the truth that was the carrier of thought through the transitions that seemed so threatening to many. If his religion was the carrier of his orthodoxy in a time of changing theology (see Chapter 1 above), it was the role of truth to provide the objective correlative of that religion. In any case it should be noted explicitly that the crisis that played such havoc in the church of the late 1960s and early 1970s was not a crisis of faith:'The crisis … is a crisis not of faith but of culture. There has been no new revelation from on high to replace the revelation given through Christ Jesus. There has been written no new Bible, and there has been founded no new church, to link us with him.'[18] One of Lonergan's great contributions to the theology of the time was his study of its new cultural context. We might page through the chapters of *A Second Collection*, see how often this is his theme, and remember that the papers of that volume cover the years 1966 to 1973, the years of 'crisis' in the church.

4. 'Sed contra …': Praise for Scholasticism

There is an important caveat to be entered before we leave this chapter: with all his critiques of Scholasticism, Lonergan never lost his respect for that phase of Catholic thought. In the very last of his published papers he wrote as follows:

Scholastic theology was a monumental achievement. Its influence on the church has been profound and enduring. Up to Vatican II … it has provided much of the background whence proceeded pontifical documents and conciliar decrees …

The defects of Scholasticism, then, were the defects of its time. It could not inspect the methods of modern history and thereby learn the importance of history in theology. It could not inspect modern science and thereby correct the mistakes in Aristotle's conceptual system. But if we cannot blame the Scholastics for their shortcomings, we must undertake the task of remedying them ...[19]

We should not, therefore, regard these twenty-five years of Scholasticism as a sadly lost period, wasted when Lonergan was at the height of his powers. If one has to choose between two sequences, in one of which a highly intellectual period comes first and a highly historicist period second, and another order in which the sequence is reversed, I would prefer the order that puts the intellectual first, and the historical second. My reason is simple: knowledge at any time makes a bloody entrance, but to go from the appealing patterns of history to the grim and unrelenting procedures of strictly intellectual thinking is, to use Peter's words in Acts 15:10, imposing a burden that neither we nor our ancestors were able to bear. In my preferred order, one gets the best of two worlds; in the opposed order one is in danger of never really mastering the intellectual world. Add to this the significant detail that Lonergan credited his years of teaching theology with his acceptance of modernity.[20]

This is a book on Christology, yet in this chapter I have barely mentioned that topic. That is true, but it is easily explained. Christology divides into a Scholastic period and a historicist period; study of the former is concluded in Chapter 8, and study of the latter, too far-reaching to be contained in a paragraph or two, awaits its turn for a full exposition. The present chapter, then, is transitional (as are chapters 9 and 10); it is an entity in motion. Such an entity, Aquinas would maintain after Aristotle, lacks determinate intelligibility; it is not something, but is on the way to being something.[21] Nevertheless, this Chapter 7 is in a deeper way profoundly Christological, for it deals with the dynamism that moves us from one type of Christology to another.

8

Modernism, Dogma, Truth

For better perspective on the recent period of turmoil in the church and on Lonergan's involvement in it, I wish now to examine his position on modernism and on the dogma of the councils (Chapter 8). I will then conclude this chaotic transitional part of my book with a study of the tantalizing work *de bono* (Chapter 9), which in some ways is equipped to play a mediating role between the earlier and the later Lonergan.

I mentioned in Chapter 4 that Lonergan interrupted his Christology lectures of 1948 to give his class an account of modernism. At that time, following step by step the papal encyclical on modernism (*Pascendi dominici gregis*, 1907), Lonergan set forth, simply as a reporter, the doctrine of the encyclical.[1] By and large he seems to identify himself with *Pascendi*, though at the end of his exposition he provides a more personal view, a summary of the historical movement that led to modernism, as well as a Catholic philosophy of truth and related issues. Such was the mentality when he began to teach theology in the 1940s.

His position twenty years later is not quite so simple. He recognized 'the fact that modern developments were covered over with a larger amount of wickedness. ... One may lament it but one can hardly be surprised that at the beginning of this century [1900], when churchmen were greeted with a heresy that logically entailed all possible heresies, they named the new monster modernism.'[2] His own later position would seem to be this: accept the features that belong to modernity (modern science, modern scholarship, modern philosophy), and reject the features that turn modernity into the heresy of modernism. But in 1948 he was not only a long way from studying the German Historical School, he was also locked into a system that he would later criticize quite severely (see Chapter 7 above). It would take some years for him to realize that

95

Scholasticism had ceased to be the ruling force in Catholic thought; even then a satisfactory replacement had not appeared. Nor could it appear without pain and turmoil.[3]

1. Dogma and the Councils

Lonergan may have come later to see more clearly the positive intent of modernism, but he never changed his conservative position on dogma: dogma was truth, and the truth is not negotiable. On the other hand, he came to realize that dogma in Scholastic form is not the word of life for the people of God. Further, there was the vexing problem of relating dogma to scripture.

Two transitions were needed to satisfy these needs. The first, a preoccupation early on, was the transition from the New Testament to dogma and Scholastic theology. The other, only later recognized as a distinct question, was the transition from Scholasticism (or, more generally, from doctrine and systematics) to communication with the people of God. A rough summary of the two might be first, from the people to the theologians, and then from the theologians back to the people. His Christology is involved in both of these questions.

For the first transition it matters little whether we are studying Lonergan's Christology or his trinitarian theology; he covers much the same ground in the relevant parts of the two treatises. There is, however, a problem of bibliographical economy, because he dealt with this question so often. My bibliography will be selective, but one work that has to be mentioned is *The Way to Nicea*.[4] Though it is specifically trinitarian and takes us only to the Council of Nicea, it deals with questions common to the Trinity and Christology. Two other works, both called 'The Origins of Christian Realism,'[5] might be consulted as samples of work Lonergan did several times. To be considered in any case is the graduate course *De intellectu et methodo*,[6] given at the Gregorian University in 1959, for it deals in exceptional depth with our first transition, and indeed with the transition as transition (an aspect treated also in *The Way to Nicea*).

It is the transition as transition that is crucial, for it studies the way 'the same' is found in the principle and the term of the transition. Validly conducted, the transition enables us to see the same Lord Jesus Christ in the Gospels, in the *homoousios* of Nicea ('consubstantial'), in the theology of Athanasius, in the decrees of the Council of Chalcedon, and in the Scholasticism of the Middle Ages. In this formidable series it is the *homoousios* on which dogma stands or falls. In the Athanasian form it means simply that in scripture the same things are said of the Son as are said of the Father, with the exception of 'Father';[7] or, in the form we have seen in Prestige, that the Son is God in the same sense as the Father is God. But those formulas apply with ease to the New Testament, to Nicea, to Thomas Aquinas, and to us today: it is the same Lord Jesus that we worship and study in all four contexts.

The other transition I mentioned is not so well documented, and Lonergan himself came to it rather late in his career. It might be indicated by the difference between the *De intellectu et methodo* and Chapter 14[8] of *Method in Theology*. The former, strong on the move from scripture to theology, has less to say on the move from theology to the people of God. But Chapter 14 of *Method* is totally on that second move; as the title 'Communications' suggests, it deals with preaching the word to *these* people here and now. Involved in that project is the move from a classicist view of culture, always the same ('semper idem'), to a view that recognizes differences and their importance. The lecture 'Dimensions of Meaning' gives a good account of the matter. Here is the way Lonergan describes the style of the classically oriented science of man.

> It is limited to the essential, necessary, universal; it is so phrased as to hold for all men whether they are awake or asleep, infants or adults, morons or geniuses; it makes it abundantly plain that you can't change human nature ... But modern science aims at the complete explanation of all phenomena, and so modern studies of man are interested in every human phenomenon ... the accidental as well as the essential, the contingent as well as the necessary, the particular as well as the universal ...[9]

The application to communications is obvious. I preach to the congregation before me in the pews, not to the people of Corinth of twenty centuries ago. 'The Christian message is to be communicated to all nations. Such communication presupposes that preachers and teachers enlarge their horizon to include an accurate and intimate understanding of the culture and the language of the people they address.'[10]

2. Transcendence of Truth

Lonergan is clear on the permanence of dogma from the New Testament through history to modern times. But how can Catholic dogma endure throughout these transitions? The question is considered in *Method in Theology.*[11] 'First … there is affirmed a permanence of meaning,' on which the council [Vatican I] quotes a famous line from Vincent of Lerins (322, 323): 'the same dogma, the same meaning, the same pronouncement' ('in eodem scilicet dogmate, eodem sensu, eademque sententia'). Next, 'the permanent meaning is the meaning declared by the church.' Third, 'this permanent meaning is the meaning of dogmas' (322). Fourth, however, 'the meaning of the dogma is not apart from a verbal formulation, for it is a meaning declared by the church. However, the permanence attaches to the meaning and not to the formula' (323).

Lonergan concludes this section of *Method* with his position on truth. It is a familiar theme, and I referred above to its use in *De argumento theologico* where Lonergan asks: What is the possibility, the foundation for a transition from context to context? He replies that it seems to be the transcendence of truth, for truth has the character of the unconditioned, the absolute; it is not tied to some determinate context. Thus, to use again the examples we have seen, a doctor, hearing his or her patients declare their symptoms, transposes the symptoms into medical categories. All are talking about the same reality and declaring the same truth with the same meaning, but in different formulas. Similarly, a judge questions the witnesses, not in order to take part in some human tragedy, but to transpose the words of the witnesses into juridical categories.

9

'De bono et malo'

In the renewal of theology that Lonergan was slowly working toward, the doctrine of redemption had a special place. In that doctrine the work I will call *de bono*, and refer to by the code letters DBM, is a new and especially puzzling factor.[1] How it fits into the full picture is not at all clear. In terms of our now familiar metaphor, it seems in some ways to be an 'outpost,' but at the same time it contains within itself traits of the 'delayed sector.' Whatever its place in Lonergan's total history, the work is of high interest and importance in his Christology; the attention it gives to the mysterious 'historical causality' is enough by itself to guarantee that.

But it has importance also for the history of his ideas on theology itself. It may be seen as an attempt, partially successful, to break from Scholasticism; for example, the thesis form is almost abandoned, new categories featuring the work of Christ are introduced, and history is a theme. Still, it retains strong Scholastic roots in the topics chosen for study in chapters 1 and 2; I shall argue for 1958, in his Scholastic period, therefore, as the date of its composition. At the same time it is a forward-looking document, and its intention is as important as its achievement. So whatever its precise date, I think we may locate it in Lonergan's thought as intermediate between the high Scholasticism on one side of *De Verbo incarnato* and *De Deo trino* in 1964, and on the other side the open shift to modernity in, say, the papers of *A Second Collection*, 1966 to 1973. But before we get to its doctrine and its place in Lonergan's thought, there are questions that regard the text, the date, and the title.

1. Text, Date, Title

First, in regard to the text. In the summer and fall of 1972, a preliminary catalogue of the Lonergan papers in the recently established (1971) Lonergan Center in Toronto was drawn up by F. Crowe, C. O'Donovan, and P. McShane, with additions in 1974 by G. Sala. It fell to McShane to catalogue Batch IX. Folder 5 in that batch was listed under the title DE BONO ET MALO (with McShane's note: 'title of first chapter'); folder 6 was listed as a carbon copy of folder 5. McShane added this commentary: 'This folder and the following were given by BL to FEC on August 12, 1972. According to FEC, BL says it dates from 1963–64 and it was to be an addition to *De Verbo incarnato*, with the specific purpose of explaining the "historical causality" of Christ.' There are 4 chapters and 25 articles in 124 pages.

For a short time it seemed possible that we had here an autograph of a new work by Lonergan, but that view was quickly abandoned once we took time to examine the work. The manuscript is seriously faulty in many respects, and though it has corrections in Lonergan's hand for 14 pages, even then it does not measure up to his kind of work. More likely it was the work of an amanuensis returned to Lonergan for corrections, corrections Lonergan soon ceased to make – one supposes this is because the manuscript was in such sad shape. But then where was the autograph of Folder 5, Batch IX, if it had survived at all?

That problem was solved upon Lonergan's death in 1984, when his papers were found to contain a manuscript with the same quasi-title, DE BONO ET MALO, and the same contents for the first 4 chapters and 25 articles; but now there are additions to make a total of 6 chapters and 45 articles. Further, it was very clearly done in Lonergan's own typing. Further still, later study of his letters from Rome in the late 1950s revealed that in 1958, after working at it for two years, he had nearly completed just such a work of 6 chapters and 45 articles (it was 'pretty well done'; see below). The 6 chapters and 45 articles of the 1958 letter have to be the 6 chapters and 45 articles of the autograph work discovered after Lonergan's death and now in the archives.

Second, in regard to the date, a question inextricably intertwined with that of the text. From 1956 to 1958, in at least three letters from Rome, Lonergan spoke of a major work he was preparing. On June 12, 1956, he wrote that he was planning a work on redemption. On November 17, 1957, he reported that he had started work on it in that academic year. On May 25, 1958, he wrote: 'I have got 6 chapters (45 articles) on the redemption pretty well done. May be able to bring manuscript to Halifax' (he was to spend the summer in that city).

The dating of 1963–64 given by Lonergan on handing over his papers in 1972 has therefore to be critically evaluated. I assume that my report is reliable enough, for my note on it was made at once, having exactly the same date of August 12, 1972; it was not, then, made from memory years later. But, if my note is to be trusted, is Lonergan's 1972 remark locating it in 1963–64 due to a memory failure on his part? Did Lonergan know in 1972 when he handed over the faulty manuscript that it was only part of the work? Did he even advert to the fact that he was handing over an incomplete text, the work of an amanuensis, instead of his own autograph? At the time he was 'house-cleaning' his files and contributing from time to time other documents for the Lonergan Center; it is possible that he noticed the file title but didn't scrutinize the contents.

Alternatively, it could also be that ca. 1963 he began to tinker with the work of 1958. The autograph does show some suggestions of an unfinished state: for example, the lack of numbering of the pages after 179. The letter of 1958 speaks of 6 chapters and 45 articles as 'pretty well done'; but 'pretty well done' does not mean finalized; in fact it suggests the opposite. We shall see more of the evidence of a break in the work after Chapter 4 (chapters 5 to 6 not included in 1972, and their pages not numbered in the autograph). Further evidence will come to light, too, in the transition from Chapter 5 to Chapter 6, for Chapter 5 concludes as if Lonergan were still unsure what he would say in Chapter 6 (see my comment on page ★236, below).

Further, there is a section in the *De Verbo incarnato* of 1964 that is lacking in 1960;[2] it is entitled 'vita humana et historica' (see Chapter 10 below) and it chimes well with the articles of Chapter 6 of *de bono*. It is possible that, between the Christology of 1960 and that of 1964, Lonergan completed his work on Chapter 6 of *de bono* and as a result introduced the section 'vita humana et historica' into the *De Verbo incarnato* of 1964 – a tenuous argument, but worth filing.

All this might justify his mistake (?) in 1972 of calling Folder 5, Batch IX, a work of 1963 or 1964. It is abstractly possible, then, that he did resume work on the manuscript in 1963–64. There is a curious lack of communication in the whole business, beginning with the fact mentioned earlier that in the manual of 1960 (repeated in 1961 and 1964) Lonergan laments a lack he may have attended to himself in 1958 (if that is the date of *de bono*): namely, the historical causality of Christ. The manuscript of 4 chapters has then to be regarded as the typing by an amanuensis as part of a work still in progress at the time. It is not entirely worthless; it has some value, for example, as proof that Lonergan took this work seriously enough to try to get it properly typed for the printer. Still, in this study of his Christology I happily leave these questions to the research of others.

The basis for my study will be the larger autograph text of 6 chapters and 45 articles, and this text has with high probability to be considered a work of 1958. Lonergan himself numbered the first 179 pages (chapters 1 to 4), and I will continue the series to include numbering of chapters 5 and 6, thus making 302 pages in all. But from 180 on I will add an asterisk (★180, ★181, and so on) to remind the reader that the numbering is not Lonergan's. My references will be to those 302 pages and will be given in the text in round brackets; unless otherwise stated, the translations are my own.

Third, let us turn to the title. Lonergan himself did not give a name to this work. In the early circulation of the manuscript it was known from the opening pages as *De bono et malo*, or simply *De bono*. That was soon seen to be naming the whole from a part, but determining the correct title for the whole was not easy. Michael Shields, the translator, calls it DE VERBO INCARNATO SUPPLEMENTUM, but adds in brackets DE REDEMPTIONE SUPPLEMENTUM QUODDAM. In favour of Shields's first choice there is Lonergan's statement to me: 'it was to be an addition to *De Verbo incarnato*'; in favour of the second there are the letters just now quoted, in which Lonergan speaks of a work in progress on redemption. For my present practical purpose I have stated my intention: to refer to it as *de bono*, or by the code letters DBM.

2. Chapters 1 to 4

It is time to consider the work itself. The first five chapter headings are as follows: On Good and Evil, On the Justice of God, On Christ Dead and Risen, On the Cross of Christ, On the Satisfaction Made by Christ ('De bono et malo' – 'De iustitia Dei' – 'De Christo mortuo et resurrecto' – 'De cruce Christi' – 'De satisfactione Christi'). Chapter 6 has no title, but from the announcement at the end of Chapter 5, I would call it On the Effects of Redemption ('De effectibus redemptionis'). There is an introductory page under the title 'De bono et malo' that seems in fact to introduce the whole work and to establish a link with the *pantôn* text of 1935. It is our task, it says, to collaborate in the restoration in Christ of all things on earth and so, Lonergan writes, we must consider what sort of thing the 'good' is ('quale sit bonum'), how the human good consists especially in order, by what law ('qua lege') the human good of order is corrupted by sin, and what finally is the human capacity ('potentia') for restoring the human good of order. If all that is kept in mind, the text concludes, we will better understand how important in the problems of daily life is that great benefit of God the Father which we receive in the Holy Spirit through our Lord crucified and risen (page 1). That paragraph establishes the pastoral orientation of the whole work.

Chapter 1 is a mine to explore for Lonergan's views on the human condition, its mutability, the process from one situation to another, communication between situations, the role of language, the higher culture, world order, and other familiar topics. It would be a mistake to regard this as irrelevant; it is a fairly thorough anthropology, and therefore background material for Christology. Further, the later, more explicitly Christological chapters will appeal to this anthropology. Thus, article 42 ('De Christo agente historico') appeals to article 2 on the cultural good and natural human desires, to article 3 on signs, to articles 5–8 on evil, to article 10 on the ultimate order, to articles 11 and 12 on the order of justice. Thus also article 45 appeals to Chapter 1 on the reign of sin. The work, in short, is a tightly knit unity.

Chapter 2, like Chapter 1, is again full of background material for Christology, but rather than an anthropology it is a theology, dealing with such topics as the wisdom of God, the permission of sin, the mystery of the divine election, the ultimate order of divine justice, and so on.

It is, however, with chapters 3, 4, and 5 that we come to specifically Christological doctrines in which Lonergan takes a new look at redemption. Then, in Chapter 6 we find at last the elusive question Lonergan will refer to, in his manuals of 1960, 1961, and 1964, as still wanting: the historical causality of Christ. I will take chapters 3 to 5 as a unit and sketch their position in the present history. (Their topics were listed above with their Latin original.) It is Chapter 6 that will mark an especially important new step for Lonergan.

Chapter 3, according to the introductory statement, means to do little more than collect the relevant passages of scripture, as Lonergan will do in 1960 for thesis 15 of *De Verbo incarnato*, or perhaps had already done in his class lectures. But it is thesis 15 as it would be rewritten; clarifying titles are added, subtopics are reordered, some ideas are expanded (for example, Christ as priest). What arouses our expectations – the resurrection – is made the topic of a distinct article:[3] Christ not only died for our sins but also rose as a life-giving spirit, an eternal priest, ever praying for us, sending the Spirit of the Father on us, and bringing eternal salvation to all who obey him (144, 'omnibus obtemperantibus sibi causam salutis aeternae').

Chapter 4, On the Cross of Christ ('De cruce Christi'), has to get more attention. The introduction contrasts the doctrine of redemption with other doctrines as one explicitly proposed in scripture with its meaning already clear (146). For the cross of Christ is not only a fact but a precept and example, and no principle in the economy of salvation stands forth more than the transformation of evil into good. Hence Lonergan will consider the meaning, the law, the mystery, the justice of the cross before treating theological questions.

The meaning of the cross is the transforming of evil into good: the evil of guilt and the evil of punishment (147). Victory over the two evils does not mean they disappear (149). But how is evil conquered? Contraries are cured by contraries. As the evil of guilt arose through a defect of rational consciousness and a turning from God, so it is conquered by conversion to God and the restoration of rational consciousness. There is a difference between victorious human justice (another's goods for me, 'alterius mihi') and the meaning of the cross (150, what is mine for another, 'meum alteri'). Further, the good arising from evil through the victory of the cross is twofold. The victory benefits the victor but also changes the human situation for the better.

Article 23 is On the Law of the Cross (151, 'De lege crucis'). The law of the cross is the meaning of the cross as it pertains to the New Testament: as precept, as example, as conformation to and association with Christ, as penetrating the whole economy of our salvation (154). The voluntary victory belongs first to Christ. We imitate his victory sacramentally, morally, and physically (155). There is, consequent to victory, a good that eye has not seen nor ear heard (1 Corinthians 2:9); it is, however, a good that can be understood imperfectly (DB 1796, DS 3016) from the fruits of the good tree and those of the evil tree (Matthew 7:17,18). First, the fruits of the evil tree, for nowadays the enemies of the cross of Christ attack the very meaning ('ratio') of the cross (Caiphas, Nietzsche, Pilate, Marx). The fruits of the good tree, however, are seen first in the risen Lord, and are manifested at his baptism and his transfiguration in the voice from heaven, 'You are my own dearly loved Son' (157). Now love is directed to a person, and so the Father's love has its term in the Son as God and equally in the Son as man, and this love is the Holy Spirit. For the Son, a person, is sent by the Father, a person, to us who are persons, that the love by which the Father loved the Son, namely, the Spirit, may be given to us. Let us note the point, so important to Lonergan, of stressing the 'person': the Father loves the person of the Son, hence loves the Son in human form with the same love, for the Son in human form is still the divine person who became incarnate (157).

Article 24 is On the Mystery of the Cross (158–67, 'De mysterio crucis'). It collects passages on mystery in the New Testament, but these need further explanation, for on the basis alone of the term 'mystery' ('vi vocis') these could all be understood as the secret counsel of God (159–60). Hence the need for a more careful study of 'mystery.' (See also below, the last section of the 1958 lecture, 'Redemption.') There are mysteries in the strict sense in our redemption, and although we can by natural means know God to be wise, generous, loving, merciful, and just, we know this only by human analogy, whereas from the Son incarnate, dead, and risen we have a far higher analogy, one that enables us to know God as God is in the divine self. But besides mysteries in the theological sense, there are mysteries in the sense of events in the life of Christ and in the sense of the mysteries of the Rosary (161).

There is at the other extreme the mystery of iniquity; it is a mistake to deal with this mystery as we do with the intelligibles. Further, in the mystery of the cross there is the 'too' intelligible of the divine, there is the 'non-intelligible' of sin, and between these two there is the mystery of death. For death has the meaning of punishment (162, 'ratio poenae'). Yet death is a means of salvation. The fact that death is both a punishment for sin and a means of salvation cannot be explained as an equivocal use of the word (163). Death is punishment but this punishment is transformed into a means of salvation according to divine wisdom, not deleting the old evil and creating a new good as Judaism believed, but by means of a man transforming into good the evils themselves that come from sin.

Five aspects enable us to recapitulate the mystery of the cross (164–67): it is symbolic, intellectual, voluntary, providential, and divine. As a symbol it acts upon our sensibility and so on our intellect and will, and with the help of grace produces such fruits that the contemplation of Christ suffering and dying becomes a school of sanctity (164). Next, the cross is an intelligible order conceived by divine wisdom; yet in two ways it is not understood, for it supposes the non-intelligible of sin and the too-intelligible of the divine. Third (165), the cross results in diversity of the voluntary, a diversity exemplified in the voluntary sin of those who condemned Christ and in the voluntary acceptance by Christ of the cross. Fourth, though there is generic identity between our cross and Christ's, the divine plan makes a difference in that the victory of Christ is the cause and exemplar and motive of ours. Fifth, there is the aspect of revelation: we gain a far higher analogy for our knowledge of divine wisdom and goodness from the analogy of the man Christ dying and rising for us than we do from the analogy of other creatures (166).

Article 25 is On the Justice of the Cross (168–79, 'De iustitia crucis'). First, the general principles on justice are recalled: what God could do and what in divine wisdom God did do, most freely, most wisely, most fittingly (168). Lonergan next considers singly the elements contained in the meaning, the law, the mystery of the cross. He begins (170) with the divine salvific intention. Then there is the decree to save the human race according to the way of the cross ('secundum rationem crucis'). A third element (172–73) was the divine intention that the salvific activity be exercised by a mediator: namely, God's own Son. A fourth element (174) was the intention that the mediator, though Son of God, should save us according to this way of the cross. Here again we find the familiar doctrine that the Father loves us with the same love that he has for the Son. This is fitting insofar as we are one with the Son, for if between man and wife, if between friends all things are shared, how could it be that Christ would not make our cross his own? And Lonergan devotes several paragraphs to the unity of Christ with us. Acceptance of the cross (176), however, is not the whole meaning of the cross, nor does the cross only assert human victory over evil; it also leads to liberal gifts from a good Father, to our resurrection and glory. Lonergan has a paragraph on the church born from the side of Christ, and on the desire Christ has to be one with us (177). A fifth element is the intention that in the order of things set up by divine wisdom, the manifestation of divine goodness should be such as to allow evil, so that out of evil good might be done (178–79, Lonergan's familiar doctrine again).

3. Chapters 5 to 6

Oddities in the sequence of articles and titles in Chapter 5 make reference awkward. Lonergan himself numbered the pages of chapters 1 to 4 consecutively (1 to 179, but 80 is missing – the number, not the page).

After that, consecutive numbering ceased, but as stated above, I will continue Lonergan's series, counting the pages to give the number he would have used, and adding an asterisk to remind the reader of my usage.

Immediately after Chapter 4 we have a kind of entr'acte between chapters 4 and 5, the four-page article 26 (★180 to ★183), with the title Division of the Question ('Dividitur quaestio'). Here, on the basis of difficulties raised by Anselm's doctrine, Lonergan lines up the several headings to be investigated in the coming chapter. There follows a page with the heading for Chapter 5: On the Satisfaction of Christ (★184, 'De satisfactione Christi'), and a kind of 'table of contents' for the chapter, with articles 26 to 34 listed, but this page itself is not called an article. Only then do we come to article 26, On the Meaning of Necessity ('De ratione necessitatis').

The whole chapter is much like *De Verbo incarnato*, except that it reads better than the thesis form of the latter, and by assigning separate sections to separate topics, it is able to treat concepts more precisely. The differences in order and style, however, are so numerous that careful comparison of particular points in Chapter 6 of *de bono* with the same points in thesis 16 of the manual becomes impossible in the space I could reasonably allow for it, and in any case is not significant. The differences in content, on the other hand, are not numerous and I will here and there add brief remarks that touch on them.

Article 31, On the Sacramental Analogy (★219 to ★222, 'De analogia sacramentali'), differs from its parallel in *De Verbo incarnato* in being assigned a separate article. It finds a basis for this analogy in the Council of Trent, and is confirmed in the tradition by Anselm, Peter Lombard, Alexander of Hales, and Thomas Aquinas. It is further confirmed by sacramental theology and by Lonergan's preceding articles which argued against understanding satisfaction on the analogy of legal justice or of reparation (by 'preceding articles' Lonergan seems to mean articles 27 to 30); there remains, therefore, only the sacramental analogy (★221).

The *de bono*, however, is rather different from *De Verbo incarnato* on that analogy; there Lonergan argues in the context of the concrete question, 'either satisfaction or punishment' ('aut satisfactio aut poena'), puts in thesis form his argument for the sacramental analogy, and adds the assertion that it is just an analogy and not a perfect similitude.[4] Which treatment remains Lonergan's choice? I should say that of *de bono*; it is hard to imagine him not revising that manuscript to accord with *De Verbo incarnato* if the latter were meant to be final, but one can easily imagine him leaving *De Verbo incarnato* without a revision that would have a domino effect on other parts of thesis 16.

Article 32 is On the Sorrow of Christ ('De dolore Christi'). Like the sacramental analogy, it is assigned a separate article. Its doctrine differs from the parallel in (DBM *223 to *225; DVI–3, 548–52) in that Lonergan invokes an almost full-page quotation from Aquinas to support his theological argument. Both works see the cross as an expression of hatred and sorrow for sin (DBM in article 32, and see *218; DVI–3, 548, 551). The quasi table of contents for Chapter 5 (*184) lists the sacramental analogy (with a reference to article 31), the sorrow of Christ for our sins (with a reference to article 32), and his expression of this sorrow (with a reference to article 33). Christ, in expression of this sorrow, accepted his passion and death that these might have the meaning and force ('ratio') of satisfaction.

Chapter 5 and article 33 in that chapter have the same title, On the Satisfaction of Christ ('De satisfactione Christi'). Turning to the article (*226 to *232) we notice that it, too, differs somewhat from the parallel in *De Verbo incarnato* (DVI–3, 510–13). It treats the interior act of Christ with reference to article 32 on the love Christ has for the Father and for us, on his hatred for sin and his sorrow for our sins, and on his determination to take away all sin.

The key word is 'interior'; Lonergan describes the ways this interior act is exercised. I pause a moment on the third way: through external sensibility and bodily movements (*226). Lonergan refers (*228) to the distinction he had drawn far back in article 3 between signs that denote and signs that express ('signa [divisa] in denotativa et expressiva'). The former pertain to communication of understanding, the latter add corresponding action. After two pages of such prolegomena ('praemissa'), he asks four questions (*228): first, whether it was fitting that Christ should exercise his internal act in an external way; second, whether to this end it was fitting that he should accept his passion and death; third, whether this accepted passion and death was vicarious; and fourth, whether the vicarious passion thus accepted was vicarious satisfaction. The answer in each case is affirmative (*228 to *232).

Article 34, on superabundant satisfaction (*233 to *236), has but a brief parallel in *De Verbo incarnato* (DVI–3, 541–42), just three short paragraphs, quoting Romans, Clement VI, and Aquinas. The article, however, concludes

(*236) with a curious look ahead: having treated satisfaction in the head, Lonergan says, it remains to treat it in the members. How this is to be understood will be stated later, when we discuss the effects of redemption ('postea declarabitur cum de effectibus redemptionis agatur'). That presumably introduces Chapter 6. The curious aspect is the word 'postea.' Since in the text that we have, the 'later' statement follows immediately, one would expect 'will be stated in our next section' ('statim declarabitur,' or some such phrase instead of the indefinite 'postea'). But we have noticed Lonergan's omission of page numbers for chapters 5 and 6. There occurred, it seems, some break in the continuity of his writing after Chapter 4, and the 'postea' might have been written without a full plan for what was to follow. Confirming this are some minor points: the very complete table of contents for Chapter 5 (*184) has no parallel for Chapter 6. Instead, the autograph shows that Lonergan scrapped what was to be his opening five-line introduction to that chapter (*239) and replaced it with a two-page introduction (*237 to *238), and even in those two pages he replaced a seven-part plan for article 35 with an eight-part plan (*238). These data point to a situation in which he was composing and recomposing as he wrote.

Chapter 6 has no title, but as was just now argued, I would call it On the Effects of Redemption ('De effectibus redemptionis'), perhaps adding 'in History.' It has 11 articles, the titles of which raise our hopes that we are about to get the question of historical causality treated in full. These titles are On the Work of Christ (Article 35, 'De opere Christi'); On Agents by Intellect (Article 36, 'De agente per intellectum'); On Social Agents (Article 37, 'De agente sociali'); On Historical Agents (Article 38, 'De agente historico'); On Christ as Agent (Article 39, 'De Christo agente'); On Christ as Exemplar (Article 40, 'De Christo exemplari'); On Christ the Head (Article 41, 'De Christo capite'); On Christ as Historical Agent (Article 42, 'De Christo agente historico'); On the Heavenly Mediator (Article 43, 'De mediatore caelesti'); On the End of the Incarnation (Article 44, 'De fine incarnationis'); and Why God Became Man (Article 45, 'Cur Deus homo'). The file has an added text of 11 pages, Article 44, On the End of the Incarnation ('De fine incarnationis' – perhaps a first draft of that article, Michael Shields suggests).

A first point to make on this Chapter 6 is a warning on what not to expect from the promised treatment of the historical causality of Christ. The reader should discard romantic ideas about such questions as the role of Europe in unfolding history, the emergence of the scientific revolution, the significance of Columbus and the Americas, the influence of Christ on the rise and fall of empires, Christianity and Icelandic culture. I pick these headings out of the blue, merely to state that, along with thousands like them, they are only remotely relevant to the historical causality of Christ in Lonergan's sense (even his relation to Jaspers' axis of history gets the briefest possible mention, *279 in Chapter 6). They are, of course, mediately relevant and would fit perhaps in the *pantôn* text of 1935, but not in the sober articles of over twenty years later, where the perspective is transcendental. Still, attending to what Lonergan actually wrote, we may discover with some surprise that the historical causality of *de bono*, while different from, is not alien to that of 1935. Let us begin with hope the study of the first article of Chapter 6.

Article 35, On the Work of Christ (*237) refers back to Chapter 3 and proceeds from that. Leaving in abeyance what pertains to understanding of the data, Lonergan turns to the data themselves of scripture as giving a foundation for the study and revealing the object we seek to understand. The data come under seven headings: (a) the kingdom of God, (b) salvation in Christ, (c) deliverance from sin and (d) from Judaic law, (e) access to a faithful and just God, (f) access in trust, (g) access by personal acts, by which (h) we are incorporated into Christ and the people of God (*238). These headings are filled out with multiple quotes from scripture.

Article 36, On Agents by Intellect (*244), has been a favourite topic for Lonergan since he wrote his doctoral dissertation, 1938–1940. The present article sets forth the difference between acting by nature and acting through intellect, the difference between the limitations of the former and those of the latter, and other related ideas.

Article 37, On Social Agents (*248), brings in another favourite topic. Here, in noting the social character of nearly all our activity, Lonergan distinguishes proportionate cause (a cook is able to prepare a meal) from actual cause (a cook actually prepares a meal). The latter involves history: using a proportionate cause but also attending to the conditions to be fulfilled if there is to be an actual result. The point is underlined in the final paragraph: 'Agents become social under historical conditions, and under historical conditions they exercise their liberty' (*251, 'Sub conditionibus enim historicis agentia fiunt socialia, et sub conditionibus historicis libertatem suam exercent').

Article 38 is On Historical Agents (*252). At last, history makes its thematic entry! After a definition – 'We call that an historical agent which causes the good of order, whether it be an external good or a cultural' ('Agens dicimus historicum quod ordinis bonum vel exterius vel culturale causat') – there follows a formidable list of subcategories: more or less historical, totally or partially historical, historical per se or per accidens, proportionately or actually historical, historical as originating or as conserving, as destructive or as restorative. The special importance of these categories for Christology becomes manifest in the course of article 42 (starting at page *278), where they will be used to define the historical role of Christ.

Lonergan repeats his familiar doctrine on God (divine transcendence, time and eternity, simultaneity, Banez and Thomas) to conclude: the simply first and simply absolute historical agent is God (*254). But men are historical and ministerial agents. It was the counsel of divine wisdom to govern all things and bring them to their end through secondary causes and according to the fittingness ('convenientia') of their natures. The distinction between what instruments do of their own power and what they do through the power of the principal agent is illustrated by the difference between a general and a soldier in a battle.

To set forth the role of single historical agents requires many distinctions. They are social agents acting through intellect but not by themselves or for themselves. Nor can social agents act without influence on the good of order, either external good or cultural good or both: 'Every human action performed under social conditions either preserves or corrupts or perfects a good of order already existing' (*255, 'omnis actio humana sub conditionibus socialibus peracta iam exsistens ordinis bonum vel conservat vel corrumpit vel perficit').

There are degrees of causal intervention: seen in those who raise their minds beyond particular goods to the good of order (*255–*256); those who move from proportionate agents to actual when by one means or another they bring a proposal to realization (*256). Lonergan now applies the distinctions with which he began: the more historical, the originating and conserving, and so on. 'Those agents are considered especially historical which have led men from a primitive culture to an urban civilization, and have then perfected that civilization even more through philosophic and scientific reflection. But among all historical agents the greatest is the Word made flesh, the Saviour of men, the Agent we have now to consider' (ibid.: '... maxime historica reputantur ea agentia quae homines ex primitiva cultura in civilizationem urbanam deduxerunt, et deinde quae hanc civilizationem reflectione philosophica et scientifica ulterius perfecerunt. Maximus autem inter omnia agentia historica est Verbum caro factum, hominum Salvator, quem iam considerari oportet'). Thus the general doctrine on historical agents will be applied to Christ as historical agent.

Article 39 is On Christ as Agent (★259–★261). After a brief account of the usual distinctions (Christ acting as God, as man, and so on) Lonergan devotes almost the whole article to the problem of the divine mandate and the obedience of Christ. He goes into the question of the liberty of Christ, replies to objections to this liberty, and posits what we have seen to be his basic principle: 'the divine precept was simultaneous as truth with the obedience of Christ' (★259, 'divinum praeceptum in signo veritatis [simultaneum] fuisse cum ipsa Christi obedientia') – the doctrine familiar to us from *De ratione convenientiae*. In sinful human beings a precept becomes known, we seek escape, finally by divine grace we are converted and submit ourselves to God. But one who is impeccable (Christ) is already converted and his love of God is not impeded; there remains an immediate and superabundant willingness to obey (★260).

Quite interesting is the extent of the power of Christ. First, we distinguish in Christ what he did by his human power as such and what he did through that same power as the instrument of God conjoined to the divinity. According to the first he did not command a movement except in his own body; but as the conjoined instrument of the divinity, the efficacy of his command was not limited to moving his own body; it was extended to command of the demons, of the winds and waves, of the sick, and even of the dead. Further, his efficacy extended to the exercise of his power through others, as when others did miracles in his name, or as when the acts of the ministers of the sacraments are a cause of grace. The article concludes with a 'table of contents' (★261) of what is to come: namely, articles 40 to 43.

Article 40 is On Christ as Exemplar (★262–★265). The topic came up in the notion of sacrifice (Chapter 3 of my essay above, under Causes); also in article 24 above, On the Mystery of the Cross. A quick scan of *De Verbo incarnato*, however, yielded little on exemplar; article 40 seems to be Lonergan's chief study of that topic. There are two senses of the word. An 'agent by intellect' is that which an agent inspects when he or she would operate by intellect, and in this way Christ is an exemplary cause when we imitate him. The other sense is an exemplar according to some economy or ordering of things (say, the economy of salvation) such that what is done in the exemplar must be done, too, in other things. In this sense Christ achieved our salvation in the way of exemplar (*262). For understanding this three factors are considered. There is the principle of the economy, which comes from God who orders and chooses. Then, there is the determination of the principle in Christ or realized by Christ in his life. Third, there is the application of that determination received in us (*262).

Pursuing the argument, Lonergan gathers a battery of texts from scripture on God as the principle of our being conformed to the image of his Son (*262–*263) and argues that these texts show Christ as exemplar in the present economy of salvation, so that what is done in Christ must be done likewise in those who are to be saved (*263). But Christ knew this, and as free and rational he so determined himself as eo ipso to determine what should be done in others. And what is true of Christ the exemplar is even more true of God who made the human Christ and so ruled him that he would be in all things a most apt exemplar (*263). Lonergan concludes with his answer to the objection that this is not true causality: it is true causality when a real dependence is understood and affirmed (*265).

Article 41, On Christ the Head (*266–*274), starts with the Pauline doctrine of the interdependence of organs in living things: only the eye sees but it sees for the whole body. This is not causal efficiency, as when we guide a blind person by the hand. Quite different also is the extrinsic and miraculous restoration of vision. Then, with vision restored the feet are freed from extrinsic help and, as naturally joined to the eyes, can in a way see on their own. Now we, though many, are one body in Christ and members of one another, with Christ the head and chief member. So what is done in Christ is done in the whole and for the whole. Hence we distinguish the proper formality and meaning ('ratio propria') of the head from the 'ratio' of the exemplar and from that of the efficient cause.

Take 'satisfaction' as an example (*266). Christ satisfied for our sins and this is an exemplar of what should be done in the members. Besides that, Christ's satisfaction is an efficient cause of our satisfaction. There is no problem about attributing this exemplary and efficient causality to Christ the head provided we do not exclude the third role *proper* to the head: namely, that through the satisfaction made by Christ we have already made satisfaction (★267). As when the eye sees, the body sees, so when Christ satisfies, the body satisfies. As the eye sees not mainly for itself but for the body, so also Christ did not satisfy for himself but for us, and did not merit mainly for himself but for us (★267). Showing again the unity of this whole work, Lonergan refers back to various earlier articles: to article 18 on the sacrifice of the New Testament, to 19 on meritorious obedience, to 20 on vicarious passion, to 5 on the satisfaction of Christ (★267).

The following points are then added. First (★268), our union with Christ is not to be so exaggerated as to make it substantial. Nor second, is his work to be so conceived as to exclude ours. Third, there is to be excluded an exaggerated distinction that would renew Pelagianism or at least deny redemption as a means: without Christ we can do nothing. But we must go further: redemption as means must not be reduced to efficiency and exemplarity (★269). The operation of Christ the head, though extended to members and requiring and producing a similar operation in us, is already, considered in itself, an operation for the members and of the members. Fourth (★269), the proper 'ratio' of the head is not to be understood in a rationalist way, as if it were demonstrated by necessary reasons in the light of reason alone. Fifth (★270), semirationalism is to be excluded, as if supposing the mystery of redemption to be revealed we could then demonstrate it. Sixth, we must exclude particular forms of rationalism and semirationalism along with the exclusion of their generic form; hence with Augustine and Aquinas we hold that the death of Christ was not necessary either for satisfaction or for merit or for sacrifice or for the intercession of Christ. Seventh, we exclude the opposite of rationalism, and maintain rather that, though the death of Christ was not necessary, it did not proceed just by divine will, for the divine will follows divine wisdom as the law of God's justice. The existence of the actual order was freely chosen by God, yet the orders from which God chose are determined by divine wisdom. Eighth (★271), we must not attend only to necessary reasons, contemning the contingent and the 'convenientes'; rather, we follow Aquinas, whose method can be seen both in a long series of articles (*Pars tertia*, questions 46–56) and in a single but outstanding article (*Pars tertia*, q. 1, a. 2).

With these points premised to exclude error in doctrine or method we proceed to the proper 'ratio' of 'head' and so to the understanding of Christ as head (★272). A first element derives from scripture: bodily members act not for themselves alone but for the whole body; so it is with Christ. A second element comes from the fact that union is the effect of love; so Aquinas explains the satisfaction of Christ not just because Christ is the head of his members but also because two persons can be one in love. A third element comes from human nature itself; for men are agents by intellect ('agentia per intellectum') and so are proportionate to all they understand and will; but they cannot act except through the body, and so they do great works only in collaboration. A fourth element is had from the sins of men (*273): as we are drawn to sin through the sins of others, so it is appropriate that we be restored to salvation through the good work of another. A fifth element is had from original sin, as scripture (Paul) declares. A sixth element is had from the very person of the reconciler and redeemer (*274); as we do not go to a cook for tailoring or to a tailor for meals, so it was fitting that through our Lord, the Son of his Father, the merit of obedience be gained on our account, satisfaction be made for our sins, and a propitiatory sacrifice be offered for us.

Joining all these we have some imperfect understanding of this great mystery by which the Son of God made man performed for us the roles of head, friend, vicar, priest, and pastor.

Article 42 is On Christ as Historical Agent (*275–*283). Now that we have considered the exemplar and the 'ratio propria' of head, we must go further and attend to that action and efficacy of Christ by which are made and perfected the members of his body and his plenitude. This action is twofold. One action is exercised from heaven, where he lives and intercedes for us (see article 43 below). The other was exercised in Palestine twenty centuries ago but has always had and always will have an influence 'modo historico' right to the end (*275). What sort of agency this historical action of Christ is appears in two interconnected factors: the effect produced, and the way it is produced. The effect produced has three aspects (*276): the effect of the whole historical action; the effect directly intended by Christ as historical agent; and the effect indirectly intended by him.

The effect of the total historical action is the whole human good of order, both external good and cultural good, past, present, and future. This good of order comprises first, the continual flow of particular goods of every kind; then, the human operations by which the flow arises; third, the internal habits and external institutions and customs whence operations come and are coordinated; and fourth, men themselves, joined by interpersonal relations, who operate according to institutions and customs and enjoy the goods thus arising.

This total effect as part of the universal order is produced by God according to the order of divine wisdom and justice. Now above, in articles 11 and 12, we distinguished the historical order of divine justice from the personal order. In this life we so act under material, social, and historical conditions that what happens to us singly is not determined alone by one's personal merits or demerits. There is another, future life where according to the just judgment of the man Christ there will be an award singly to each according to their personal works. Though that future life is outside the historical field, what it will be for each singly is determined in the historical field.

So we must distinguish the total historical effect as it is in itself and as it is as ordered to a future heavenly life (★277). This ordering is first according to the divine intention, and next according to the effect received in us: grace, virtues, motions of the Spirit. As argued above (articles 5–8), unless this effect is received, people so tend to the good of this life that sooner or later internal disorder declines into multiple evils. Hence the total historical effect in itself is good insofar as it is ordered to the future life, and so one who directly intends this true ordering eo ipso intends indirectly the promotion of the total historical effect.

All this enables us to discern the historical effect directly intended by Christ and the effect indirectly intended. The action of Christ directly tends to the ordering of human earthly life to the future heavenly life. But since this ordering frees us from evils and converts us to good and greatly promotes the human good of order in itself, it must be that this ordering is indirectly intended by Christ as historical agent (★277).

It follows that Christ is an historical agent by reason of the effect he intends (★278). For an agent is historical when it causes the good of order, external or cultural (article 38). But the cultural good regards the natural desire to see God by the divine essence, the natural desire for moral rectitude, the natural desire for beatitude and immortality (article 2), all of which are attained insofar as the effect directly intended by Christ is produced. Further, since the other human goods depend on right internal ordering and since this right internal ordering is not had without the direct effect of Christ, it is clear that all human goods depend directly or indirectly on Christ as agent.

After the concept comes the application: Lonergan brings forward article 38 with its many aspects of a historical agent in general and applies them one by one to Christ (★278–★279). Thus Christ is the historical agent par excellence. He is the total historical agent, and the historical agent per se. More important for Lonergan, it seems, Christ is the restorative historical agent (a link here with the *pantôn* paper), directly intending to restore the image of God in man (*279).

But Christ was an historical agent not only because of the effect intended but also because of the way he produced the effect (*279). For every social or historical action supposes some stable good of order. This is seen in the relation of Christ to the Jewish people (long preparation, messianic expectation, cultural heritage, the law as our pedagogue in Christ, and so on). It is seen also in the nations coming to a higher culture while also learning their impotence. Therefore, though discovery of the higher culture could be called a historical axis because it developed the idea of the good in a conscious and reflective way (a reference to Jaspers, surely), still the coming of Christ is the centre and principal axis of human history, since through our Lord and through him alone we so will the good that we also do it.

Further, every social and historical action is had through others who understand and consent. This, too, is found in Christ whose kingdom is propagated through the gospel, through faith, through penitence; but the gospel preached supposes mission, faith supposes hearing, penitence is had through the baptism of Christ and the gift of the Spirit. Further, these others who understand and consent are not just anybody at all; they are members of Christ (*280). As Christ our head merited, satisfied, offered sacrifice for us, so also we as his own members bear responsibility for the historical work of Christ.

Again, Christ acts socially and historically through his members not as individuals taken singly, but as forming one body, socially, historically, and spiritually (*281, 'sed qua socialiter, historice, et spiritualiter unum corpus sunt'), for we are one body in Christ. Further, though the action of Christ is mediated socially and historically, it is personal and accommodated to human persons. The Word was made flesh that there might be an expressive sign for human persons (see article 3). Human knowledge begins with sense and the Word made flesh is sensible. The sensible leads to knowledge of intelligible and spiritual truth; so the whole life of Christ, with every word and action of his, conspires to the end that what is manifested in the flesh may be received in the spirit. Add that some signs are merely denotative, but the sign or mystery of Christ is expressive par excellence, for he loved me and gave himself up for me: Galatians 2:20 (with a quotation of Aquinas and Augustine).

Further, the historical action of Christ, by the mediation of his body, the church, not only instructs minds and attracts hearts, but also effects and increases the renovation of human interiority (★282). Thus the seven sacraments have power to confer grace, but as they originate from Christ and are conferred by his members, so they have from Christ the power to confer grace.

Finally, Lonergan recalls the distinction made (article 39) between what Christ does by his human power and what he does as instrument of the divinity (★283). For the human power of Christ by his social and historical action produces a contingent effect, directly or indirectly intended. But the same human power, as instrument of the divinity, effects that which God infallibly knows is being done, efficaciously wills to be done, irresistibly causes to be done. And Christ knowing everything through the beatific vision and intending his total effect, also knew and obediently willed himself to be the instrument of that divine intention which operates infallibly, efficaciously, irresistibly.

Article 43 is On the Heavenly Mediator (★284–★287). After a page of the usual quotations from scripture and the linking of Christ's heavenly mediation with the image of it that we have in the Eucharist (see Chapter 3 of this essay, above) Lonergan gives special attention to the doctrine of the reconciliation of all things with God and among themselves, which reconciliation comprises the whole work of Christ. For as the human good of order bespeaks a flow of particular goods as well as coordinated operations and internal habits and external institutions (in such a way, however, that all these are collected and vivified in a concrete synthesis by interpersonal relations), so it is with the supernatural good of order where are found all the particular gifts of grace and glory, the operations in which we do all in the name of the Lord, the infused virtues and gifts of the Spirit, and the institutions of the church – all this is contained in interpersonal relations, what Paul calls being in Christ and the Spirit (★287). Through Christ we have access in one Spirit to the Father, and we are loved by the Father as is his proper Son, with the proceeding love which is the Holy Spirit.

Article 44 is On the End of the Incarnation (★288–★292). An apparent conflict in the scriptural data on this question leads Lonergan to undertake an analysis of the notion of end. There are two ways of being ordered to an end, and so a twofold end, primary and secondary, and so likewise two ways of choosing and loving an end. For a means to an end is relatively good. Now one kind of the relatively good is being useful to gain an end; another kind is participating or communicating the goodness itself of the end. The first kind (*289) is only a means, abandoned as soon as the end is attained. But the other kind, possessing in some way the goodness of the end, is not a means but a secondary end. Further, the will of a means and the will of a secondary end are two different things: a means is not loved but is chosen only as related to another, but a secondary end can be loved from the superabundant love of the primary end.

Further, a secondary end can comprise many ordered parts, and this ordering can super-order or co-order or sub-order the parts in relation to one another. Hence to will the secondary end properly is to will the parts also and to will them in their ordering. There is one end that is simply primary and is to be loved above all things. The secondary end is another matter. It includes all created things duly ordered among themselves. One who loves a secondary end in this way does so out of superabundant love for the primary end, and loves all the parts in the ordering which divine wisdom and divine goodness gave them.

Further (*290), this secondary end is also called the external glory of God, or the order of the universe, which is the most excellent in created things, and more perfectly than any other creature participates in and represents the divine goodness. Further still, this secondary end according to the sacred text is the body of Christ, head and members, according to which everything is restored and reconciled (Ephesians 1:10; Colossians 1:20). Christ, therefore, God and man, with both divine and human wills, loves God above all things as primary end and also, because of divine goodness and out of superabundant love for that goodness, loves also the secondary end, the external glory of God and the body of Christ, head and members.

But the divine will of Christ is really identical with the primary end, so Christ with his divine will loves himself above all things and loves other things because of himself ('propter se') and out of the condescension of his goodness. But the human will of Christ is identical with the secondary end, and the created humanity of Christ is not the totality of this end but a part of it. And so the human will of Christ loves his humanity ('se'), not above all things, nor on its own account, but from superabundant love for the divine goodness and as a part of the secondary end ('voluntas Christi humana se diligit, non supra omnia, neque propter se, sed ex superabundante dilectione erga divinam voluntatem et tamquam partem quamdam secundarii finis'). So that which in the divine will of Christ is the condescension of goodness is in his human will obedience and subordination of self.

So the question is solved (★290 – the question, presumably, that was raised in the first two paragraphs of article 44, 'De fine incarnationis'). Christ as God and Christ as man wills and loves the same things ordered in the same way among themselves. But (★291) Christ as God is one good and Christ as man is another good. Christ both as God and as man loves the whole body of Christ, head and members, as secondary end for the glory of God. Loving the body he eo ipso loves the head and members, and as he loves the members because of the body so he loves the head because of the body, for the part is because of the whole. Further, as he loves head and members as parts of the body, so he loves them as duly ordered among themselves, and so loves the members as subordinate to the head.

Insofar, then, as Christ is said to hold the primacy in all things, we are dealing with the subordination of the members to the head. Likewise, when it is said that all are yours and you are Christ's and Christ is God's, we are dealing with the subordination of other things to the members, and of the members to the head, and of the head to God.

Insofar, however, as Christ is said to have come to serve and to give his life and to redeem those who were under the law that we might receive the adoption of sons, we have to distinguish the person coming and the nature assumed (★292). The person coming acts from the condescension of the divine goodness, but the assumed nature acts from obedience. The person coming is ordered to the mission of the Holy Spirit, which, however, transcends the order of end ('ratio finis') and shows the intra-trinitarian order. But the assumed nature is subordinated to the external glory of God, and to the order of the universe, and to the whole body of Christ, as part to the whole; and since this subordination to the whole redounds to the good of the members, therefore for us and for our salvation the life ('anima') of Christ is given and his blood poured out.

There is obscurity here, Lonergan concedes, when the divine person in human nature is considered separately ('divisim') according to the person and according to the assumed nature. But the obscurity is to be ascribed to the mystery, due to the fact that we cannot at the same time hold in thought ('cogitare') an infinite person and a finite nature.

Article 45 is entitled Why God Became a Human Being (★293 to ★302, 'Cur Deus Homo'). The word why ('cur') asks for the cause, so

Lonergan reviews the causes of Christ, in particular the final cause, which he has just set forth. But now he goes further to ask why a divine person is required and why another, who may be finite, would not suffice to this end. He is not asking generally about the end of the incarnation but more particularly why God became man, ('cur Deus homo'). The answer is *that divine friendship might be communicated in an ordered way to enemies* ('*ut amicitia divina inimicis ordinate communicetur*' – italics in original).

Friendship is the mutual love of benevolence in the sharing of some good. To love is to wish good in general ('velle bonum alicui'); benevolence is to wish good to another ('velle bonum alteri'); mutual benevolence is had when several singly wish some common good to others. Divine friendship (*294) is the mutual love of benevolence in regard to what is good by essence. This is proper to the divine persons, but it is communicated to intellectual creatures contingently and temporally, first in hope, then in our heavenly home ('in patria'). The enemies of God are sinners; they are held in the nets of impotence, both singly in not doing the good they wish, and all together to constitute socially and historically a kingdom of sin and to exist under the power of darkness. Divine friendship is communicated to enemies in an ordered way according to the free counsel of God conceived by divine wisdom and chosen by divine goodness. Since this counsel is free, we abandon the views of rationalists and semirationalists, and so we seek neither necessary reasons nor such reasons of 'convenientia' as would be perfectly understood by us. We seek only the understanding lauded by Vatican I (DB 1796; DS 3016), and since the counsel conceived by divine wisdom leaves the divine will free to consider other counsels, much less is our imperfect understanding fixed on one counsel as definitive (*295).

So much for the terms. We must now declare more in particular the nature ('quale fuerit') of this free divine counsel that the Son should become a human being. First some principles, then their application (*296). There are three principles: cause, continuity, diffusion of friendship. *Cause*: God generally acts through secondary causes, so it was fitting that there be one human being among others on account of whom divine friendship would be communicated to human enemies. *Continuity*: God generally acts according to what is fitting ('conveniens') to created nature, and so it was fitting that the communication be made not by upsetting the common course of things (as with the apocalyptic eschatology of the Hebrews) but for the most part observing all laws, both natural and human, psychological, sociological, historical. *Diffusion of friendship*: this is found in a friend loving the friends of a friend, and is extended even to loving enemies because of a friend.

The application of these principles may be considered according to the term *for* which ('ad quem') and according to the term *by* which ('a quo'), and in each case with conclusions that are only 'convenientes' (*297). In regard to the term 'ad quem': a human being is required who is an intermediate friend, a friend of God according to divine friendship, a friend of human beings on whose account divine friendship might be extended to other human beings. But to be a friend of God according to divine friendship, a person should be ordered to possession of the infinite good of God and hence adorned with grace, virtues, and the gifts of the Spirit. This, however, is absolutely supernatural, so no mere creature by its own right ('iure quodam suo') is a friend of God according to divine friendship.

True, a mere creature can be a friend to God by divine pleasure or by the merit of another, but an intermediary by divine pleasure would set aside the principle of cause, and one by merit of another would begin a regress to infinity (*298). Hence there is needed one who by personal right ('iure suo') is a friend of God. This excludes mere creatures. So the intermediary must be a divine person in a human nature who by personal right is a friend of God.

'The first reason, therefore, why God became a human being is that there might be a human being who by personal right is a friend of God according to divine friendship' ('Prima ergo ratio cur Deus homo est ut habeatur homo qui iure suo sit Dei amicus secundum divinam amicitiam'). To this may be added at once another reason, for the one we postulate will have all supernatural gifts and be a proportionate exemplary cause for sharing these gifts with others. Lonergan answers a possible objection according to which divine friendship is due a divine person as subsisting in the divine nature, but not to a divine person as subsisting in human nature. The answer is that friendship is the mutual love of benevolence, and the love of benevolence is not diminished when a person-friend assumes another nature.

Further, our intermediary must be a friend not only of God but also of human beings (*299). So he or she must love human beings and they must love him or her. The first (need to love human beings) follows from what has been said, but that they must love the intermediary adds to it. For a friend of God is bathed in love ('caritate perfunditur'), and so friends of God love God above all things and also, because of God, love their neighbour. But human beings are enemies of God and sinners, and do not love a friend of God but hate such a person. So this friend of God, in order to become an intermediary, must convert human beings from enmity to friendship, so that loving a human being who is God they may come to love of God.

Here emerges a third reason 'cur Deus homo.' If a divine person is a human being, the love of this human being is the love of a divine person. For this divine person made human is the intermediary friend on whose account God loves human beings, even though they are enemies, and the same one, being a divine person, is the intermediary through whom human beings come to love of God. But how should an intermediary convert enemies to friendship? By the principle of continuity it is fitting that this be done, not by upsetting the ordinary course of things, but by observing the general course of events and for the most part keeping human and natural laws. But alienated human beings, though they can will the good, do not so will it as to do it, and though they can bring to high perfection both the external and the cultural good of order, they pervert this good by their sins (*300, with a reference to Chapter 1). Hence, if the human and psychological and social laws are not to be suspended (the principle of continuity would forbid that) men cannot be converted from evil to good except according to the way ('ratio') of the cross, and then it is fitting that the intermediary friend not only teach and prescribe the law of the cross but also make that law his own or her own, and being afflicted by the hatred of their enemies, turn this evil into good.

Besides, the intermediary loves God above all with the most perfect love, and loves neighbours because of God (*301, 'propter Deum'). But those who truly love not only share the good they have but also bear the evils their friends bear, counting them not as another's but as their own (*301, 'non aliena ... sed quodammodo sua'). Further, the task of the intermediary is to convert human enemies to friendship, and there is no greater invitation to love than to take the initiative and be the first to love. So it is fitting for the intermediary to show the greatest love and to manifest it in the most effective way (John 15:13: 'no greater love'; and 12:32: 'if I am lifted up').

Besides, this demonstration of love and invitation to love achieves only an initial and dispositive love in human beings. It is one thing to love as a human being the divine person made human and another to love the same one as God. For the former, the demonstration of love and invitation to love suffices; for the latter, supernatural gifts of grace are required. Now, according to the principle of cause, the intermediary ought to cause the supernatural gifts, too, so we must consider how the intermediary causes supernatural gifts in human beings, even while they are enemies of God (★302). Lonergan's reasoning is that the intermediary human being is a divine person and must act with a certain divine munificence: where sin abounds, grace superabounds (Romans 5:20). But grace superabounds if the divine person not only brings it about that human beings act for themselves, but also that he himself acts for them as head for members, priest for the people, shepherd for the flock, king for the subjects, vicar for those represented, friend for friend. And this is fitting because commonly, human beings act through others, being led to sin not only by their own vices but by those of others. Even when, elevated by grace, they act for themselves, they do so only imperfectly.

It is fitting, therefore, that the intermediary friend satisfy for sins superabundantly.

At the end of this long paraphrase of *de bono*, I return to the questions I posed at the start: on the date of this work, and on the place it holds in the Christology of Lonergan. On the date: I have given some testimony from the year 1972, when Lonergan turned a faulty text of *de bono* over to the archives, attributing it to 1963–64 and stating that it was to be a further thesis in *De Verbo incarnato* with the specific purpose of explaining the 'historical causality' of Christ. I have granted the possibility that ca. 1963–64 he brought *de bono* out of hibernation and was considering further work, or had done further work on it, and so gave it that date. But the letters of 1956, 1957, and 1958 are so clear that we are forced to consider *de bono* the work the letters speak of, and so to give it the date of 1958. That is my somewhat tentative final position.

I have dwelt on this bit of history, relying, too, on scattered clues from conversations, because the notion of historical causality seems to have been very much on Lonergan's mind as he pondered his new Christology. We need to determine the sequence of his thinking, and in the scarcity of data we must take clues where we find them.

Our next heading asks for the place *de bono* holds in Lonergan's history. From the perspective of his last years we might see it as an intermediate stage between the still largely Scholastic theology of 1964 and a new approach that was still only in potency. He himself seemed to see the work as entering a new phase, adding to but not departing radically from his early Christology. In any case this intermediate phase was never pursued: God intervened in the form of lung cancer. Lonergan never returned to Rome, and his later Christology was in a new style. One could see this as providential, for 1965 is a kind of dividing line in his life work, and returning to pre-1965 interests might have turned out to be a backward step.

That reference to divine providence suggests some reflections on *de bono* rather different from the more academic approach I have taken in this chapter. There is an attraction in this long and enigmatic work – this warmed-over Scholasticism, as it will appear to some – this work that is so forbidding at first, but exercises a growing attraction as one reads.[5] I ask myself what the attraction is. I believe one factor is the devotion to Christ that pervades the whole long argument. A similar question occurs in regard to the myriad quotations from scripture. How different from the 'search for the historical Jesus' Lonergan's search is. Text after text from scripture – Lonergan seems to know the whole New Testament by heart, and in Latin, together with chapter and verse. There is little attention to differences between John and the synoptics and to all the other questions that engross or vex so many authors. This can be read in a pejorative way; I read it rather as a sign of a whole approach to Christology: something like a lover saying, 'How do I love thee? Let me count the ways.' It is the attitude of John's Gospel, of Paul's letters, of Mary Magdalene at the tomb on Easter morning.

Another theme to challenge the academic reader: there is a tremendous reverence for the wisdom and goodness of God. How often the phrase recurs, 'conceived by divine wisdom and chosen by divine will.' This underlies his respect for the councils and church doctrine and brings home the relevance of my first chapter on Lonergan's personal piety and religion. It also links with phrases like 'the natural desire to see God by his essence' – words that have such a depth of meaning for Lonergan, both religious and theological.

4. 1958 Lecture on Redemption

There is one more act to be fitted into the drama of Lonergan's thinking on Christ and redemption: a lecture he gave in the late summer of 1958 on 'The Redemption.'[6] I have quoted his letter of May 25, 1958, where he wrote: 'I have got 6 chapters (45 articles) on the redemption pretty well done. May be able to bring manuscript to Halifax.' Whether he brought it to Halifax I do not know, but his main work that summer in Halifax would have been the lectures on *Insight* that became *Understanding and Being*. In his Christology, however, the Montreal lecture would have followed directly on the *de bono*, which was 'pretty well done' when he wrote his letter of May 25, so I see the lecture, too, as intermediate between his high Scholasticism and the new approach taking shape in the 1960s. Thus it presents the same puzzle as *de bono* on its relationship to the Christology manuals of 1960 and 1964. It is a matter, perhaps, of the salients and tardy pockets in my favourite metaphor of trench warfare.

Like the *de bono,* the Montreal lecture precedes the *De Verbo incarnato* series. But again like the *de bono,* it is more forward-looking. It seems to represent personal work that the more rigidly structured classroom courses did not easily assimilate. Further, it seems to be independent of the manual he would issue in 1960, for over a year after the lecture he implies that the manual had not yet been decided on.[7] In any case, on its own merits I award the lecture of 1958 its own mini-section in the history of Lonergan's theology of redemption.

The very first point in the lecture takes a pastoral line, considering the redemption as communication where *De Verbo incarnato* will consider it as the kindred theme of revelation. The link is the notion of expression: 'The redemption is the outstanding expression of God to man. ... We express ourselves, we communicate, through the flesh, through words and gestures, the unnoticed movements of the countenance, pauses, all the manners in which, as Newman says, "cor ad cor loquitur," the heart speaks unto the heart. And the incarnation and the redemption are the supreme instance of God communicating to us in this life' (5–6). It is a personal communication 'directed to each individual soul ... accessible to everyone' (7).

There follows a longish section (8–14) on the intelligibility of the redemption. The redemption is a mystery, yet it 'involves things that profoundly trouble the mind of man: suffering and death and sin, forgiveness and law, and so on' (8). What kind of intelligibility? Lonergan lists some of its features. It is not a necessity (8) but a dynamic intelligibility (9), an incarnate intelligibility (10), a complex intelligibility (12), a multiple intelligibility (13). Sub-section 3.3 (10–11) enlarges on this incarnate intelligibility:

[It is] not an abstract but an incarnate intelligibility. It exploits all the subtle relations that hold between body and mind, between flesh and spirit. Christ crucified is a symbol of endless meaning, and it is not merely a symbol but also a real death. It is again in the concrete, in the flesh of Christ, in his blood, and in his death that punishment is transfigured into satisfaction (10).

Turning to more traditional language Lonergan speaks (14–24) of sacrifice, of the word 'redemption,' of vicarious satisfaction, of merit, and of efficiency. Under that heading of efficiency (24) he refers to the historical causality of Christ in the redemption: 'What he has done as a historical person who founded a church and down the ages has exerted an influence on the lives of countless millions, more intimate and more profound than any other historical figure.' This short passage of only seven lines is significant for the whole study we are making. With only a smattering of history we can name a hundred great historical figures, people whose lives made a difference, not only in their family circle or neighbourhood and during their lifetime but in the wider world and over the centuries. It has been Lonergan's aim in all his thought on historical causality to see Christ as such a person, making a difference, not on the level of wars or politics or literature, but on the level of sin and repentance, of anguish and faith, of evil and hope, of love and forgiveness, and thus exerting an influence 'more intimate and more profound than any other historical figure.'

The last section of the lecture, 'Redemption as Mystery' (24–28), is again a departure from the usual approach. For a total view Lonergan suggests 'that the fundamental category is the word *mystery*, not in the theologian's sense of a truth that we cannot adequately understand in this life, nor in the sense of Christian piety that speaks of the mysteries of the life of Christ … but in the sense of the New Testament, where it refers to the secret counsel of God' (24, with references to Mark 4:11-12 and Romans 16; see, however, *de bono*, article 24 above, on a needed specification of 'secret counsel'). Lonergan then develops this point in terms of the kingdom of God, the body of Christ, and the foundation of the church, turning finally to the passage in which 'Christ speaks of giving his soul in redemption for many' (27).

'The New Testament … in such a passage and in many others provides the clue to the intelligibility of the redemption. It is the victory of suffering, of accepting the consequences of sin, the evils of this world, in the spirit that animated Christ. It is the transformation of the world that arises when evil is transformed into good by the Christian spirit' (28). That last remark links this lecture with Chapter 4 of *de bono* and Chapter 17 of *De Verbo incarnato* on the familiar 'law of the cross.'

Approaching the critical period in Lonergan's thought, his break with Scholasticism and engagement with modernity as represented especially in the idea of historicity, I return to the more benign attitude of Chapter 7 above. I would make the point that Lonergan's Scholasticism was not a dull rehashing of dead doctrines. I would insist even that his Scholasticism was innovative. On his beginning to lecture at the Gregorian, and before he came to terms with the new historicity, his students already labelled his courses 'una parola nuova.'[8]

10

'Una parola nuova'

If even Lonergan's Scholasticism was 'una parola nuova,' the term must apply still more appropriately to his newly emerging modernity; that is the development to be studied now. The somewhat scattered materials for this chapter can be given a semblance of order if they are gathered under two headings: a kind of Ariadne thread for an overview of the journey, and halts on the way to illustrate our progress.

1. The Thread: From 'De methodis' to 'Method'

A good number of Lonergan's followers, and I among them, have tried to pin down the change his thinking underwent in the 1960s. The jury is still out on most of our ideas, and this uncertainty on what really happened means uncertainty to the same degree on what the revolutionary factors were and when they became effective. It may be quixotic even to search for a series of clearly fixed turning points. It is possible that only at a much later time, history will show what was going forward, as *Insight* clarified *Verbum* and *Method* clarified *Insight*. So as I continue the search, some points seem to emerge as especially significant. This chapter will attempt to define a few of them.

In my view, historicity represents the fundamental development in this period. Can we pinpoint the entry of that new force into the world of Catholic thought? And how are we to handle the transition in Lonergan himself from the two great works of Scholastic theology, *De Verbo incarnato* and *De Deo trino*, to the position taken, say, at the Laval lecture of 1975 (see Chapter 11 below)? For my limited purpose of discerning elements for a new Christology, I propose a thread to follow, with nodules here and there to make it more visible. The thread is the series of graduate courses and institutes on method from 1955 to the book of 1972; the nodules, the points of pause, are provided fairly well by the tables of contents in the published collections of his occasional papers. Meanwhile, a continuing third factor, his basic degree courses in theology at the Gregorian, is contrasted with these two to give a curious duality to his work during the Roman period of 1953–65. I do not wish to belittle his courses in basic theology – they carried the weight of tradition and are studded with little gems to admire – but my plan calls for concentration on our Ariadne thread and its nodules. The first part of this chapter will follow the thread; the second will pause here and there to examine determinate samples of history, concrete evidence of the change going forward.

The series of graduate lectures began in Lonergan's second year in Rome, probably in the second semester of 1954–55. The first course was listed as 'De methodis universim, inquisitio theoretica' ('On methods in general, a theoretical inquiry'). He himself, however, called it 'a course on Insight': that is, not the act of insight, but on the still unpublished book.[1] In fact, he seems to have followed the book rather closely, for he remarks about the course that he 'was able to get only as far as end of Chapter XIII.'[2]

There is no record of courses in this series for the next three years, but in the spring semester of 1958–59 he gave a course 'De intellectu et methodo' ('On understanding and method'), followed in 1959–60 by a course 'De systemate et historia' ('On system and history'). 'De intellectu et methodo' was offered again in the spring semester of 1960–61, but a year later in 1961–62 the course offering was 'De methodo theologiae' ('On the method of theology'). Both courses are well documented. We have a carefully done 'reportatio' of the 'De intellectu et methodo' of 1958–59; the 'De methodo theologiae' is available also in audio and in English, for it was repeated at Regis College, Toronto, in the summer of 1962, and of this course we have a tape-recording and its transcription. A graduate course with the same title ('De methodo theologiae') but different content was given at the Gregorian in 1963–64, and we have a 'reportatio' of this. Summer courses at Moraga, CA (St Mary's College) in 1961, at Spokane (Gonzaga University) in 1963, and Washington, DC (Georgetown University) in 1964 bring us to the interruption due to surgery in 1965. The series resumes at Boston College in 1968; Regis College, Toronto, in 1969; Boston College again in 1970; and Milltown Park, Dublin, in 1971. There is abundant material on most of these, and they all, directly or indirectly, pursue the same thread, showing the 'new' Lonergan emerging. I will delay a moment on select courses to show the direction and character of his thinking.

The *De intellectu et methodo* of 1959[3] is foundational, I would say, for the 'new' Lonergan, and essential to an account of his later Christology. It is, in effect, an analysis of the historicity that distinguishes the later Lonergan. The heart of the matter is found (pages 11–24) in his presentation of the threefold problem of foundations, historicity, and the chasm that historicity creates between theology and its sources. The role of wisdom (16–22) is of high interest, as are the five precepts of method (37–68), but my interest centres on the transition from the symbolic mentality of the scriptures to the scientific understanding that is the aim of theology. How Lonergan finally solves the problem of that transition we shall see in due course; for the present I continue to follow the thread of his series of attempts to deal with it.

The course 'De systemate et historia' of 1959–60 was recorded with great care by Fr Rossi de Gasperis, and our archives have a photocopy of his script.[4] Unfortunately for us, Fr de Gasperis had his own system of writing and abbreviating that no one so far has ventured to transcribe into something readable. The archives, however, have Lonergan's autograph of 18 pages for what seems to be the beginning of the course.[5] These pages contrast the Greek mind with the modern and are concerned with overcoming the dialectical opposition between them. But the bulk of the 18 pages deals with history, with the difference between history conceived as a matter of believing witnesses and history conceived as understanding what was going forward, even despite false witnesses and fabricated clues. Lonergan attends to the specific problems of the history of science, the history of art, the history of philosophy, the history of theology. He is concerned especially with the question whether the history is scientific, and applies to the question his heuristic strategy of the upper blade (systematic ideas) and lower blade (data). Already in 1960, the historicity of all things human is well delineated in this manuscript.

The 'De methodo theologiae' of 1962[6] (at the Gregorian University and at Regis College) is an advance on the courses of 1959 and 1960. Lonergan begins with a 50-page 'chapter' on method, in which the first two sections, significantly, are on operations and the subject; only in third place do objects become the heading.[7] After this chapter on method, Lonergan turns to the human good (the order ten years later of *Method in Theology*). Other topics are three antitheses (sacred and profane, internal and external, visible world and the intelligible), historical consciousness, extrinsicism, meaning, hermeneutics, history. The categories of transition in *De intellectu et methodo* are expanding and finding expression in new forms.

I conclude this part of the chapter with two notes. First, the Georgetown University institute of 1964 has the neat tableau: data, data with a meaning, and meaning that is true.[8] Another is a word of caution: we should not regard these institutes as a planned series in which Lonergan would unfold his thought year by year in orderly fashion. On the contrary, in several of them he responded to invitations and lectured under headings suggested to him. It is true, however, that despite the variety of assigned headings he managed to make the institutes serve the purpose of his own developing thought.

2. Some Nodules

Besides the thread there are the nodules, indicated as I have suggested in the published collections of his occasional papers. For the rest of this chapter I will select five of these papers for brief study, and conclude with a glance at themes that are touched on in the papers of *A Second Collection* and are representative of the later Lonergan; they show him emerging from Scholasticism and making his way to *Method in Theology*.

2.1. The Human and Historical Life of Christ

For a brief description of Lonergan's interest in the human and historical life of Christ we may borrow from the 1975 lecture at Laval University, when he contrasted the medieval approach (through soul, essence, potencies) with the one needed today: 'If we are to think of Jesus as truly a man, we have to think of him as a historical being, as growing in wisdom, age, and grace in a determinate social and cultural milieu, as developing from below the way other human beings do and from above on the analogy of religious development.'[9]

Returning now to the order of chronology, we find that this theme was developed several years earlier in the *De Verbo incarnato* of 1964. Thesis 12 of that work (332) speaks of Christ eliciting those cognitive acts that constitute his human and historical life. A few pages later (344–48), this human and historical life of Christ ('vita humana et historica') is identified with that part of the life of Christ the man that pertains to a pilgrim on earth. Though the topic can claim Thomas Aquinas as patron, for he deals extensively with the course of Christ's life on earth, it had not been a major theme in Lonergan's previous Christology. The 1964 work reveals new thinking, which I paraphrase as follows.[10]

A human life, Lonergan wrote, is the life in which by stages one so advances from infancy as to make oneself the human being one would later be found to be before God and fellow human beings. It is not a matter of simple growth and size but of the developmental process that is at once physical and psychic, at once apprehensive and affective, at once intellectual and gifted with free choice. One learns not only in order to know, but first of all in order to coordinate and govern one's body, to walk, to feed and dress oneself, to make one's sensitive operations more distinct and efficacious, to combine them in many advancing ways, to explore and use at will the whole field of possible combinations.

This learning process is perfected in body and sense in such a way that the faculty of understanding is neither otiose nor a perfectly conjoined instrument, but has the purpose of forming such an instrument. The more this instrument is perfected, the more one's will and personal choices will influence the process; and therefore on the contrary side it belongs to parents and tutors so to give the reins to their charges that children can act for themselves, adolescents can understand for themselves, youths can decide for themselves.

We affirm then, says Lonergan, that Christ received not adult humanity but that of an infant, that he made himself an adult through his acts of experiencing, knowing, choosing. We say that he not only had but formed for himself his own personal manner of acting ('indolem'), his own character, his personal way of making, doing, speaking, living. We affirm that he formed himself, not merely by natural activities, as if he were in a state of pure nature, and not by the light of faith either, as if he were not the head but a member of his body, but by the immediate knowledge of God through which he so revealed the divine mystery in an incarnate way that he was able to say to all, 'Follow me' (Luke 2:52).

Second, this life of Christ is historical because it was lived in a human world and under the conditions of a human world. For as a human life is constituted also by cognitional and voluntary acts, so human beings living together constitute, by their apprehensions and choices, a human technological, economic, familial, political, social, cultural, religious world. Further, there are as many of these human worlds as there are races, languages, localities, climates ('tempora'). And these worlds, according to their origin, evolution, crises, decadence, hybrid character, affiliations, natural similarities ('apparentationes'), are investigated indeed by the more profound historians, but are constructed individually by those who live in them, even if they do not know they do so.

We affirm, then, that Christ did not only receive the humanity of an infant, but also one derived from the line ('stirpe') of David, in the region of Palestine, in the time of Augustus, so that he would speak Aramaic, be educated under Hebraic law and grow to adulthood ('adolesceret') among the people of Galilee. We say he was not only born in that determinate human world but that he made it his own, with its language and culture. Lonergan's phrase 'made it his own,' as it implies acceptance and assimilation (the language of Piaget, whom Lonergan read in 1959), affirms a certain personal adaptation and trans-formation ('recreationem') of that world. Jesus therefore avidly questioned the doctors of the law in Jerusalem that he might learn ('acciperet'); further, this twelve-year-old prodigy ('mirabilis') not only learned but also penetrated and transformed what he learned. Nor did he return unwillingly to Nazareth (Luke 2:41-52), since he was not only learning from the Old Testament but also had the New to think out in effable terms.

Such was the human historical life of Jesus as Lonergan saw it, not expressed in the style of a novelist, but in his own descriptive and ex-planatory way. Lonergan goes on to note the difference of the medieval problematic from the more recent. The former studied the perfection of knowledge in the intellect of Christ, and so considered primarily habits and possible acts, rather than the acts actually elicited. More recent thinkers consider acts as forming part of life, and consider individual human life as forming part of human history. Lonergan points out the ineptitude, either of attributing error to medieval theologians because they did not consider modern questions, or of affirming a medieval thesis yet trying to satisfy the difficulties of the recent theologians.

2.2. Historical Causality: The Question Raised

A second illustration of Lonergan's breaking away from Scholasticism is his discussion of the historical causality of Christ. Outcroppings of this interest appear in the pre-Scholastic *pantôn* paper of 1935; it gets explicit attention in article 42 of the *de bono*; and there is the enigmatic raising of the question in the *De Verbo incarnato* of 1960 ('desideratur consideratio de causalitate historica'). Finally, there is all the material we shall collect and discuss in Chapter 14. It is difficult to find an intelligible sequence in all this. Perhaps the fault lies in seeking such a sequence; perhaps Lonergan's sustained interest results in the spontaneity of unorganized references, and the 'sequence' exists only in an underlying carrier of interest.

I have already (Chapter 9 above) drawn attention to the puzzle of Lonergan's call in 1960 for a work on the historical causality of Christ, a work that he himself had written two years earlier in *de bono*. Returning to that question I fall back on the view that ca. 1959 Lonergan was caught in the bind of having to provide a manual for his students, and not being ready yet to incorporate into it all the work of 1958, he simply provided an updated version of the Boyer manual that he had been teaching. The question of the very format of a *De Verbo incarnato* that would include *de bono* was inhibiting, for *de bono* was a series of articles not well suited for transfer to a volume written in thesis style.

What is certain is that historical causality was very much on Lonergan's mind at this time and remained one of the key questions of his Christology.[11] His interest is documented in *De Verbo incarnato*, with its already oft-quoted one-liner on the gap in Christology: 'Further, there is lacking study of the historical causality which Christ the man obviously exercises.' The context was a scholion on the power of Christ ('De potentia Christi hominis'). There is a reference to treatises on the causality of the sacraments that allows us to subsume here our earlier work on that topic, but the scholion itself is exasperatingly brief: only our one-liner, preceded by three lines of bibliography.[12]

The notion, however, turns up again in the same treatise when Lonergan is dealing with the death of Christ and states that John shows its historical causality.[13] This is not explained at any length, but it is contrasted with the role of secondary causes. The latter are illustrated by the betrayal, the chief priests, Pilate, and so on. But John, Lonergan says, does not merely narrate the continual opposition of the Jews but also goes behind secondary causes and proposes higher principles that suggest that this opposition is an almost necessary element in the common course of human affairs.[14]

Besides this written documentation there is the oral communication of Lonergan with his followers and students. I have given my own testimony on a meeting with Lonergan in 1972, when he called *de bono* a work of 1963–64. Adding to the data on this matter, Joseph Komonchak reports a conversation he had with Lonergan in the early 1960s: 'One day when I asked him about the theology of the redemption, he disabused me of the idea that Aristotle's four causes were adequate, sending me instead to the idea of historical causality.'[15]

2.3. Incarnate Meaning

Lonergan's thinking took a long step forward in the early 1960s, when meaning was added to intelligibility as a governing concept. Of course, his earlier work was full of references to meaning.[16] But now there is a new angle: there emerges the fundamental concept of meaning as constitutive (due, it seems, to his having read Dilthey) and of the world as constituted by meaning.[17]

This new interest naturally entered his Christology. 'Time and Meaning' (1962) lists some varieties of meaning: intersubjective, symbolic, incarnate, artistic, linguistic.[18] Our interest is caught by 'incarnate meaning,' but in this lecture that phrase does not refer to the meaning incarnate in Christ but rather to Georges Morel's three volumes on the meaning of existence in John of the Cross.

> [Morel] has written a penetrating, profound account of what he calls the symbol, and to distinguish it from symbols as considered by Durand or Jung or Freud, one may call it incarnate meaning, namely, meaning in the sense of the meaning of a man's life, the meaning of a decisive gesture in a person's life. The meaning resides *in* the person, in everything he has done leading up to this moment.[19]

The application to Christ is soon made, however; it occurs in a lecture on 'The Analogy of Meaning.'

> From intersubjective meaning one can move on very easily to what might be called incarnate meaning. A person, either in his totality or in his characteristic moment, his most significant deed, his outstanding achievement or sacrifice, *is* a meaning. That meaning may be cherished, revered, adored, re-created, lived, or it may be loathed, abominated, contemned. The persons in the drama of the passion and death of Christ all have that embodied and incarnate meaning. Such is the meaning of the crucifix, the meaning of our Lady standing at the foot of the cross, the meaning of Judas, of Peter's denial, and so on. They all contain profound meanings: there is a meaning contained simply in the person, in the person's actions, in the person's deeds. I have given you a religious example, but the same can be verified in national heroes. That type of incarnate meaning is perhaps the fundamental theme in Georges Morel's three volumes ....[20]

Lonergan goes on to contrast Morel with Heidegger. Morel's work is on the meaning of existence in John of the Cross, whereas Heidegger 'had given us an apostate's view of the meaning of existence ....'

After considering various types of meaning (somewhat expanding the earlier list), Lonergan adds a short section on 'Meaning in Theology.'

> ... theology goes a step further; it adds something on to human science. Human science arrives at its goal when it knows correctly what men mean. But what men may mean may be true or false, right or wrong ... But the word of God differs from the word of man. It is a datum, and it has a meaning, as have the data of human science. But it adds something on to that. The meaning of the word of God ... has a fundamental ... validity, a truth; it is something not to be refused, not to be rejected.[21]

Lonergan sets this in the context of divine revelation. 'Revelation is God's entering into the world of human meaning.'[22]

2.4. Mediation of Christ in Prayer

The idea of mediation appears with a relatively new application in the Gonzaga University lectures of the summer of 1963 and later that same year in a lecture at the Thomas More Institute. As is regularly the case, it is preceded by a sustained effort to get ideas straight. This Lonergan attempts under these headings: mediation in general; mutual mediation; the functional whole; self-mediation; mutual self-mediation.

> We have considered a long series of applications of the notion of mediation in a way that has no dependence on Hegelian logic with its idealist presuppositions, that rests simply on generalizing the notion of mediation found in Aristotle. Aristotle conceived only necessity, evidence, truth as a field in which there is the immediate and the mediated. By considering any factor, property, aspect to be immediate in one location and mediated in other locations, I have attempted to show how the notion of mediation can develop into a pattern of structures of mutual mediation, self-mediation, and mutual self-mediation.[23]

Our question is not about all the ways mediation may be applied, but about application to the mediation of Christ in prayer. The obvious ways Christ mediates come under the heading 'objective application'; what is significant in prayer Lonergan puts under 'subjective application.'

First, objective application.[24] The mediating role of Christ has already come up, notably in article 43 of *de bono*, and in thesis 15 of *De Verbo incarnato*. The present interest is limited to the objective aspect as preliminary to the mediation of Christ in prayer. It is found in the example of Christ: 'The example of Christ in his life, in his suffering and death, is set before us through all our religious teaching; and the work of Christ – in his redemption, in his sacrifice, in his satisfaction, and in the church that carries on his work – is all before us.' Lonergan then turns to trinitarian theology, and collects several texts of scripture on Christ and the Spirit as mediating. That Christ mediates between us and the Father we find in 1 Timothy 2:5: 'There is one God and there is one mediator between man and God, the man Jesus Christ.' That the Spirit mediates between us and Christ we find in 1 Corinthians 12:3: 'No one can say that Jesus is Lord except in the Holy Spirit, and no one in the Holy Spirit says anathema to Jesus.'

Next comes the subjective application,[25] where we can see Christ both as immediate and as mediator.

> Each of us is to himself something immediate: oneself as one is, oneself as *Existenz*, as capable of a decision that disposes of oneself and yet incapable of an absolute disposition; all that is to be known about oneself by analysis, by insight – yet not as so known, but rather as lived, as the *vécu* not the *thématique*, as the *actus exercitus* not the *actus signatus*. It is oneself as a prior given to oneself, all the data on one's spontaneity, one's deliberate decisions, one's living, one's loving. It is not one's thinking about all that but each of us in his or her immediacy to himself or herself. (178)

In that immediacy there are supernatural realities that result from the communication to us of Christ's life. There is identification between Christians and Christ (178).

> That is our reality, the higher part of our reality. It is something in us that is immediate and becomes mediated by the life of prayer. It is not immediate in the sense in which our bodies and our souls are immediate in us. They are ours by nature. Being a temple of the Holy Spirit ... is something that is ours essentially by a gift. Still ... it is part of our concrete reality, and in that sense it proceeds through the mediation of prayer from being a sort of vegetative living to a conscious living. ... It is not a matter

of study of oneself ... It is a living, a developing, a growing, in which ... a new whole emerges. That transformation is the mediation of what is immediate in us ... (179)

What is immediate can be mediated by our acts, and gradually reveal to us ... the fundamental fact about us: the great gift and grace that Jesus Christ brought to us (179–80).

This mediation is potentially universal; it can regard every act, thought, word, deed, and omission of the subject. And not only is there the mediation of the subject by his acts, but the acts have an object, and in that object the centre is Christ. It is Christ, not as apprehended by the apostles, or by the church, or by Christ himself, or by the Spirit. It is our *own* apprehension of him; we put on Christ in our own way; it has its foundation in tradition and revelation, but it arises from what is immediate in the subject (180).

It is, then, a self-mediation (180). There is the mediation by our acts of what is immediate in us through the grace of God. Further, 'it is not merely a self-mediation in which we develop, but it is a self-mediation through another ... one is carried along ... not in isolation, but in reference to Christ' (10). Again,

This development of the person in relation to another person is not only a self-mediation through another; it is a mutual self-mediation ... because Christ himself, as man, developed; he acquired human perfection. The human perfection that he acquired could have been quite different from the perfection that de facto he did acquire. Christ chose and decided to perfect himself in the manner in which he did because of us. We think of the way of the cross primarily as the cross of Christ. But primarily the way of the cross is the way in which fallen nature acquires its perfection ... It was because he was redeeming a fallen humanity that Christ chose ... to become the perfect man ... he was thinking of us and thinking of what we needed to be able to attain our own self-mediation. Just as ... we attain our own self-mediation with reference to him in this life of prayer, so also the life of Christ himself was a self-mediation with reference to others, and the others are we and all men.(180–81)

... One can think of attaining perfection through suffering ... in terms of abstract principles ... But instead of an abstract principle we have a mutual self-mediation ... We think of the cross as the cross of Christ; but primarily the cross is something that belongs to all humanity; Christ chose it because of us, and we choose it because of him.(181)

Lonergan now turns the matter over to each of us personally: 'To carry the point further is, in a sense, a matter only of private meditation ... The life of prayer is something on the level of what is lived ... and any talk about it is thematizing it.' Still Lonergan feels he has developed some notions that may be applied to our own subjectivity, to what is immediate in us. Initially, in a very obscure fashion, he did so in terms of objects. 'These objects are the immediate in an ontological immediacy. And that ontological immediacy is promoted to a psychological, an intentional immediacy through the life of prayer' (181–82).

The life of prayer, then: Christ is mediator in the life of prayer insofar as the life of prayer itself is a transition from the immediacy of spontaneity through the objectification of ourselves in acts. The acts of living and the acts within prayer are referred to Christ. By that process we perfect ourselves ... There is a similar process in the becoming of Christ as man; and in that case he was becoming himself with reference to us. In both cases the fundamental theorem ... is transforming evil into good .... (182)

I have quoted Lonergan at great length in this chapter, as I will do in the next chapter as well. Readers, I feel, will approve. The doctrine in both cases is too precious to be filtered through an abbreviating interpreter.

2.5. 'Being in Christ Jesus'

This scriptural phrase was exploited in a talk Lonergan gave in 1964 at Regis College, Toronto, under the title '*Existenz* and *Aggiornamento*,' which raised the question What kind of persons must we be to implement the *aggiornamento* Vatican II decreed? '... what it is for a Catholic, a religious, a priest, to be himself today.'[26] The question then focused on being oneself.

Being oneself is being, and by being is not meant the abstract but the concrete ... It is substance and subject: our opaque being that rises to consciousness and our conscious being by which we save or damn our souls ... [L]ove shows itself more in deeds than in words; but being in love is neither deeds nor words; it is the prior conscious reality that words and ... deeds reveal.(229)

That prior and opaque and luminous being is not static; it is precarious. And its being precarious is the possibility not only of a fall but also of a fuller development. The development is open; we are open to God. Implicit in our inquiry is a natural desire to know God. Implicit in our judgment on contingent things is the formally unconditioned that is God. Implicit in our choice of values is the absolute good that is God (229–30).

'In Christ Jesus we are not only referred to God, as to some omega point, but we are on our way to God. The fount of our living is not … desire of an end that uses means but love of an end that overflows.' God created not to get but to give. Christ did not will means to reach an end, but possessed the end and 'overflowed from love of the infinite to loving even the finite' (230). So, too, 'those in Christ participate in the charity of Christ,' as temples of the Spirit, as adopted children who can say *Abba*.

> But this being in Christ Jesus may be the being of substance or of subject. Inasmuch as it is just the being of substance, it is known only through faith … it is being in love with God without awareness of being in love. Without any experience of just how and why, one is in the state of grace or one recovers it, one leaves all things to follow Christ, one binds oneself by vows of poverty, chastity, and obedience, one gets through one's daily heavy dose of prayer, one longs for the priesthood and later lives by it. Quietly, imperceptibly, there goes forward the transformation operated by the *Kurios*, but the delicacy, the gentleness, the deftness, of his continual operation in us hides the operation from us. (230–31)

> But inasmuch as being in Christ Jesus is the being of subject, the hand of the Lord ceases to be hidden. In ways you all have experienced, in ways some have experienced more frequently or more intensely than others, in ways you still have to experience, and in ways none of us in this life will ever experience, the substance in Christ Jesus becomes the subject in Christ Jesus. For the love of God, being in love with God, can be as full and as dominant, as overwhelming and as lasting an experience as human love. (231)

> Being in Christ Jesus is not tied down to place or time, culture or epoch. It is catholic with the catholicity of the Spirit of the Lord. Neither is it an abstraction that dwells apart from every place and time, every culture and epoch. It is identical with per-

sonal living, and personal living is always here and now, in a contemporary world of immediacy, a contemporary world mediated by meaning, a contemporary world not only mediated but also constituted by meaning.

In personal living the questions abstractly asked about the relations between nature and grace emerge concretely in one's concern, one's interests, one's hopes, one's plans, one's daring and timidity, one's taking risks and playing safe. And as they emerge concretely, so too they are solved concretely. Such concrete solutions, whether doing a job or exercising a personal role, divided from the viewpoint of the challenge to which Pope John XXIII initiated a response, may be solutions thought out in Christ Jesus for an archaic world that no longer exists or for a futurist world that never will exist; they may be thought out for the world that is now but only at the price of not being thought out in Christ Jesus; they may be for the world that is now and thought out in Christ Jesus.

Our time is a time for profound and far-reaching creativity. The Lord be with us all – *ad maiorem Dei gloriam* – and, as I have said, God's own glory, in part, is you (231).

2.6. The New Lonergan Emerging: Various Papers

The five sections just concluded are samples of the Lonergan emerging from Scholasticism and exploring new ways of thought. They belong to a fairly well-defined period in his life, a period defined not just in years, but also by experiences and events and achievements. It found him, I would say, at the height of his powers. At its close he was just opening up what we believed would be a magnificent new era in theology, presaged by the breakthrough of February 1965. It suffered an abrupt and agonizing interruption under a surgeon's knife in the summer of 1965. Before going on to the post-1965 period I wish to set this preceding period in relief, considering 1958 to 1965 as a unit and in contrast to the period that follows.

Let us start from the five works cited in this chapter. They show through specific examples the general trend of Lonergan's thinking up to 1965. In a wider sweep the trend is roughly represented by the later papers in *Collection* (the three last papers there are dated 1964, 1964,

1965) and by the papers in *Philosophical and Theological Papers 1958–1964*, where the title itself of the volume conveniently provides the date of the contents. Then there is a break in progress that can be marked in several ways. The breakthrough to the eight functional specialties came in February 1965.[27] His near encounter with death occurred with the lung surgery in the summer of that year. The summer institutes were correspondingly interrupted.

But his period of slow convalescence had a positive side, too. It meant freedom from classroom obligations; from now on he could teach when he chose. More to the point, it provided a needed delay in his thinking as he struggled to come to terms with the German Historical School; the struggle was rewarded when his reading ca. 1969 of Peter Hünermann enabled him to use history in the way set forth in chapters 8 and 9 of *Method*.[28] The new factors at work are operative in the eighteen papers of *A Second Collection*,[29] the book that is my present concern. These papers are a record of Lonergan's growing mastery of a new *Begrifflichkeit* as he applies it to the emerging church of the 1960s and 1970s.[30] Many of the papers mediate between his state of mind in 1965 and his near definitive position in *Method*, 1972; in between he was working out his ideas for dealing with what had long been a major question for him: history. We do not therefore expect lengthy discussions of Christology.

Still, the references we do find are worth our attention. Thus, in the context of that key triad, progress–decline–redemption, a passage in the paper 'The Transition from a Classicist World-view to Historical-mindedness' reads as follows: 'This analysis fits in with scriptural doctrine, which understands suffering and death as the result of sin yet inculcates the transforming power of Christ, who in himself and in us changes suffering and death into the means for attaining resurrection and glory.' There follow a number of scriptural references in regard to sin, death, the first and last Adam, Christ's death and resurrection for our salvation. Lonergan continues: 'As Christ's death is a principle of salvation, so also are our own deaths, whether understood physically ... ascetically ... morally ... sacramentally' (8–9).[31]

A question rather new for him is discussed in the paper 'The Future of Christianity' (149–63): namely, the question on what is distinctive of Christianity (156). The question will return in Chapter 16 in the context of world religions but it belongs here too. Lonergan first quotes with approval C.F.D. Moule, to the effect that the Christians did not stand for an original philosophy of life or an original ethic. Rather, they bore witness to an event, the resurrection of Jesus. To which Lonergan adds, 'What distinguishes the Christian, then, is not God's grace, which he shares with others, but the mediation of God's grace through Jesus Christ our Lord.' This leads Lonergan to an important slant on the social character of Christianity.

> In the Christian, accordingly, God's gift of his love is a love that is in Christ Jesus. From this fact flow the social, historical, doctrinal aspects of Christianity. For the gift of God's love … is not so private as to be solitary. It is given to many through Christ Jesus that they may be one in him. They need one another to come to understand the gift that has been given them, to think out what it implies and involves, to support one another in their effort to live Christian lives. … The need of teaching and preaching, of rituals and common worship, is the need to be members of one another, to share with one another what is deepest in ourselves, to be recalled from our waywardness, to be encouraged in our good intentions. (156–57)

There is a helpful overview in the 1970 paper 'The Response of the Jesuit as Priest and Apostle in the Modern World' (165–87). Here is his own list of headings: authenticity, the Spirit, the word, sending, followed by two sections more pertinent to the audience he was addressing: the Renaissance Jesuit, and the Jesuit today. Section 2, The Spirit (170–73), is all about love: the love of intimacy, the love of one's fellow human beings, the love of God. The focus is on the latter, which is unrestricted love, love that is the proper fulfillment of our capacity. Lonergan expands these points, taking a position that corresponds to Chapter 4 of *Method*. That chapter must have been written almost simultaneously with the 'Response of the Jesuit' paper, but not being specifically Christian it did not speak in terms of Word and Spirit.

Section 3, The Word (173–75), shows the complementarity of Word and Love. Love must be declared. 'If a man and woman were to love each other yet never avow their love … [t]here would be lacking an interpersonal component, a mutual presence of self-donation' (173). Lonergan continues with further statements on love and comes to the relation of Son and Spirit in the gift of our salvation, a point of great interest for his Christology.

But there is a notable anonymity to this gift of the Spirit. Like the Johannine *pneuma*, it blows where it wills; you hear the sound of it, but you do not know where it comes from or where it is going (John 3:8). What removes this obscurity and anonymity is the fact that the Father has spoken to us of old through the prophets and in this final age through the Son (Hebrews 1:1-2). His communication is twofold; it is both by linguistic meaning and by incarnate meaning. By linguistic meaning he rebuked those that give scandal, announced redemption for sinners, provided for the forgiveness of sin, established the bond of the Eucharist, promised the gift of the Spirit, and set before men the destiny of eternal life. But all such linguistic meaning was endlessly reinforced by the incarnate meaning to be contemplated in the life and ministry and, above all, in the suffering, death, and resurrection of Christ.(174–75)

Section 4, on sending, follows (175–81). The Spirit can be everywhere, but Christ's communication was circumscribed in time and in place; hence, 'the challenge of the Word radiates to the ends of the earth only through human mediation' (175). There follows an essay of several pages on that human mediation – remarkable, but only tangential to our Christology.[32]

2.7. *Method in Theology*

In chronological sequence, *Method* picks up where chapters 1 to 15 of *A Second Collection* leave off, following on all but the last three papers in that volume. As Lonergan kept reminding us, *Method* is not a book of theology and even less one of Christology. '... I quote scripture, the ecumenical councils, papal encyclicals, other theologians ... sparingly. I am writing not theology but method in theology.'[33] Moreover, *Method* was more ecumenical than most of Lonergan's previous work: 'The method I indicate is, I think, relevant to more than Roman Catholic theologians. But I must leave it to members of other communions to decide upon the extent to which they may employ the present method.'[34] Thus we should not look for a Christology here, and the elements for one that we may find are subordinate to a wider purpose. A good example of that is his brief section on incarnate meaning (73); it is but a subordinate part, one of ten, in a general discussion of meaning. When he would illustrate the efficacy of this meaning he refers to Marathon, to Christian martyrs, to Hamlet, but not to Christ.[35]

145

Granting, then, that *Method* is not a Christology and not a book of theology, I still find in it passages that suit our purpose. One of these is the section on the word (112–15). I have noted the expressly Christian account of the 'word' that Lonergan gave in his 1970 lecture 'The Response of the Jesuit,' but *Method* gives the background in terms of religion in general. Its carrier is likewise various, though language is a privileged case. (The term 'word' is not capitalized here, for it is used generally: 'By the word is meant any expression of religious meaning or of religious value.')

Important is Lonergan's doctrine on the inner and outer words. 'Before it enters the world mediated by meaning, religion is the prior word God speaks to us by flooding our hearts with his love. That prior word pertains ... to the world of immediacy ... The outwardly spoken word is historically conditioned ...' (112). But do not regard the outward word as something incidental; it has a constitutive role. As we just now saw, love must be declared; unspoken love is not completely love (112–13). The mini-treatise on the word continues. 'The word ... is personal ... The religious leader, the prophet, the Christ, the apostle, the priest, the preacher' all announce what is congruent with God's gift of love. 'The word, too, is social ... The word, finally, is historical ...' (113).

Lonergan adds two corollaries: 'Faith is the knowledge born of religious love' (115), and 'Among the values that faith discerns is the value of believing the word of religion, of accepting the judgments of fact and the judgments of value that the religion proposes' (118). All this is set forth without special reference to Christ. But it is easy to link the outward word with Christ and the inner word with the Holy Spirit within us, as Lonergan did in 'The Response of the Jesuit.'

A more explicitly Christian chapter is the one on doctrines (Chapter 12, 295–333). Lonergan discusses the nature and functions of doctrines and writes on their development, their permanence, their historicity, and related questions. He illustrates his argument with copious references to the history of church doctrines on Christ, but concludes toward the end of the chapter (332): 'Though a Roman Catholic with quite conservative views on religious and church doctrines, I have written a chapter on doctrines without subscribing to any but the doctrine about doctrine set forth in the first Vatican council. I have done so deliberately, and my purpose has been ecumenical.'

For the rest I may simply point to the Index of *Method*: it has only a few entries under Jesus Christ (none under Christ) but has multiple entries under 'Christian ... Christianity ... and Christology.' Thus, Lonergan's examples are often Christian, but the book is only indirectly Christian. Let me illustrate that point with samples provided by the index. Christians have varying views on the data relevant to Christian theology (150). The Christian church results from the outer communication of Christ's message and from the inner gift of God's love (361–62). 'The Christian tradition makes explicit our implicit intending of God in all our intending by speaking of the Spirit ... of the Son ... of the Father ...' (291). On the personal entrance of God into history: 'Such was the religion of Israel. Such has been Christianity' (119). In summary, Lonergan uses Christian examples to illustrate his position but he generally intends those examples to apply more widely.

11

The New Christology, 1971–1975

The dates 1971–75 are meant to cover three areas of research: first, the courses at Harvard, 1971–72, and Regis College, 1972–73; next, a short but valuable question session at Boston College, 1974; and third, the Laval University lecture of 1975.

1. Harvard and Regis, 1971–73

Lonergan was Stillman Professor at Harvard Divinity School in the academic year 1971–72. In the spring semester he gave a course there called Method in Christology. On his return to Regis College, Toronto, he planned to give the same course there in the spring semester, 1973; he did in fact give some lectures but was unable to continue, and the course was completed by Fred Crowe. Is it a course in Christology or a course in method? The title calls it a course in method, but if we regard the content and his remark that his purpose was to give meaning to Chalcedon, we might incline rather to call it a course in Christology. And though it proves nothing, that option would accord with my giving method a contrapuntal role in the course (see my Prologue above): I find it easier to think of Christology as carrying the theme and method accompanying it, than to think of the roles reversed.

That question really does not matter: *materialiter*, as the Scholastics say, it is a course in both method and Christology. A more important question asks how seriously Lonergan took the opportunity to test his method in an actual field of theology. I am inclined to say that much of the testing had been done long before, that his method had grown out of the double 'experiment' of more than thirty years of teaching and lecturing, double because the exigences of seminary theology forced him to attend to the tradition, and the exigences of the times forced him to the *aggiornamento* achieved in his independent writing and lecturing. (See above, note 20 to Chapter 7.)

In any case, at Harvard the time was not yet ripe for a formal and deliberate testing. First of all, the book on method was not yet published. Then, he was old, and weary from the long struggle in poor health to finish the book; the time was not propitious for new ventures. But somewhere in the course (I have lost the reference) he stated his purpose: to give meaning to Chalcedon. That serves rather well as a pointer to the roles that method and Christology have in the course. For Chalcedon is central in a Christology, and meaning is central in method. Materially, then, the course offers a Christology, structured in a pattern that, except for the omission of redemption, is broadly the same as that of the Gregorian *De Verbo incarnato*. Formally, one may say, it is governed throughout by principles of method, but the references to method are scattered and, after the opening lecture, rather brief; one would have to collect and order them to create a mini-course on method. The place to look for the present question is not the Harvard course but the preceding history. During thirty years and more he refined the instrument he would present in *Method*. His course *De intellectu et methodo*, dealing explicitly with transitions in theology, would illustrate the refinement of the instrument, while his seminary courses, *De Verbo incarnato* and *De Deo trino*, were providing the material elements of the testing.

Fortunately, however, I am not writing a book on methodology, but one on Christology. Records of Lonergan's Harvard Christology exist. There are two autograph files in the Archives, both numbered 602. The first (let us call it 602–1; in R. Doran's catalog, A2390–A2402) is Lonergan's lecture notes for the Harvard course. This file, however, is not complete; it seems that a year later Lonergan was using these notes, somewhat reworked, for his Regis course and so removed them from the Harvard file as they were needed. The second file (call it 602–2; in the Doran catalog, A2370–A2388) is his Regis lecture notes (with materials transferred from the Harvard file) as far as he got. There are tapes of the Harvard Christology, numbers 665–74 in the Archives, and of the Regis Christology, numbers 731–37 in the Archives. There is a transcription of the first two Regis lectures (call it 602–2T), but it needs editing.

The work of collating all these documents and making a coherent report on the lectures remains to be done, but a few soundings will suffice for present purposes. Lonergan begins with the distinction of Christology from soteriology (602–2, page 2), providing an answer, at least verbally, to the question some have asked: where in his Christology is his soteriology? The former, he says, is the doctrine of the person of Christ, the latter the doctrine of the work of Christ. The course is on Christology and so does not treat soteriology or the redemption. The distinction perhaps served to reduce his task to what was manageable in a semester course; still, redemption had been part of his Christology in *De Verbo incarnato*, and one misses it here in the Harvard lectures.

The lectures begin with and are heavily slanted to the New Testament. In fact, a striking difference of the Harvard-Regis lectures from the Gregorian *De Verbo incarnato* is the position accorded scripture. I have remarked that, though Lonergan had come to admit in 1955 (LETTER– 5, above) the principle of the new exegesis, he was much slower to implement it in practice. Now he does so with a vengeance. Fully recognizing, however, that scriptural scholarship is not his specialty, he relies on Reginald H. Fuller[1] and, following him, treats the three stages of early Christology: Palestinian Judaism, Hellenistic Judaism, and Hellenistic Gentile thought, setting forth in each the 'tools' – that is, the language – of that stage.

From scripture the lectures proceed through the history of Christology in the usual manner. Lonergan dealt with his materials in a thorough way only as far as Chalcedon (confirming the view that his purpose was to give meaning to that council) and rounded off the course with a hurried mention of other topics usual in Christology. The last pages treat briefly Chalcedon, the consciousness of Christ, the metaphysics of the hypostatic union, and conclude with a half-page on differentiations of consciousness with sweeping application to Scholasticism and Chalcedon, and to Constantinople II and III.

2. Boston College, 1974

There is a fair amount of documentation on Christology for the seventeen years of active life that remained to Lonergan after 1965, the year functional specialties came on the scene, but one radical development is badly documented. The best exposition I have found is his sketchy reply to a question asked at the June 1974 Boston College Workshop. In the third question session (page 14 of a transcript by an unknown person) Lonergan was asked: 'Would you say something about what you are now doing in Christology as distinct from what you did in *De Verbo incarnato*?' His reply to the question was brief, categorical, and off-putting: He was doing nothing in Christology at the moment! He was too busy with other things! But then he relented and went on, 'However, what I would do ...' And it is the hypothetical Christology of that 'what he would do' that is of the highest interest.[2]

What he would do regards first the use of the New Testament. The world of thought dominated by Aristotle's speculative intellect looked for truths and attended principally to that factor in the New Testament. But when you have sublated orthodoxy by orthopraxy you get a different emphasis. What before was taken as a sort of confirming evidence [becomes primary] – the high opinion people had of Christ; the extraordinary demands he made on people, 'He who loves father and mother more than me is not worthy of me'; [factors] that regard orthopraxy; that supreme exigence with regard to orthopraxy – these would demand first and fundamental emphasis. And you understand the later development in terms of grounding that demand in the New Testament. 'That's just an idea; working it out I leave to [others].' But Lonergan himself returned to the idea briefly the next year in his Laval lecture, and I use that written document to fill out and clarify the Boston College sketch: 'An implicit Christology does not attribute to Jesus himself any of the titles the New Testament ascribes to him but does find Christological doctrine implicit in his preaching the kingdom of God and in the authority and power he displayed.'[3]

Let us return to that badly recorded but invaluable question session at Boston College, 1974. Lonergan goes on to mention two other angles he would use in his hypothetical Christology ('what I would do'). One regards Christ as subject (15), and a somewhat disorderly statement seems to be saying the following: if the human subject is something that develops, as seems most likely, well, you have questions that come up about Christ as subject, the development in Christ's [subjectivity], and that can make things a lot more complex. On this matter Lonergan appeals to the Jungians: 'If they are right in saying that the self is the real center of the human being, very few people have that as their subject, the psychological subject that you reach to, approximate towards, is a great stage in the process of individuation.'[4] (This is surely to be complemented by Lonergan's reference a year later at Laval to Jungian thought on becoming oneself.) The point here seems to be that in Christ the subject is divine; we do not therefore speak of development in Christ the subject, but only of development in the human subjectivity of Christ. That, too, is confirmed if we look ahead again to the Laval lecture of 1975.

… we need a distinction between subject and subjectivity. For man's self-realization is by self-transcendence. Without difference there is no self-transcendence. Without identity it is not one's own but some other self that is realized. So we shall reserve the term, subject, to denote the identity. We shall employ the term, subjectivity, to denote the intelligible unity that already is teleologically what it eventually is to become.[5]

Thus, in God there are three subjects but one unchanging subjectivity; in Jesus there is one subject and two subjectivities, one of them human and changing.

The other angle he would exploit, Lonergan says in answer to the Boston College question, is the now familiar theme of the historical causality of Christ (page 15 of the Boston transcript, question session 3). It is most interesting that this keeps cropping up in Lonergan as a *desideratum*, while he persistently fails to bring in not only his work of 1935 (that is understandable) but also his work *de bono*. At the Boston workshop he even makes a sort of apology for his failure to treat the question in his textbook.

When you write a textbook in theology you do what you can … One of the things that I wanted to treat and worked towards treating but never got around to actually putting it in a treatise form, is the historical causality of Christ. It is the sort of thing where you need a theory of history and Christ as historical cause. Even to communicate the notions connected with it in Latin would be a matter of some difficulty, which I did not altogether surmount, didn't get around to doing when I was teaching. But it is a fundamental question, a fundamental issue, and it's perhaps the expression in our time of Christ the King, Christ the historical cause, [an expression that] fits in more with the way people have been thinking. Categories that have meaning are more than a symbol, [more than] seeing something as a symbol.(ibid.)

Lonergan seems to be saying:'The King as a symbol was suitable for other times, but historical causality is a category for understanding in our time what the King once symbolized.' I find this disjointed response at the Boston workshop in 1974 suggestive of a new approach in Christology, and can only hope that further research in the archives will shed stronger light on the matter.

3. Laval University, 1975

Less than a year after these events at Boston College, Lonergan gave one of the two major talks at a 'Colloque de christologie tenu à l'Université Laval.' His contribution was 'Christology Today: Methodological Reflections.'[6] Like the hypothetical Christology of Boston College 1974, the essay did not declare a fully determinate position but is rather looking forward to a future Christology. Still, it is the nearest the new Lonergan ever came to an explicit Christology, and so I impose on my readers a rather detailed report on the talk, near verbatim at times. In what follows, unless the contrary is clear, it is Lonergan who speaks.

First he sets the essay in context. We are in a new age of theology which puts forth new expressions of an old faith to meet the exigences of the new times. This applies to Christology as well as to other areas of belief; hence, our concern is what is new in Christology. In this situation one function of method is to determine what was inadequate in former procedures and discover better procedures to replace them; but another is to discern deficiencies to which the new age itself is exposed. Lonergan proposes to refer occasionally to these deficiencies; his purpose, however, is not controversial and negative but positive and didactic. He will deal with seven related topics, which he proceeds to list.[7] Three are prolegomena that deal in turn with psychology, philosophy, and history. As for Christology, he will treat it first as a religious question, then as a theological question. There follows discussion of two specific doctrines: 'The Meaning of Chalcedon' and 'Person Today.' The latter identifies and attempts to meet the main issue: 'Can one be truly a man without being a human person? It is an issue that is all the more grave now that we have set Scholasticism aside without as yet putting in its place any commonly accepted doctrine.'[8]

3.1. Psychology

The first prolegomenon discusses psychology. Scholastic psychology was a metaphysical psychology dealing with soul, potencies, habits, and acts, and the objects of those acts. 'So little did consciousness enter into this psychology that Aristotle treated in the same work the psychology of men, of animals, and of plants' (75). It is this psychology that has underpinned theological accounts of the person of Christ, his human perfections, his grace. This basically metaphysical approach stems from the Aristotelian view that other sciences were subalternate to metaphysics, the terms and principles of which held for all beings and were the nucleus around which particular sciences constructed their further determinations (76).

To meet the contemporary challenge one must go beyond a metaphysical view, not to reject it but to include it within the dynamic unity of a foundational methodology where all cognitional procedures would be retained and related within the critical architectonic of transcendental method. That method refers not only to objects but also to the a priori of the subject; that is, to the a priori of the subject's questions and to the range of objects disclosed in answers (76).

Now when psychology is conceived as a science in its own right, then it proceeds from the data of consciousness. 'Its basic terms name conscious operations. Its basic relations name conscious processes. Its account of truly human development is of conscious subjects moving cumulatively through their operations to the self-transcendence of truth and love' (76).

Ordinarily, this advance is from below upwards, from the sensitive level through understanding and judgment to evaluation, decision, action.

> Still the ordinary process is not the exclusive process. Man's insertion in community and history includes an invitation for him to accept the transformation of falling in love …

> Moreover, in the measure that this transformation is effective, development becomes not merely from below upwards but more fundamentally from above downwards. There has begun a life in which the heart has reasons which reason does not know …

> It is on the analogy of such transforming love that perhaps we can gain some imperfect understanding of the mystery that the life lived by Jesus of Nazareth really was the fully human life of the second person of the Blessed Trinity. (76–77)

I have touched on notions that are fundamental in any account of Lonergan's history: above all, the transition for basic science from metaphysics to the data of consciousness. Then, the addition of the downward movement of development to the upward movement; this had become a recurrent theme, adopted with alacrity, a year or so earlier.[9] Other factors, like the primacy of transforming love in the analogy for a divine person leading a truly human life, are likewise contributions to be studied in their own right.

3.2. Philosophy

The second prolegomenon deals with questions raised from the side of philosophy. When one deprecates the intrusion of philosophy into theology, the result is 'not no philosophy, but unconscious philosophy, and only too easily bad philosophy.' This is illustrated in a Christology of presence, where 'presence' is not thought through. What is presence? It means one thing in a world of immediacy, a world we all have lived in from infancy, and another in a world mediated by meaning. The two worlds differ vastly in their content, in their cognitional procedures, in their criteria for valid procedures. 'The world of immediacy is a world of data, of what is given to sense and given to consciousness. It is a world as yet without names or concepts, without truth or falsity, without right or wrong' (78). In contrast, the world mediated by meaning goes beyond experiencing, through inquiry to understanding, through understanding to truth and reality, beyond mere knowing through deliberation to free courses of action, finally to the point where consciousness becomes conscience (78).

This background eliminates some of the current confusion about presence. 'Besides the presence of parents to their infant child, there also is the presence of the parents to one another. No one would fail to notice the difference between these two instances of presence.' But to argue for a Christology of presence without clarity on presence itself makes confusion inevitable. For 'the presence of Christ to us is not presence in the world of immediacy … The fact is that divine revelation comes to us through the mediation of meaning. It comes through meaning transmitted by tradition, meaning translated from ancient to modern tongues, meaning here clarified and there distorted by human understanding, meaning reaffirmed and crystallized in dogmas, meaning coming to life in God's grace and God's love' (78–79).

Taking issue with those who would proceed from this world up to God but not in the opposite direction, Lonergan argues for a two-way traffic. While one-way traffic may suit a Christology of presence, 'it runs counter to the structure and procedures of the world mediated by meaning' (79). Human development proceeds from below upward but also from above downward. This applies to contemporary science and to theology, where 'one proceeds not only from the data of revelation to more comprehensive statements but also from an imperfect, analogous yet most fruitful understanding of mystery to the syntheses that complement a *via inventionis* with a *via doctrinae*' (79–80).

3.3. History

The third prolegomenon concerns history, a major issue in modernity but only belatedly acknowledged by the church. 'The meaning of Vatican II was the acknowledgement of history,' Lonergan claims.[10]

> There is the history that is written and the history that is written about. Today the history that is written is the work of an ongoing community of professional specialists, developing their proper skills and techniques, setting their own standards, and making their standards effective through a long and exacting apprenticeship of graduate studies. History in this contemporary sense largely was the creation of the nineteenth century, and its acceptance in the Catholic church has occurred only slowly and gradually in the present century (80 – pagination again that of the Laval lecture).

Lonergan's present interest is the history that is written. 'Where earlier history was a matter of believing testimony, contemporary history is a matter of understanding evidence …' This contrast, between 'precritical belief in testimony and critical understanding of evidence is of the greatest theological significance.' On the older view, 'the greatest emphasis will be placed on the words of Jesus Christ himself … But when the New Testament is viewed as evidence … what Jesus really said and did belongs to a stratum still earlier than any to be verified in the successive contributions to the synoptic tradition, and the Jesus of history becomes … the hopefully fuller figure that is the objective of the new quest of the historical Jesus' (80–81).

'In the light of this shift from history as belief to history as science, one is to find in the New Testament in the first instance evidence on the language and the beliefs that were current' when the New Testament books were written. 'At a second instance evidence is provided for earlier times and places' through earlier strata found in later writings. 'In a third instance what antedates established strata and origins is a matter not so much for historical science as for historical inference' (81). For theology 'this means that scripture as inspired is mainly evidence on the faith of the early church,' though 'it provides premises for inferences on still older knowledge or belief' (81).

Moderate conservatives speak of implicit and explicit Christology in the Jesus of history. Implicit Christology does not attribute to Jesus any of the titles the New Testament ascribes to him, 'but does find christological doctrine implicit in his preaching the kingdom of God and in the authority and power he displayed'; explicit Christology would attribute to Jesus some of the less significant titles. Moderate conservatives themselves are divided on this question (81).

There is a presupposition in scholarly history that may be dealt with at once. Older theology conceived the psychology of Christ as man, not merely in ontological terms but also a priori on the basis of the perfections befitting a divine person. Today we have to attend more to the words 'similar to us in all things save sin.' So 'we have to think of [Christ] as a historical being, as growing in wisdom, age, and grace in a determinate social and cultural milieu, as developing from below as other human beings and from above on the analogy of religious development' (81–82; see Chapter 10 above on the 'vita historica' of Jesus).

This relates to Lonergan's third point at Boston College in 1974: namely, the historical causality of Jesus; for Christ has to be a historical being before he can exert historical causality. But this little excursus on history also justifies Lonergan's omission of detailed study of the human life of Jesus: it is because the New Testament gives us matter not so much for historical science as for historical inference, and this, as a 'still tentative reconstruction of the thought and language of the Jesus of history,' is open to radical change (86).

3.4. Christology: A Religious Question

History has invaded the interpretation of scripture, Lonergan says in his fourth excursus, so that it is seen not as 'a static pool of information but a moving stream of cumulative and progressive investigation' (82). This results in a variety of views on Christ, and method has to find what is valid in current views without becoming involved in positions open to radical change. Lonergan will now attempt such a study, describing four steps in his approach and culminating in the question 'Who is this Jesus?'

A first step embraces both man and his world: man with his four levels of consciousness, and the human world as structured by intelligence, by judgment, by decision and action; that is, by what Lonergan will refer to as post-Kantian transcendental method.

The second step: though all human behaviour involves attention, intelligence, reasonableness, and responsibility, 'different inquiries have different emphases and so different goals and different presuppositions.' Thus, 'the textual critic, the exegete, and the historian proceed from the same data to three quite different conclusions.' But historians, too, differ, and do so in three ways. One way is from von Ranke, telling how it really happened. Another is from Lord Acton: passing moral judgment on deeds of societies and their leaders. A third is religious history 'that would discern in facts and moral actions what pertained to the salvation of mankind' (82–83). Thus, our second step yields five different genera of inquiry, and all five can be applied to the New Testament. But clearly the main concern of the New Testament is religious history; the New Testament is first and last a book with a message: 'it challenges us with a last word about last things.' Saul heard a voice on the way to Damascus; each of us will hear that same voice with either of two verdicts.

So far we have considered two steps: the exigence of post-Kantian transcendental method; and the common view that the New Testament pertains to religious history, that it centres on a *kerygma* addressed to *Existenz*. Now we add a third: that the message is 'simple, radical, and intensely personal, that it stands in correlation with the response it elicits, that in that response there emerges the message as message-for-us' (83–84). Lonergan's distinction of the second and third steps is not altogether clear; can we say in clarification that his second point regards the character of the New Testament message, and that his third regards the message as addressed to us personally?

We are approaching Lonergan's fourth step, which again lacks his usual clarity. 'The third step placed the New Testament in the genre of salvation history,'[11] and it placed our response to it on the existential level. To such a message (simple, radical, personal) the essential answer is action, and the answer begets further answering action: as in the response of those hearing Peter's first sermon, 'Friends, what are we to *do*? as in acclamations that 'Jesus is Lord,' and in confessions that God has raised him from the dead; as in the gospels, written to clarify the acclamations and preclude misinterpretations (84).

In this context Lonergan brings us to the fourth step. For the New Testament not only is a religious document calling for religious living; it also is a personal invitation, and the appropriate response to it is a personal commitment. 'So ineluctably there arises the question, Who is this Jesus?' This is Lonergan's fourth question, it seems, and it adds to our existential response a personal commitment to Jesus.

3.5. Christology: The Theological Question

As a religious and personal question the question of Christology antedates New Testament times. But in our time it also is a theological question, and it has to deal with certain prior issues. There is the contrast between the Jesus of history and the Christ of faith. There is the suggested option between a functional and an ontological Christology. There is the problem of uniting the concern of the inquiring subject with the objective wealth of scriptural scholarship (85).

Lonergan deals with the first question, the contrast between the Jesus of history and the Christ of faith, by referring to the three kinds of historical writing: writing on historical fact, on moral issues, on matters pertaining to salvation. Different writing supposes difference in competence. One writer may be competent on questions of fact, but not on questions that require moral sensibility or religious concern. Similarly, a religious person will readily discern the Christ of faith but may be a fundamentalist in interpretation. Still, there exist those who are religious persons, committed to the Christ of faith, and yet are familiar with scientific history. 'And so they not only present the Christ of faith but also join in the new quest for the historical Jesus' (86). The opposition tends to vanish when religious persons learn to deal with history, and historians come to recognize in the New Testament firsthand evidence on the beliefs of the early church.

This gives us our clue to christological method, enabling us to select what is valid in current views without becoming involved in positions open to radical change. What is open to radical change is reconstruction of the thought and language of the Jesus of history. What can be valid in current views is based on the evidence we possess on the beliefs of the early church. 'By discerning Christian tradition in that evidence, by coming to grasp its immanent structure and intelligibility, by leaving open the questions still to be settled by the reconstruction of the Jesus of history, the theologian ... will find a first and basic component in a methodically developing Christology' (86).

On the second question (ontological or functional?) Lonergan answers that it is neither merely functional nor yet strictly ontological. A merely functional Christology acknowledges no more than a series of religious events, like the acts of believing in the early church. But salvation history 'is not a factual history of acts of believing. It is history of what happened on the evidence believers discern in the light of faith.' There was no question for them that Jesus rose from the dead. 'At the same time New Testament Christology is not strictly ontological. It purports to deal with persons that really existed and with events that really occurred. But it does not go into the hermeneutics of its message,' least of all when that involves cognitional theory, epistemology, and metaphysics (86–87).

The third of the 'prior issues' had been formulated as the problem of uniting the concern of the inquiring subject with the objective wealth of scriptural scholarship (85). It is the same problem in a slightly different formulation now when he comes to that third issue and introduces heuristic structure (87), for the heuristic structure involves data on the objective side ('objective wealth') and an operative criterion on the subjective side ('inquiring subject'). An example of the structure familiar to Lonergan's readers is the history of thought on the nature of fire. In the course of the ages, quite different views on fire have been accepted, but they were answers to the same question. On the side of the object there were the data on fire. On the side of the subject there was inquiring intelligence, wanting to know, moving from answer to answer as a new answer seemed to cover the data better.

> A heuristic structure, then, is a conjunction both of data on the side of the object and of an operative criterion on the side of the subject. Accordingly, a christological heuristic structure will be a similar conjunction giving rise to the succession of christologies set forth in the New Testament writings and further developed in the formulations of individuals and of communities down the ages. (87)

On the side of the data there are three points (88): first, Jesus is named Son of God passim in the New Testament, from different viewpoints and in different contexts; next, through faith we are sons of God, as is proved by the Spirit in our hearts crying 'Abba'; and third, the Spirit in us knows all and is given that we may know all God gives us. Lonergan locates these three on the side of the data, where 'data' seems to refer not to religious experience but to 'the objective wealth of scriptural scholarship' (85).

On the side of the subject there arises in the Christian his or her heuristic structure: question and criterion for an answer.

There is a question: 'the problem of uniting the concern of the inquiring subject with the objective wealth of scriptural scholarship.' The
question arises from the New Testament usage of Son of God: namely,
how are we in our own minds to understand Jesus as Son of God? as
mythic? as Messiah? as God in Jesus; 'does it point to an inner reality
such as is our own divine sonship through Christ and in the Spirit, so
that as God in us is the Spirit, so God in Jesus is the Word?' One gathers
that, without saying it in so many words, Lonergan rejects all these views,
to come instead to his own orthodox position: 'Or does the sonship of
Jesus mean, as the church for centuries has understood it, that Jesus was
truly a man leading a truly human life but his identity was the identity
of the eternal Son of God consubstantial with the Father?' (88).

But 'there is not only question; there is also criterion' for an answer.

> Our own experience of our own sonship provides a first criterion,
> for if the Spirit in us is God, surely God was in Jesus too. Further
> the Spirit of God in us enables us to discern what the spirit of
> the world cannot discern. It is in the progressive clarification of
> Christian experience and in the continuous exercise of spiritual
> discernment in the Christian community that Christological
> doctrine developed.(88)

Lonergan concludes this section with a synoptic view of the many
Christologies over the centuries: from those conformed to the diverse
strata represented in the New Testament, through the vicissitudes of the
first centuries, down to those finding for fifteen centuries a static equilib-
rium in the great councils from Nicea to Constantinople III. 'But in our
time of hermeneutics and history, of psychology and critical philosophy,
there is an exigence for further development. There are windows to be
opened and fresh air to be let in.' And he asserts his optimistic personal
stand on a genuine new Christology. 'It will not, I am convinced, dissolve
the solid achievement of the past. It will, I hope, put that achievement on
a securer base and enrich it with a fuller content' (88–89).

3.6. The Meaning of Chalcedon

Lonergan does not delay on the meaning of Chalcedon; as he says,
the meaning is not obscure. Still 'the clarity of Chalcedon has an essential
condition, for it can be clear only if it has a meaning, and it can have a
meaning only if dogmas have a meaning' (89). Lonergan takes issue with

those who, in various degrees, belittle dogmas. Some do not even advert to the very notion of dogma, to the notion that propositions can be true or false. Thus Fr Schoonenberg discusses not the dogma of Chalcedon but the pattern of Chalcedon. Lonergan does not doubt the significance of patterns or of what he called in *De Verbo incarnato* schemata (compare 89–90 with Chapter 6 above on schemata in the New Testament), but their significance is only preliminary. Do different patterns mean more than different occasions or different contexts? Further evidence is needed before we can make that assertion. 'So from the nature of the case a discussion of patterns has to face deeper issues. The deeper issue at Chalcedon is that its decree is dogmatic and that its pattern results from earlier dogmatic decrees' (90).

3.7. Person Today

Despite deficiencies in Fr Schoonenberg's position, 'he raises an issue – very real in systematic theology and very urgent in pastoral theology – when he asks whether one can lead a truly human life without being a human person' (90–91). The dogmas teach one divine person in two natures. In earlier ages it was enough to adore the mystery; in medieval times some metaphysical account of person and nature was enough; but, Lonergan repeats, 'in our age of psychology and critical philosophy, of hermeneutics and history, something both different and more exacting is required. We have to be able to say what it means for a divine person to lead a fully human life' (91; I refer the reader again to Chapter 10 above on the 'vita humana et historica' of Christ).

Lonergan states his thesis: 'The person of Christ is an identity that eternally is subject of divine consciousness and in time became subject of a human consciousness.' He explains his terms. *Identity*: there are three meanings of 'one'; 'one' in the sense of 'instance'; 'one' in the sense of intelligible unity; 'one' in the sense of Chalcedon's 'one and the same': identity is the third of these. *Consciousness*: our sensitive, intellectual, rational, and moral operations are intentional and conscious; as intentional they make objects present to us; as conscious they make us present to ourselves. But 'present' is used here in two senses. 'Intentionality effects the presence of an object to the subject, of a spectacle to the spectator. Consciousness is a far subtler matter: it makes the spectator present to himself, not by putting him into the spectacle, not by making him an object, but while he is spectator and as subject' (91–92).

In the context of Christology, the question of self-realization is especially important. Lonergan refers to Jungian thought and the 'individuation process from a life centered on the *ego* to a life centered on the self' (92, and see the section on the Boston Workshop of 1974, above in this chapter). I have already quoted a short passage of his own thought on self and self-realization; it is worth seeing at greater length.

> In brief, we cannot conceive subject and object as fixed and immutable things. The world mediated by meaning is not just reality but reality as known, where the knowing is ever in process. The subject that mediates his world by meaning similarly is in a process of self-realization through self-transcendence. So in man we have to distinguish and verify all three meanings of *one*: a man is one as an instance of the human species; he is one as an intelligible unity in an ongoing process; finally, he is one as one and the same, as identity, as himself and nobody else. Further, as we distinguished three meanings of *one* in man, so too we need a distinction between subject and subjectivity. ... So we shall reserve the term, subject, to denote the identity. We shall employ the term, subjectivity, to denote the intelligible unity that already is teleologically what it eventually is to become. (92)

Now, in a truly human life there is identity despite the great differences that accrue over a lifetime, even involving the becoming and the stability of my *ego*, my personality, what I call my self. 'For such differences regard not the identity of the subject but his subjectivity' (93). This explains the second point Lonergan made at Boston College in 1974. It enables us to speak of the human personality of Christ while denying that he is a human person, for here personality is used not in the sense of personhood but in the sense of subjectivity. (Lonergan continues with a discussion of divine subjectivity and trinitarian theology, a topic I omit.)

So much, then, in answer to the question whether one can lead a truly human life without being a human person. Lonergan affirms an imperfect understanding of the possibility of a single divine identity being at once subject of divine consciousness and also subject of a human consciousness. The paradox of living a truly human life without being a human person is removed by the distinction between identity and subjectivity. Jesus' identity is divine but he had a truly human subjectivity that grew in wisdom and age and grace, that was similar to ours in all things save sin (94).

A final paragraph shows the conformity of the human subjectivity to the divine. He is Son, and introduced 'Abba' into our prayer language. 'Again, as the eternal Word is the eternally true expression of the value that God as *agape* is, so the Word as man by obedience unto death again expressed that value by revealing how much God loved the world.' In his resurrection he beckons us to the splendor of the children of God, when up to now the universe groaned as if in childbirth. We discern in this not only the ground of our hope but also the cosmic dimension in the new creation of all things in Christ Jesus our Lord (94).

3.8. Conclusion

Such high matters 'awaken perplexity as much as satisfaction'; hence Lonergan concludes with a statement on the root differences between Schoonenberg's position and his own. Schoonenberg had two premises and one conclusion. The premises: Jesus was a man, Jesus was a person; conclusion: Jesus was a human person. But his conclusion presupposes not two but three premises; the third, not to be admitted by a Catholic: Jesus was only a man (94–95).

I will not conceal my admiration for the brilliance of Lonergan's solution to a problem that he saw as 'very real in systematic theology and very urgent in pastoral theology.' Yet new questions arise. If a modern Arius came on the scene today, would it suffice to quote Nicea against him? I believe Lonergan would ask, Do you understand your doctrine in the sense in which Arius understood it, the sense that was condemned at Nicea? If so, you stand condemned as Arius was. Similarly, if a new expression for Nicea were proposed on the orthodox side, for example, in the words of George Prestige, 'The Son is God in the same sense as the Father is God,' Lonergan would ask, Do you understand your doctrine in the same sense as Nicea understood it? If so, we extend to you the right hand of fellowship.

Such questions are by no means foreign to the spirit of the Laval lecture, and Lonergan believes his method can deal with them. 'In an age of novelty method has a twofold function.' One is to indicate what was inadequate in past procedures and suggest better ones available. 'But it may also have to discern the exaggerations and deficiencies to which the new age itself is exposed' (74).

Lonergan's main concern, however, was not polemical; it was, as he stated in his introduction, for a renewed Christology (74). And his special contribution is on the method to use to achieve the new. It is still the way that was followed in the past. 'It is in the progressive clarification of Christian experience and in the continuous exercise of spiritual discernment in the Christian community that Christological doctrine developed.' In other words, not the logic of conclusions-theology, but the pursuit of Christian discernment.

4. Elements of a Might-have-been Christology, 1975–82

I have said that 'Christology Today' is probably the nearest we will get to an explicit position in Lonergan on a new Christology. Nevertheless, he did not stop thinking in 1975; seven years of active life remained to him and, just as he kept refining his thought on method, so also he kept adding elements that would have entered into a new Christology, had he ever concentrated again on that branch of theology.

Many of these elements are contained in other papers (besides 'Christology Today') of *A Third Collection*.[12] It would be worth our while to study the interests of Lonergan as he thought out these last writings. There is still a pastoral concern: the next-to-last chapter, 'Pope John's Intention,' has for its section headings 1 to 3, 'Pastoral,' 'A Pastoral Council,' 'The Relevance of the Pastoral Council.' But the exigences of understanding are not abated, as may be seen from a study of the three preceding papers: 'Natural Right and Historical Mindedness,' 'Theology and Praxis,' and 'A Post-Hegelian Philosophy of Religion.' For purposes of Christology one might notice also Chapter 3, 'Mission and the Spirit,' and Chapter 5, 'Prolegomena to the Study of the Emerging Religious Consciousness of Our Time,' which concludes with reflections on the dialogue of Christianity and other religions (see Chapter 16 below). But perhaps it is time to move on. With this brief report on elements of a might-have-been Christology I finish my 'opus compilatorium' and now, to justify the title of the book, I must make the transition to the idea of Christ and history.

12

Lonergan and History in General

In the prologue to this book, I took as a working hypothesis the view that history is the key to the unity of Lonergan's Christology. I would go even further now and specify the hypothesis to say that Christ and history are co-extensive, are perhaps, if each is plumbed to its depths, interchangeable topics. That means that the role history played in Lonergan's Christology is a sprawling topic, reaching from 1935 to 1982. To prepare for it, I will introduce a chapter on the general role of history in Lonergan's work, to be followed by four chapters that study specific aspects of the matter.

I have not forgotten Lonergan's remark on the need for a study of the historical causality of Christ; we saw a special article on that topic in *de bono*, and Chapter 14 below will take up the question from a fresh viewpoint. But I believe the importance of history reaches beyond that particular question. In bringing my essay under the title 'Christ and History,' I commit myself to examining the place of Christ in the whole vast ambit and groundswell of history.

1. The History That Happens

The position here is that history is a unifying theme that captured Lonergan's early interest and pervades his work throughout his life. I mean the history that happens, of which the history that is written forms a part. The question regards his attitude toward the sum total of human thought and activity: What makes it a unity? What is the inner dynamic of the whole Lonergan engagement with life and its problems? We could think of the question in terms of intentionality. What is the total in-tended goal of the total intending activity of Bernard Lonergan? What lies behind all his particular intendings, and all his achieved results? Behind all his labour to construct an organon, and all his efforts to apply it?

Rivals for that honour must be set aside with unfair brevity. One obvious candidate is method, as the key concern of the two-volume work *Insight* and *Method*. But method, while it occupied him throughout life, could hardly be said to have captured his mind and heart; method is a means, not an end; its study was a withdrawal that anticipated a return; and the great two-volume work takes its place in thought as a monumental organon for study of the universe rather than as the key constituent of the universe itself. Secondly, Lonergan's Thomism could be a candidate, as illustrated in his *gratia* and *verbum* studies and numerous lectures. But he regarded his eleven-year study of Thomas as serving an apprenticeship, and while his Thomism endured and was forever part of him it was not a lifelong field of study. A third possibility, his formidable studies *De Verbo incarnato* and *De Deo trino*, might claim consideration, but they were particular fronts in the broad campaign of theology and in any case were the result of teaching assignments and not simply of personal choice. Again, cognitional theory was for a time a focal interest, but the limiting phrase is 'for a time'; his position on knowing and its justification was settled at an early stage and afterward taken for granted.

The real rival to history as our unifying theme would in my view be sociology or some aspect of social studies, or perhaps the socio-cultural pair. The social has its own a priori claim in that it too was an early interest (sharing that advantage, however, with method and cognitional theory) and early interests seem to endure in Lonergan; further, there is his explicit early declaration (see Chapter 2 above) that he regarded a *Summa sociologica* as the great need of the times.[1] With that as tacit context we will find in page after page of his writings references that show an enduring interest in social studies. A sample passage describes the times and the challenge they presented and by the same token gives us a clue to the spread of his social interests.

> The new scene is one of technology, automation, built-in obsolescence, a population explosion, increasing longevity, urbanism, mobility, detached and functional relations between persons, universal, prolonged, and continuing education, increasing leisure and travel, instantaneous information, and perpetually available entertainment.[2]

In a related approach, the close connection of the social and the cultural suggests that that pair could be taken as a unit pervading his thought. This is a suggestion well worth careful study, but it in turn suggests that values, a category that includes 'vital, social, cultural, personal, and religious values in an ascending order'[3] would make the sociocultural idea its subordinate. Values itself as a pervasive theme came on the scene rather too late to win a place on our list of candidates, so I return to history as my choice.

It is important, however, to specify this as the history that happens. The history that is written is a second-order category that emerged as a scientific study with the German Historical School in the 1800s (von Ranke, 1795–1886); it became a challenge to Lonergan and an object of his special study with his transfer to Rome in 1953.[4] The history that happens, however, began with Adam and Eve and continues into an unforeseeable future. Of course it is closely linked with the history that is written, which in fact is an item in the history that happens. In any case we know what happened largely through an historical account of it, and historical accounts in their turn have it as their aim to mediate the event to us.

One might ask whether history as account finds a place in the hierarchy of values I just listed, and my answer would be that it doesn't fit into the list as having a slot of its own in the schema, but that it belongs to all of them together, as a specific aspect of each: history and vital values; history and social values; history and cultural, personal, and religious values. On the other hand, the history that is written has an especially close link with the culture of a people.

2. History and the 'Essential' Lonergan

My task is to investigate the full role of history in Lonergan's thinking. I can fulfill it most conveniently by wholesale use of what I said on the topic in the Lonergan Workshop at Boston College in 2000.[5] My claim then was that the need to understand history, basic history, the history that happens, is the chief dynamic element in his academic work: not insight, not method, not economics, not emergent probability, but history. I will call it the 'essential' Lonergan, not in the sense of those books that collect the chief writings of an author (*The Essential Augustine, The Essential Confucius, The Essential Darwin*), but in the sense of the key to all those writings, the principle of any collection of them, and the single idea or set of ideas that unlocks the secrets of someone's mind and life and works. I would claim that there is a similar intention of universal history latent throughout his writings, even in the great *Insight* and *Method*, which function, then, not as the goal, but as an organon to move him toward the goal. This, I submit, is the essential and characteristic Lonergan.

In support of that I would adduce, to start with, the evidence of his casual usage. The idea emerges, like the outcroppings of a hidden lode, in certain little phrases that now take on special meaning: 'the transition from feudal to bourgeois society';[6] 'systems on the move';[7] 'ongoing discovery of mind';[8] 'the emergence of ethical value';[9] the 'long transition from primitive fruit-gatherers, hunters, and fishers to the large-scale agriculture of the temple states';[10] 'from the compactness of the symbol to the differentiation of philosophic, scientific, theological, and historical consciousness';[11] 'how is there effected the transition from one level or stage in human culture to another later level or stage';[12] and so on.

'On the move,' 'ongoing,' 'transition,' 'emergence,' 'from … to' – they are all outcroppings of a lode, signs of a mindset, pointers to the essential Lonergan. Aristotle and Aquinas say that character is manifested in sudden reactions to the unexpected, 'ex repentinis.'[13] These phrases have the same effect. They show us one whose second nature is to think in terms of change, development, history.

Next, to these casual instances I add a pair of more formal statements, one from the start, the other from the finish of his career. There is that letter of 1938 when he said to his Religious Superior, 'Philosophy of history is as yet not recognized as the essential branch of philosophy that it is,' and asked for freedom to work on that needed branch.[14] Likewise, at the end of his career (in 1982), in the last paper he gave, he was still deeply challenged by history: 'It is cultural change that has made Scholasticism no longer relevant and demands the development of a new theological method and style, continuous indeed with the old, yet meeting all the genuine exigences both of Christian religion and of up-to-date philosophy, science, and scholarship.'[15]

In between these bracketing statements are others that clinch the matter. In his 1959 lectures on education he stated that 'reflection on history is one of the richest, profoundest, and most significant things there is. In the past few centuries any great movement has been historical in its inspiration and its formulation.'[16] Almost twenty years later he stated that 'to understand men and their institutions we have to study their history. For it is in history that man's making of man occurs, that it progresses and regresses, that through such changes there may be discerned

a certain unity in an otherwise disconcerting multiplicity';[17] I draw attention to that last clause, the role of history in giving 'unity in an
otherwise disconcerting multiplicity.' Even the two great works of his
organon are linked to a theory of history: 'I have a general theory of
history implicit in *Insight* and in *Method*.'[18] He sees history as explaining
doctrinal development: 'the intelligibility proper to developing doctrines
is the intelligibility immanent in historical process.'[19] And he expressly
relates his 1938 position to that of twenty-five years later.[20]

Christ and History: 'Via receptionis'

On beginning Chapter 12, I spoke of the sprawling topics that should be considered under the heading of Christ and history. As my prologue introduced the whole book, so Chapter 12 introduced my theme of Christ and history, giving special attention to the overall relation of history to Lonergan's life work. My sequence now is from history and Lonergan to history and Christology as he conceived the matter.

Still striving for unity in multiplicity, I call on a pair of ideas that figured frequently in the psychology of Thomas Aquinas: the 'via receptionis' (from things to soul) and the 'via motionis' (from soul to things).[1] Taking some liberty with the Thomist couplet I will adapt it to organize first the data on God's entry into history, in which our race receives from God ('via receptionis'), and then the data on the historical causality of Christ ('via motionis'), in which Christ manifestly exercises an influence on the world ('de causalitate historica quam Christus homo manifeste exercet'). The latter, under the heading of historical causality, will be a topic in Chapter 14. The 'via receptionis' is the topic of the present chapter.

Some preliminary notes may obviate difficulties and objections. History may refer to what happens or to what is written about what happens. Basically it is what happens: Christ as event, then, rather than the Christology of that event. Christology, however, as mediating the event to us is the immediate reality, while the event is always what is ultimately intended.

It is more important to identify some questions of substance that may arise. For example, we see the Christ-event as happening not only in thirty short years under Augustus and his successors, but as happening in the preparation for those thirty years that began two millennia earlier; in fact, we see it as happening not only in the time period of four millennia accessible to us, but in the countless prehistoric millennia of the past, and the millennia, possibly countless, of the future. Again, a full Christology must relate itself to a Pneumatology, and indeed to what for the time being I call a Patrology, where that term refers not to the Fathers of the Church but to the first person of the Trinity. Further, we must remember, when we talk about Christ in his singularity, that a strong influence on Lonergan was the Catholic doctrine on the mystical body of Christ, which is a doctrine on us his members. And that doctrine brings us to universalist thinking and the collective activity of our race.

With those caveats I proceed to a study of the entry of God into history, or salvation history as initiated by God and received by the human race ('via receptionis'). I will return from time to time to particular items in the 'opera omnia' that we have seen in previous chapters, but concentrate now on their relevance to Christ and history.

1. God's Entry into History

For this question I return to my second chapter above and the *pantôn* paper of 1935. That essay is expressly concerned with historical questions: church and state, Bolshevism, liberalism, and so on. Moreover, it is concerned also with theological questions, with Christ as historical agent in conflict with alien historical agents. It was the first of Lonergan's efforts to pull it all together, and I believe its message is still a clue to his life work: all history is brought to unity in Christ. It contains in brief the dynamism that was operative in the years 1935 to 1982.

While all that is true, it remains that the motif of the paper is contained in the passage from Ephesians quoted in the very title, and that that passage describes not the historical causality of Christ but the 'historical' causality of God the Father. It is the Father who initiates salvation history, and it must therefore be studied from God's side as well as from ours. Lonergan's theology, beginning regularly from the Father, easily accords with this order.

From God's side, then, salvation history is the work of what we call the economic Trinity. Christ is with us, as the divine Word, as one of the Trinity, bringing with him the meaning he has in eternity and taking on the meaning of the earthly economy as it is directed by God's infinite wisdom. But there is a wider context. We have to situate the Word–with–us in the totality of the economic Trinity; that is, the Spirit, too, is with us as God, as one of the Trinity, bringing with him the meaning he has in eternity and taking on the meaning of the earthly economy as it is directed by God's infinite wisdom. The Father, too, is with us in hope, as God, as one of the Trinity, bringing with him the meaning he has in eternity and taking on the meaning of the earthly economy as it is directed by divine wisdom.

Parallel, therefore, to the doctrine on the Word is the doctrine affirmed by Lonergan on the Father and on the Spirit: 'there is a threefold personal self-communication of divinity to humanity; first, when in Christ the Word becomes flesh, second, when through Christ men become temples of the Spirit and adoptive sons of the Father, and third, when in a final consummation the blessed know the Father as they are known by him.'[2] This accords with the trinitarian text from Ephesians, which defined the doctrine of the *pantôn* essay and encapsulates our position on Christ and history. But the whole 'economy' of the divine entry into human history, of our human reception of that entry, and of the historical causality exercised by Christ have to be thought out in relation to the primary historical causality that God the Father exercises.

Now, the economic Trinity as such is new both to Scholasticism in general and to Thomas in particular. When, before turning to creatures, Thomas is rounding off his trinitarian doctrine, he deals with the comparison of the three in two questions: one in regard to their equality and similarity, the other in regard to the divine missions.[3] This is where Thomas might have introduced the economic Trinity, had that been a question of the day. But Thomas had never heard of the economic Trinity. His context for these two questions, even for question 43 on the divine missions, is wholly intra-trinitarian, and so he has left to us this splendid opening, enabling us to talk of the economic Trinity in a context he has supplied.

The *Tertia pars* of the Thomist *Summa theologiae* has been much criticized as making Christ and Christology a mere appendix to theology. But it is important to note that the *Tertia pars* is about Christ as man, Christ 'secundum quod homo';[4] if we were to add the economic Trinity to the questions on the missions we would have a study of Christ as God on earth, Christ 'secundum quod Deus in terris.' A full theology of the economic Trinity would then complete the treatise with a study of the given Spirit 'secundum quod Deus in terris' and a study of the hoped-for Father 'secundum quod Deus in terris.' Then it would give the Spirit and the Father their own *Tertia pars*, with treatises on the given Spirit as given, the Spirit 'secundum quod datus,' and on the hoped-for Father 'secundum quod speratus.' I do not, therefore, see the Thomist *Tertia pars* as invalidated now, but I do see it as no longer sufficient. We have to create a new division in the *Prima pars* for the economic Trinity 'secundum quod Deus in terris,' and we have to extend the *Tertia pars* to include, along with the treatise *De Verbo incarnato* 'secundum quod homo,' a treatise *De Spiritu dato* 'secundum quod datus,' and a treatise *De Patre sperato* 'secundum quod speratus.'

For the way this would work out in history we have a foundation and model in the letter to the Ephesians. Let me summarize what I said on that letter in my prologue. Chapter 1:3-10 states the Father's plan, which was to bestow on us in Christ every spiritual blessing. 'He has made known to us his hidden purpose': namely, that the universe, all in heaven and on earth, might be brought into unity in Christ. Then, chapter 4:9-13 states more particularly the logistics of the divine plan: Christ descended to earth and ascended to heaven that he might fill the universe. And he gave gifts 'to equip God's people for work in his service.' So shall we all at last attain to the unity inherent in our faith and our knowledge of the Son of God.

Repeating my second chapter, I would say that even in this summary form Ephesians offers an all but explicit endorsement of my thesis on Christ and history. In choosing for his title the restoration of all things in Christ, Lonergan makes the argument and message of Ephesians his own argument and message. All history is unified in Christ; Christ permeates all history. We are just short of identifying the fullness of Christ with the fullness of history.

2. Dialectic in Human Reception

From God's side, therefore, we have the divine background for a doctrine of Christ and history. But there is, from the side of creation, a counterpart to God's side, one directly pertinent to Christ and history. We are coming to the 'via receptionis,' and for that we need to understand the character of the 'receiver.' Two characteristics are fundamental: dialectic and development.

Dialectic is found in the same *pantôn* essay. In statements that introduce a lifelong interest, Lonergan describes a threefold dialectic in the historic progress of intellect. In the dialectic of *fact,* an incomplete idea is put into execution as though it were complete; when its incompleteness is revealed there is the emergence of a compensating idea. In the dialectic of *sin,* false situations lead to the phenomena of depraved polytheism, liberalism and religious wars, and communism. In the dialectic of *thought* there is a pure dialectic in the development of the perennial philosophy, but as contaminated with the dialectic of sin it gives the actual course of abstract thought since Socrates.[5] We are indeed deep into Lonergan's view of history and must keep reminding ourselves that Ephesians establishes it as the history whose culmination is Christ.

The *pantôn* essay had therefore introduced the idea, so central to history, of dialectic, and a few years later, in the essays of 1937–38, that theme is made the organizing principle for progress-decline-redemption, which is Lonergan's basic structure of the divine-human economy. Still later, in his 1973 paper on *Insight*, he is able to apply the same idea to history, writing as follows.

> In my rather theological analysis of human history, my first approximation was the assumption that men always do what is intelligent and reasonable, and its implication was an ever increasing progress. The second approximation was the radical inverse insight that men can be biased, and so unintelligent and unreasonable in their choices and decisions. The third approximation was the redemptive process resulting from God's gift of his grace to individuals and from the manifestation of his love in Christ Jesus. The whole idea was presented in chapter twenty of *Insight*.[6]

The course of this dialectic recalls Lonergan's metaphor of the broken continuity of the front in trench warfare: there are salients and there are pockets of delay in the general line of battle. If it is true that Lonergan's Scholasticism, for all its value, delayed his entry into modernity, that it continued for some years after his graduate courses and summer institutes had established elements of a new theology, then the unity in his moving series of positions can be seen as the rather broken continuity of our metaphor.

3. Development in Human Reception

Nevertheless, his theology courses did make their contribution to the theme of Christ and history. They did so through the second characteristic of the 'receiver,' the factor of development, in which Lonergan's Scholasticism had its own internal corrective. Development is a strong feature of his Christology from the New Testament to Chalcedon, and it is history in the making. Moreover, it is history with Christ as centre. Chalcedon does not mean simply a doctrine; it means Christ, Christ in that year of 451 and in that place named Chalcedon. The historical causality of Christ is exercised just as much in the ecumenical councils as it is in the martyrs of the first centuries. Christ is the fullness of history; but the fulness is on the way, in the succession of 'Christs' that time brings to birth. Hopkins, with whom Lonergan could claim some affinity, saw this and wrote: 'The just man justices ... Acts in God's eye what in God's eye he is – Christ – for Christ plays in ten thousand places ...' (no. 14 in collection made by W.H. Gardner). Lonergan saw it and wrote his synoptic view of the many Christologies over the centuries (Chapter 11 above, end of section 5).

The purpose of his Christology as stated in his Harvard course was to give meaning to Chalcedon. At a deeper level, it was to give meaning to Christ; at a still deeper level, it was to make Christ present through his meaning; and, of course, his meaning grows. Readers will expect a more apodictic statement on *De Verbo incarnato* as linking Christ with history, but I cannot deliver that; by my hypothesis Lonergan has not caught up to his own forward thrust here. Nevertheless, by finding meaning in Chalcedon he is finding Christ present then and there, and thereby identifying Christ with history. Nor must we overlook the fact that Lonergan, with his notable work on Christian doctrine (the metaphysics of the hypostatic union, the consciousness of Christ, the liberty of Christ, the redemption, and so on), is not just providing elements for an account of history; he is also in the forward march of thought and thereby making Christian history happen. Lonergan's part in that, however, is only a part, and we have to study the question in the larger context of what is going forward in the times.

4. Changing Times, Changing Church, Changing Thought

I am presenting Christ and history in the 'via receptionis,' and the order of my presentation so far has been the agent of all movement, namely, God, and the character of the receiver, which is revealed in the two phenomena of dialectic and development. Those two samples offer a springboard to the concrete history of the times and to Lonergan's part in it.

I have sketched the general state of intellectual decline in which, so Lonergan felt, the church had fallen behind. This is revealed in the simple logic of his remark at the prestigious 1967 congress on *Theology of Renewal*, 'Obviously, if theology is to be brought up to date, it must have fallen behind the times.'[7] Lonergan made his own the development of the time. He began his theology with Scholasticism solidly entrenched in church teaching, and he contributed his own impetus to the place of Aquinas in theology. Still, as mentioned above (Chapter 4), from the beginning and in a general way he accepted Newman on development and, from his doctoral dissertation on, gave his own slant to Thomist studies. If today medieval questions get short shrift in theology, still Lonergan has given us light from the Middle Ages on how to deal with transitions.

His 'The Future of Thomism' paper is useful here as a transition piece. Thomas's commentaries on Aristotle, Lonergan says, bring to light the manner in which Aristotle can be transposed from his Hellenic to a Christian context. Transposition is an operation of special importance at this stage, because it counters the discontinuity that our metaphor of trench warfare would set up between phases of development. Thomas's commentaries on scripture are theological: 'they express Scriptural doctrine in the categories of the theology he was doing so much to develop. The endless *quaestiones* raised in his work … put Thomas in the mainstream of medieval thought …'[8]

But what of Thomas in the modern world? Lonergan lists five shifts needed for the Thomism of tomorrow: 'from logic to method … [F]rom the conception of science in the *Posterior Analytics* to the modern conception of a science … [F]rom soul to subject … [F]rom human nature to human history … [F]rom first principles to transcendental method.'[9] Of special interest for my purpose is the fourth shift, from human nature to human history: '… meaning … is subject to change; cultures develop and cultures decline; meaning flowers and meaning becomes decadent. Finally, Christianity is an historical religion; it is a statement of the meaning of human living; it is a redeeming statement that cures decadence and fosters growth.'[10] Comparing this with Lonergan's 1954 essay on 'Theology and Understanding'[11] shows how far 'The Future of Thomism' of 1968 has advanced beyond that.

I have used 'The Future of Thomism' as a marker for changes in an especially significant area, but the changing times bring new approaches to theology on a wider front. What that concretely means for Lonergan is illustrated in a series of essays and lectures punctuating his move away from Scholasticism and into the twentieth century. Considering the matter from a broad perspective, I may repeat my warning: do not expect 'Christ and History' to follow the path opened by Toynbee, Dawson, Jaspers, and the other students of history that Lonergan refers to. For examples of Lonergan's topics, think rather of those mentioned above in Chapter 10: the 'vita humana et historica' of Christ, the role of incarnate meaning, the mediation of Christ in prayer, the state of 'being in Christ Jesus,' and so on. His type of contribution is revealed in the following general remark: 'The challenge of history is for man progressively to restrict the realm of chance or fate or destiny and progressively to enlarge the realm of conscious grasp and deliberate choice.'[12] And the extent of his contribution is seen in such places as Chapter 20 of *Insight*, which he originally called 'The Structure of History.'[13]

5. 'Philosophy and the Religious Phenomenon'

The preceding pages raise a problem. To speak of dialectic, development, the structure of history, and so on is to speak in very general terms. But the samples I gave in Chapter 10 of the newly emerging cast of Lonergan's thought are particular cases chosen from many, as the term 'samples' implies. And so my problem is this: How does one move from the broad context of, say, *Insight*'s Chapter 20, to the particular samples of new thinking I illustrated by the 'vita humana' of Christ, incarnate meaning, and other such topics? Can we find a mediating factor between the universal structure of progress–decline–redemption and the uncountable items of particular history?

I think we can, and I would draw on Lonergan's 'Philosophy and the Religious Phenomenon,' where the 'issue in hand is the need of some account and ordering of the various contexts in which, first, religious living occurs and, secondly, investigations of religious living are under-taken.' The theme may be the particular case of religion, but Lonergan is ever the generalist and from the particular case provides the general mediating categories we seek. They are four: linguistic, literate, logical, methodical. These relate on one side to the broad sweep of history and on the other to the humdrum of everyday life.

In the dialectic of this ordered account, Lonergan discerns 'the terms whose meaning shifts in the course of time and ... the terms that denote the factors bringing about such shifts in meaning.' The former are social contexts (family and mores, community and education, state and law, economics and technology) and cultural contexts (art, religion, science, philosophy, history).[14]

Applying his mediating categories, Lonergan distinguishes four states in this social and cultural history, identified in reference to language and its use: the linguistic (where people speak and listen), the literate (where they read and write), the logical (where they operate on propositions, promote clarity, coherence, and rigour, and move toward system), and fourth, the methodical (where systems yield to better systems, where method discerns invariants and variables in the sequence of systems). There are, of course, complexities (139) that I omit.

Such is the general picture, but Lonergan's topic in this paper is religion, which he locates within these varying social and cultural contexts as a specific case where 'religion discovers itself, works out its identity, differentiates itself ...' This appears in the linguistic stage as myth and ritual, in the literate stage as religion of the book, in the logical stage as a reflection on itself that seeks systematic theologies. Stage four follows: 'In the methodical stage it [religion] confronts its own history, distinguishes the stages in its own development, evaluates the authenticity or inauthenticity of its initiatives, and preaches its message in the many forms and styles appropriate to the many social and cultural strata of the communities in which it operates' (140–41).

This is applied to Christianity. Christianity is a religion that 'began and spread through the words and deeds of Christ and his apostles' (linguistic stage); by 200 A.D. there was 'an elite that studied the scriptures and read Ireneus ... Hippolytus ...' (literary). Then the truth that was already a concern in the New Testament issued through apologetics into the (logical) stage of the councils. Speaking the truth led to a concern for understanding (Origen, Gregory of Nyssa, Augustine), and understanding led to Anselm, the Scholastics, and systematic theology, and so to the methodical stage (141–42).

From the economic Trinity to 'Philosophy and the Religious Phenomenon' – those two themes stake out the boundaries of this Chapter 13. The former shows God entering our history; the latter shows our reception of the gift of God's presence among us. Instead of following Lonergan's works one by one, I provided a set of concepts for mediating between the fundamental structure of history and the many historical factors that make up human living. The sequence calls for a chapter now on the influence of the divine presence on the world, on society, on the church, on the people of God: historical causality, history operating in the Thomist 'via motionis.' That will be the theme of Chapter 14.

14

Christ and Historical Causality: 'Via motionis'

The 1958 lecture on the redemption spoke of 'the efficiency of the death and resurrection of Christ ... [of] what he has done as a historical person who founded a church and down the ages has exerted an influence on the lives of countless millions, more intimate and more profound than any other historical figure.'[1] That sentence could serve as an epitome of the present chapter.

The materials in Chapter 13 found a certain unity under the Thomist notion of the 'via receptionis.' The materials in the present chapter come under the heading of 'via motionis.' As such, they respond directly to Lonergan's 'desideratum' of a treatise on historical causality, adding another dimension to our comprehensive theme of Christ and history: namely, of Christianity as a religion that is domiciled in and exercises an influence on those lands and cultures and religious ways in which it takes root. There are two steps: historical causality as exercised on the level of the cultural, and historical causality as exercised on the level of religion.

1. Christianity and Culture

In this section I understand culture broadly. I will not study the influence of Christ on economic, on political, on social areas, or on related areas of thought and practice; it is enough that these fall under the general headings Lonergan uses in his 'Philosophy and the Religious Phenomenon.' Further, for Lonergan on this topic I cannot do better than multiply quotations from his own work; these for once speak for themselves. Here is one of especially broad coverage and application.

> [The Catholic religion] expressed itself in the New Testament,
> but it kept adding further expressions in the Apostolic Fathers,

the Apologists, the Greek and Latin Fathers. An entirely new mode made its appearance with Byzantine Scholasticism, and this recurred on a universal scale with the medieval canonists and theologians. Humanism, the Renaissance, the Counter-Reformation brought in another style, a new mode of concept formation, a different mentality.[2]

Here is another passage to the same effect, of Christianity exercising historical causality: '... the fact of the matter is that the ancient Church set about transforming Greek and Roman culture, that the medieval Church was a principal agent in the formation of medieval culture, that the Renaissance Church was scandalously involved in Renaissance culture.'[3]

Again,

Always in the past it had been the Catholic tradition to penetrate and to christianize the social fabric and the culture of the age. So it entered into the Hellenistic world of the patristic period. So it was one of the principal architects of medieval society and medieval thought. So too it was almost scandalously involved in the Renaissance.[4]

There is a negative way of making the same point: namely, by noting the church's failures. The 1960 lecture on 'The Philosophy of History' tells of grand-scale ideas like the Hegelian and Marxist dialectics, and the Rosenberg myth behind the Nazi movement, and of the failure of the church to provide matching thought. 'There is very definitely a problem here. ... Dawson speaks of these movements going on and of Christians having very little influence because of largely passive attitudes.' Voegelin suggests

that the Christian view of this world, as waiting for the second coming of Christ, left a vacuum of meaning in that merely day-to-day aspect of human meaning which these modern philosophies of history are attempting to fill. When they fill it, they obtain stupendous results, stupendous influence over human life in all its aspects, as is illustrated by nineteenth-century progressivism ... and the influence of Marx ...[5]

The same failure that Dawson notices in our time, Lonergan notices in ancient and medieval times.

... the healing process, when unaccompanied by creating, is a soul without a body. Christianity developed and spread within the ancient empire of Rome. It possessed the spiritual power to heal what was unsound in that imperial domain. But it was un-accompanied by its natural complement of creating ... So when the Roman empire decayed and disintegrated, the church indeed lived on. But it lived on, not in a civilized world, but in a dark and barbarous age in which, as a contemporary reported, men devoured one another as fishes in the sea.[6]

It was in the context of that remark that Lonergan pleaded for a more creative economics and morality. It is indeed his work on economics that provides the most concrete model of what he means by the historical causality of Christ and the realization of the divine plan of Ephesians. As one more quotation will show, historical causality is not a matter of sweetness and light but the way of Christ in his example of suffering and death. Let me transcribe more fully the passage I cited at the start of this chapter.

Finally, the possibilities of resisting the mechanisms and the determinisms that can emerge historically are heightened almost to an unlimited extent by Christianity. The death and resurrection of Christ express the victory of truth and goodness in spite of every kind of suffering: physical, in reputation, and in every other way. The example of Christ and the grace of God that comes to us through Christ constitute a historical force that, in Christ's own words, amounts really to this: Fear not, I have overcome the world. Christ himself overcame the world by resisting the powers of evil in suffering everything they would inflict upon him. And he rose again the third day. It is this Christian hope that is a supreme force in history. It is a fundamental and unchangeable ground that enables ordinary mortals to stand by the truth, and stand by what is right, no matter what the consequences.[7]

As some of these texts show, the causality we mean will be a causality not only in art, law, technology, and the other social and cultural contexts, but also in ideas; ideas, in fact, rank high in the achievements of culture. An outstanding example is the way that the theology of the incarnation contributed to the philosophy of existence.[8] The doctrine of the con-sciousness of Christ may serve as a second instance. When Lonergan responded very sharply to a critique of that doctrine that effectively, he claimed, made him a teacher of heresy, he said 'The notion of the subject is difficult, recent, and primitive,'[9] whereby subject is meant a conscious person. But, as with 'knowing,' so with 'conscious.' Everyone knows a good many things, but to explain 'knowing' is the arduous task of the philosophers. So it is with 'conscious.' It is one thing to be conscious and altogether another to explain consciousness. From Lonergan's viewpoint the difficulty philosophers have is due to thinking of consciousness as perception and as therefore having an object. But think of consciousness as internal experience and much of the difficulty vanishes.

It is difficult now to measure the historical causality of his influence on other matters that once engaged his attention but are now taken for granted. Such are his recovery of the Thomist *actio*, his intellectualism, the trinitarian intelligible emanation ('emanatio intelligibilis') and other notions. Instead of listing particular contributions, therefore, I point rather to his sweeping program: 'a total transformation of dogmatic theology,'[10] and 'a complete restructuring of Catholic theology.'[11] It is hardly necessary to remind readers that, though my examples may appeal to ideas of theologians, they are Christian theologians (such as Leeming and Lonergan) and are part of the influence Christ has been exercising for twenty centuries.

Studying the historical causality exercised by Christ, I have been led to speak of variations in that exercise and in particular of the systems of thought that over the centuries have exerted their influence. All systems give way eventually to better systems, and so did Lonergan's Scholasticism. As patristic theology gave way to medieval, so did medieval give way to modernity. But, if transitions are the order of the day, in what new direction may we expect Lonergan to lead us in this new millennium? What is the new system that will replace Scholasticism? It will be, in Lonergan's view, not so much a system of theology as a system for *doing* theology: 'When the classicist notion of culture prevails, theology is conceived as a permanent achievement, and then one discourses on its nature. When culture is conceived empirically, theology is known to be an ongoing process, and then one writes on its method.'[12]

From many angles, then, we fill out the high view that the *pantôn* essay took of the historical causality of Christ. In the world of thought, Christianity is linked to history by the transitions that carry it through the four stages of the linguistic, the literate, the logical, and the systematic. In the world of action, Christianity learned from experience, in the dialectic of failure and success, what was involved in restoring all things to unity

183

in Christ. We are dealing with the history of a culture, the history of the Christian culture, and so the history of Christ in the fulness of his mystical body. These reflections lead to the second section of this chapter: history and religion.

2. Christianity and Religion

In this section on the Christian influence on religion, reference will be made to institutional religions, and especially to the Christian religion, but by 'religion' in the title I mean first the religion of everyone, the religion of the people, religion therefore as a way of life, and only secondly of world religions or the religion that is an institution.

As Christianity exercises historical causality on the broad scale of general culture, so too it exercises historical causality in the particular field of religion. This field is further divided so that various more particular contexts emerge: 'world,' church, evangelization, religious orders, media of communication, and so on. All these impinge on Christology, and Lonergan has something to say on all of them.

Now, Christ does not work alone; he has his agents in the transforming work, and the most notable of these is the Christian church. As we shall see, 'The Christian church is the community that results from the outer communication of Christ's message and from the inner gift of God's love.'[13] Reflecting on this community and its mission leads to the historical causality Christ exercises through his agents. In a multiplicity of New Testament references in his essay 'Response of the Jesuit,' Lonergan spells out the logistics of the 'sending' in which the church is involved.[14] Fortunately, he also provides the equivalent of headings that help us organize the multiplicity.

The first heading is the need for the sending. 'Both Christ's communication by linguistic meaning and his communication by incarnate meaning were circumscribed spatially and temporally. The gift of the Spirit can be everywhere at once, but the challenge of the Word radiates to the ends of the earth only through human mediation' (175). This mediation may be institutionalized (for one example, in the Twelve) or not institutionalized (for example, in non-followers of Christ casting out devils in his name). We are inclined to think of the institutional as impersonal, but the New Testament institutionalization of mediation is quite personal: 'to receive you is to receive me' (Matthew 10:40).

'Next, the early mediators are described as wonder workers' (Matthew 10:7-8). 'Thirdly, institutionalized mediation slowly developed': choosing the Twelve to be permanent companions (Mark 3:14) is the beginning of an institution; telling them after the resurrection that they were to bear witness to the ends of the earth (Acts 1:8) goes further. 'The sending of the Seventy-two … set a precedent to the effect that others, not of the Twelve, could perform the same mission as the Twelve performed' – as happens with the Seven (Acts 6:3). 'A further development may be discerned in Paul's companions, helpers, deputies …' (178). 'After untitled companions, helpers, deputies there come titled elders and titled bishops and deacons' (179).

Lonergan continues his little essay on 'sending' with remarks on the functions of the elders (179), the qualities required of them (watchfulness), their duty to lead, to preach, to teach (180). He concludes the essay with a few notes on language usage ('elders, bishops, deacons,' 180–81), and on translations of the Greek.

3. Christianity and Preaching

I take special note of the relation of this question to preaching. It is illuminating to examine the *De intellectu et methodo* of 1959 side by side with Chapter 14 of *Method*, dated 1972. Both deal with transitions and so are involved in history. The former struggles with the question how to make the transition from scripture to dogma. The latter deals with the transition from dogma to preaching the word and shows a new awareness of a problem in communication.[15]

We see the relevance of this to the historical causality of Christ when we apply the concept of historicity to communication. Communications, we are told, 'is a major concern, for it is in this final stage that theological reflection bears fruit.'[16] It is through meaning that we communicate, and so, after sketching the functions of meaning Lonergan turns to common meaning, which is the 'formal constituent' of community, calling for 'a common field of experience … common or complementary ways of understanding … common judgments … common values' (356–57). Leaping over details we arrive at the application of community in the religious field. As defined a moment ago, 'The Christian church is the community that results from the outer communication of Christ's message and from the inner gift of God's love. Since God can be counted on to bestow his grace, practical theology is concerned with the effective communication of Christ's message' (361–62). So we come to the point: 'There are real problems of communication in the twentieth century, and they are not solved by preaching to ancient Antioch, Corinth, or Rome.'[17]

> The Christian message is to be communicated to all nations. Such communication presupposes that preachers and teachers enlarge their horizons to include an accurate and intimate understanding of the culture and the language of the people they address ...

Here the basic distinction is between preaching the gospel and, on the other hand, preaching the gospel as it has been developed within one's own culture ... (362).

And so Lonergan, in preaching as in doctrine, rejects the classicist's position: the classicist 'would feel it was perfectly legitimate for him to impose his culture on others. For he conceives culture normatively, and he conceives his own to be the norm' (363).

Chapter 14 of *Method* and more generally Lonergan's Christology apply to preaching the principle already established for theology. The very first line of the Introduction to *Method* states that 'A theology mediates between a cultural matrix and the significance and role of a religion in that matrix.' So conceived, method also broadens the category of signs of the historical causality of Christ; I have mentioned the church as preeminent sign, but there are others to notice, and among them religious orders present an outstanding challenge.

4. Christianity and Religious Orders

It would be strange to write a Christology and omit all reference to that way of following Christ which we call the consecrated life, the life of religious orders and congregations. Yet Lonergan has no treatise on that topic (one that Aquinas studied repeatedly and extensively). We might argue that his own life was such a treatise, *vécu* but not *thématique*. We might collect scattered remarks of his and expand them into a little essay, but the essay would hardly approximate to the importance of the topic. For in terms of historical causality, the life and work and influence of Anthony of Egypt, of Benedict of Nursia, of Francis of Assisi and Ignatius Loyola, of Teresa of Avila, and of those who have followed them is beyond all proportion to their numbers.

A mini-treatise on this aspect of Christology might take as point of departure Lonergan's account of the realm of transcendence, for 'Western religion cultivated the realm of transcendence through its churches and liturgies, its celibate clergy, its religious orders, congregations, confraternities.'[18] Such outward signs of the effect Christ has had on the world and on religion are numerous after Constantine, in the taking over of Europe (one grants something to Belloc's famous *Europe Is the Faith*) and impregnating its social and cultural contexts with Christian symbols and customs, in the enduring meaning of Christmas, Easter, All Souls, Pentecost, in a thousand ways familiar to readers. An essay on religious orders and the historical causality of Christ would have to find place for such signs of Christian presence.

Let us not, however, grow triumphal and forget the dark side: religious persecutions and wars, some of the crusades, and other aberrations perpetrated in the name of Christ and as much opposed to his spirit as Francis of Assisi is representative of it. They belong in our history as much as its glories, though they are hardly an exercise of the historical causality of Christ.[19]

Let us return to a line of thought more specifically related to religious orders: the relevance of the 'world' in our history. The word has many senses. One of them entered Lonergan's language when, in his lectures on existentialism, he spoke of 'world' more or less in the sense of the existentialist philosophers. And note that scripture gives two sides: God's love of the world (John 3:16) and the world as seated in wickedness (1 John 5:19). Very much to the present point is the way Christians leave the world in transcending it, in the sense of flight from the world, as seen in Anthony of Egypt and a long tradition down to our time. Influence, however, operates in two directions, from Christ to religious orders and from religious orders to the people of God. So, too, with 'world.' Christians return to the world not only to preach the gospel but also to create a better world. Leaving the world is not the same for a hermit as it is for a missionary order.

But this sign of transcendence is a costly benefit. Earlier I spoke of Christians failing to counter the Marxist account of history with their own philosophy, of their withdrawal from the world and leaving the field to their opponents. And I quoted Voegelin on the vacuum of meaning in the world that this flight from it has left. There are various possibilities we could realize, but I leave the topic as part of the might-have-been that characterizes Lonergan's whole Christology.

This section on religious orders suggests a fuller listing of areas for the exercise of historical causality, a broadening to include diverse functions of the church. I have not spoken here of sacraments and sacramentals, not because I overlooked their importance for the historical causality of Christ, but because it is obvious. The same may be said of sacred ministers in the church: the episcopacy, presbyterate, diaconate. Liturgy and canon law also belong in the field of historical causality. Likewise the importance of the non-ordained laity is now recognized: a new field for the historical causality of Christ. The category of the might-have-been is limitless. Before leaving it, however, there is one more area to examine: that of the virtues.

5. Christianity and the Virtues

This subtitle regards a theme that often surfaces in Lonergan's writings without ever becoming, so far as I know, the topic of an essay or the title of a section in a book. It deserves better treatment. I refer to the specific role of the theological virtues in counteracting their opposite numbers among the evils. It belongs to the interior gifts that are meant, so Ephesians 4:12 tells us, 'to equip God's people for work in his service.' It is this specific theme as an instance of historical causality that I propose to investigate now.

The theme is emergent early (ca. 1937–38), in the student paper 'Analytic Concept of History,' where three virtues are invoked to offset major decline, 'against self-justification ... penance, against ... unintelligibility and chaos ... justice-transcending charity, against the discrediting of reason ... faith,' and to offset minor decline, the evangelical counsels.[20] That contains the germ of the later doctrine. Lonergan's main interest, however, in his early work on grace is not directly the historical causality of the virtues but rather the personal transformation they effect. Historical causality emerges directly some years later in 'The Role of a Catholic University' (1951).

> The supernatural virtues of faith, hope, and charity ... possess a profound social significance. Against the perpetuation of explosive tensions that would result from the strict application of retributive justice, there is the power of charity to wipe out old grievances and make a fresh start possible. Against the economic determinism that would result were egoistic practicality given free rein, there is the liberating power of hope that seeks first the kingdom of God. Against the dialectic discernible in the history of philosophy and in the development-and-decline of civil and cultural communities, there is the liberation of human reason through divine faith ...[21]

Another passage that deserves extensive quotation is dated 1966.

If human historical process is such a compound of progress and decline, then its redemption would be effected by faith, hope, and charity. For the evils of the situation and the enmities they engender would only be perpetuated by an even-handed justice: charity alone can wipe the slate clean. The determinism and pressures of every kind, resulting from the cumulative surd of unintelligent policies and actions, can be withstood only through a hope that is transcendent and so does not depend on any human prop. Finally, only within the context of higher truths accepted on faith can human intelligence and reasonableness be liberated from the charge of irrelevance to the realities produced by human waywardness …[22]

A few years later, *Method in Theology* (1972) makes the same point.

It is not propaganda and it is not argument but religious faith that will liberate human reasonableness from its ideological prisons. It is not the promises of men but religious hope that can enable men to resist the vast pressures of social decay. If passions are to quiet down, if wrongs are to be not exacerbated, not ignored, not merely palliated, but acknowledged and removed, then human possessiveness and human pride have to be replaced by religious charity, by the charity of the suffering servant, by self-sacrificing love.[23]

My last quotation will be from The Queen's University lectures (1976), specifically from the 'Third Lecture: The Ongoing Genesis of Methods.'

Can a people, a civilization, recover from such decline? To my mind the only solution is religious. What will sweep away the rationalizations? More reasoning will hardly do it effectively, for it will be suspected of being just so much more rationalizing. And when reasoning is ineffective, what is left but faith? What will smash the determinisms – economic, social, cultural, psychological – that egoism has constructed and exploited? What can be offered but the hoping beyond hope that religion inspires? When finally the human situation seethes with alienation, bitterness, resentment, recrimination, hatred, mounting violence, what can retributive justice bring about but a duplication of the evils that already exist? Then what is needed is not retributive justice but self-sacrificing love.[24]

Thus, over a good part of his life Lonergan repeatedly came back to the social significance of the theological virtues: faith, hope, and charity. He was regularly content to make his point in the context of another theme, with the result that these scattered gems tend to get lost. It seemed worthwhile to collect some of them and see them in a series.

6. 'What Am I to Do?'

This essay is a work of research on Lonergan's Christology, accompanied here and there by my efforts at interpretation, and sprinkled with bits of history. Readers will be well aware, however, that in Lonergan's intentionality analysis history is followed by dialectic, which sets before them the choice of a way of life, or of a system of thought, or of some measure being debated. The next concern of my essay in natural order would therefore be dialectic as it pertains to Lonergan's Christology.

At this point we must take care to know what we are doing. If I were to state what Lonergan's view of dialectic is I would not be 'doing dialectic' but probably applying an earlier specialty to his position; so I would still start with research on his dialectic, to which I would then add some interpretation of his dialectic and the involvement of his dialectic in history. But this would all be first-phase theology, on the model 'What X says on the topic Y.' And as a referee of an article I wrote remarked in commentary at the end, 'So what?' That little 'So what?' is the sixty-four-thousand-dollar question pointing to second-phase theology. It has the power to turn a mere theological observer into an 'engaged' theologian.

So what indeed? The generic 'What am I to do?' can be specified in a dozen ways, depending on the context. If the article described corruption in the government, my 'what' might take the form of my vote in the next election, or of my contribution to a candidate's funds, or of a letter to the local newspaper, or of joining a protest march, or of standing for election myself – as I said, there are a dozen ways.

Scripture reinforces the challenge. Our question is the repeated evangelical question, What am I to do? John the Baptist was asked that question (Luke 3:10). Peter and the apostles were asked it (Acts 2:37). Paul asked it of the Lord (Acts 22:10). Above, in this chapter, I presented Lonergan's description of a theologian or believer or inquiring human being confronted with the New Testament: 'So ineluctably there arises the question, Who is this Jesus?'[25] Then, just as ineluctably there arises the question

'What am I to do when confronted with Jesus?' In our day this has become specified for millions in the form given it by Bonhoeffer, 'What is Christ for us today?'

Lonergan's 'ineluctably' has a supposition. It supposes an openness to the interior dynamism of spirit. One can brush aside the 'So what?' One can admit it but do so cautiously, wary of any commitment it might challenge me to make. One may respond to the challenge but keep a rein on the response. Or, finally, one may respond with complete abandon, in the manner that the Spiritual Exercises of Ignatius Loyola teach and promote. To do less might be a legitimate goal of objective impersonal first-phase theology; it would not, however, fully exploit the dynamism and intentionality of my spiritual resources, which propel me into the second phase.

With the Bonhoeffer question, one which I must ask myself and be the first to do so, I enter a totally different ball game. My theology has become a hybrid: the question who Christ is has become also the question who Christ is for me. I am no longer an 'intellectual' just asking about some object of thought; I am a human being confronted with Jesus Christ, asking an existential question about myself, and not to learn about myself either, which might leave me still an academic, but to decide what to do with myself. We are back to the question I raised in Chapter 1: must the theologian be a believer? From another angle the question might be: How do non-believers handle second-phase theology? How do theologians handle it? Often, I suggest, by turning it into a first-phase question, and arguing about theologies.

Is my present discussion appropriate in this essay? At the International Lonergan Congress 1970,[26] efforts were made to include all points of view, and Daniel Berrigan was invited to contribute a paper. This he graciously did, paying tribute to Lonergan's honesty in pursuit of the truth wherever it might lead him, and then presenting his own position.[27] It is not exactly a position paper but rather a plea for the 'intellectuals' to stand up and be counted on the injustices 'wreaked by war-making governments, by racism, by pandemic poverty, by denial of civil and human rights.' Without such involvement, 'the mind of man is amputated from the historic hope of man.' In such a case 'the amputated intellect is of no more service than the amputated limb. Both are dead.'

Any account of theology must consider and accept the challenge of the second phase or admit frankly to being a truncated form. Any full theology of Jesus Christ has likewise to reckon with Berrigan's plea, whether in the form and application he gave it, or in some other. The alternative is to say 'Jesus Christ means nothing to me,' or at least, 'I'm not discussing the matter here.' What then would Lonergan reply?[28] The question has moved from thought to values, and very specifically to one's own values *presently operating in what one is doing*. Berrigan puts the matter in terms of humanity, but for both him and Lonergan humanity means Christ. A favourite quote says, 'Homo sum; humani nil a me alienum puto' ('I am human, and I regard nothing human as alien to me' – a dictum of the Roman writer Terentius); it might well be quoted by Christ, and be followed by the opening paragraphs of the Vatican II document *Gaudium et spes* (The Church in the Modern World). It is here and now operative for me, but in the terms of reference of this essay it is operative hypothetically for a hypothetical Lonergan.

A first step is clear enough, though still academic: ideas have consequences, and Lonergan's ideas may in the long run contribute as much as Berrigan's activism to the correction of injustices. A remark by Lonergan is typical: 'The church in Europe lost the workers in the nineteenth century, but would the church have lost the workers in the nineteenth century if she had not lost the intellectuals in the eighteenth?'[29] Regularly he cited Marx as witness to his case: Marx regarded in his lifetime as an old fool frequenting the British Museum, and now a century later dominating half the world with the impact of his ideas.

Next, what concretely were Lonergan's ideas bearing on the correction of abuses in the world? There are two approaches. One is in the natural order and is illustrated by Lonergan's work on economics; if his economics is valid and becomes accepted it will do more than a thousand protest marches to aid the poor, but its validity can only be determined by the intellectuals. The other is in the supernatural order. Lonergan would appeal to the transforming action of the theological virtues (see above). More basically and with recurring emphasis he appealed to the law of the cross: overcoming evil by submitting to it. He detested the violence and destructiveness of the new generation.[30]

So the Berrigan question returns: what active resistance should the intellectuals make against the forces of evil? Do we expect Lonergan to march with the resisters and protesters? Here there is a strange opposition between Lonergan and Berrigan, not so much in personal viewpoints – Berrigan might well agree that Lonergan should stay at his desk à la

Marx instead of marching with the activists, but would Lonergan approve of illegally burning government papers with napalm? We can make the question more concrete: in the late 1960s and the 1970s, crowds of students were in rebellion against the curriculum of studies imposed on them; crowds of young religious were in revolt against religious authority. Lonergan was severely critical of what he saw of this at Regis College, where he lived most of the years 1965 to 1975. At the same time, he was as revolutionary as any of the students and young religious on the need for change (see Chapter 7 above). Though I do not remember any position he took on the deliberate courting of civil punishment by the Berrigans, I believe he would be critical of their efforts there, sharing with them the same genuine concern for ends, but differing widely on the means to achieve them.

The solution is clear in the abstract: with the passing of classical culture, Lonergan says in a much quoted passage, 'There is bound to be formed a solid right that is determined to live in a world that no longer exists. There is bound to be formed a scattered left, captivated by now this, now that new development, exploring now this and now that new possibility. But what will count is a perhaps not numerous center, big enough to be at home in both the old and the new, painstaking enough to work out one by one the transitions to be made, strong enough to refuse half measures and insist on complete solutions even though it has to wait.'[31]

Both 'solid right' and 'scattered left' were anathema to Lonergan, but it was easy for partisans of both to claim him or denounce him according to their different perspectives. In the context of historical causality, two questions arise for those of us who are moved to accept Lonergan's teaching, for me who writes this book, and for you who read it. One is the idea-question: how to find and support the 'perhaps not numerous center' where we desire to be. The other is the praxis-question: how concretely to join or support the activists. The first question is open to debate. The other involves a personal decision in the context of the Christian message for all of us who believe and ponder the signs of the times. All of us must ask the same question and face the same decision. But each must ask and ponder alone, and decide alone, though the decision may be to join others. As Lonergan remarked in 'The Mediation of Christ in Prayer' (Chapter 10 above), to carry the point further is a matter of private meditation.

The activist question remains unanswered for me till I myself answer it. No matter how or when I answer it, it will be kept in play by that other context, wider, more urgent, universal for the human race: the context of the poor and downtrodden, of the tortured political prisoners, of the starving children of the world, of the mentally disturbed (let us not forget that they, too, are numbered among God's poor), those who suffer the agony of scruples and doubt and psychic torment. It is a context in which the whole human race is called to minister to the whole human race. Who is my neighbour (Luke 10:29)?

15

History, Faith, and the
New Fundamental Theology

This chapter hearkens to a precept St Peter gave us (1 Peter 3:15): 'Be always ready with your defence whenever you are called to account for the hope that is in you,' which means also being ready to give an account for the faith that is in us. Such accounting was once called 'apologetics,' but that term is now being abandoned as too suggestive of rationalism; instead, theologians speak of a 'fundamental theology.' My argument could, however, be called an 'apologia' in the sense in which Newman wrote a history of his religious opinions and called it an '*Apologia pro vita sua*.' He did so as an act of personal defence; my aim is rather to give an account of the faith of Christians, and only incidentally of my own. And further, my aim is not so much to defend an established position as it is to follow Lonergan in the working out of his new fundamental theology to replace the old apologetics.

The question is especially important for Protestant theologians, who once found their basis in the historical facts about Jesus related in the scriptures, but now feel that modern views on history and modern scriptural scholarship have destroyed that foundation, so they struggle to replace it. Catholic theologians, of course, face the same problem, but fall back more readily on tradition as a second line of defence.

My focus remains specifically the Christology of Bernard Lonergan, but at this point I wish to enlarge the field of data. There are two steps in my task, corresponding to two articles of the Apostles' Creed: 'I believe in God, the Father Almighty,' and 'I believe in Jesus Christ, his only Son, our Lord.' The first step was studied more than once by Lonergan, thematically and in detail, but in a trinitarian context. The second step has not been studied with the same concentration; we must therefore repair the omission now, and do so in union with fellow believers.

Up to his later years, writing as a Catholic and mainly for Catholic readers, and carried in his own faith by his upbringing and his community, Lonergan does not seem to see dialogue with other churches or religions as an urgent need. About the time of Vatican II this changed quite notably, especially with regard to world religions (see Chapter 16 below). Now he could no longer take his Christian faith for granted, but must add to his (largely philosophic) *apologia* for God an *apologia* also for his Christian and Catholic faith. Belief in God is not Christology, of course, but to treat it separately reminds us of the distinction and clarifies it. Let me treat these two steps in order.

1. Belief in God: The Old Apologetics and the New

On our first step in fundamental theology Lonergan has stated his position briefly but clearly, and done so in contrast to the old apologetics, but also in a certain continuity with it. Thus he indicates 'an analogy and a difference between the old *theologia naturalis* of the Thomist tradition and the new natural theology desired ... if we are to meet the challenge of secularism.'[1] It is not my task to write a history of apologetics, but only to describe Lonergan's position. In the traditional conception, he writes, fundamental theology was concerned to present the reasonableness of faith, and to do so not just for those who already believe, and not as a matter either of persuading those who do not believe; rather this theology would speak to both classes, and would proceed, not by rhetoric, but rigorously and scientifically by logic.

> It has a threefold structure (and this) threefold structure involved demonstrations, first, of the existence of God and of religion, secondly, of the Christian religion, thirdly, of the true Church. A natural theology established the existence of God. A natural ethics established the obligation of worshipping God. The prophecies of the Old Testament and the miracles of the [N]ew established the divine origin of the Christian religion, and the Christian message settled the identity of the true Church.[2]

There is, however, an obvious difficulty to this procedure: '... a valid argument has nothing in its conclusions that is not contained in its premises. But here the premises are presented as within the reach of human reason, while the conclusion contains what may lie beyond the reach of human reason,' the mysteries of faith. Somewhere in this apparently simple and coherent and ineluctable series we seem to have made a radical jump from what is natural to what is supernatural.

Something more, then, is obviously needed. For his own answer to his secularist opponents Lonergan enlists the aid of Congar, who maintained that 'the main task facing the theologian today is to appropriate an adequate anthropology.' Lonergan, of course, agrees wholeheartedly with the need for an adequate anthropology; he is all for 'the appropriation of one's own reality as existential subject.'[3] It is on that basis that he confronts the secularists.

> The secularist, who denies God that he may affirm man, who rejects institutional religion because he finds it blocking human development, can hardly reject the existential subject's discovery of himself, acceptance of himself, realization of his own potentialities. He cannot but share the effort to apprehend the workings of human understanding … He cannot but distinguish between the merely bright ideas of understanding and the affirmations of sound judgment … From such objective realms he will turn in upon the subject … he will derive an epistemology (and a) metaphysics. Further, the secularist is neither premoral … or amoral … He is aware of his feelings, of the values they can reveal, of the moment of moral truth in which he finds himself when he asks himself whether this or that course of action is truly good …
>
> But the appropriation of one's own reality as existential subject can lead one further still. One can observe that the whole development of science and scholarship rests on two pillars. The first is the rejection of obscurantism … The second is the empirical principle, that answers to questions be verified in the data of experience … But one may ask whether science is the only knowledge man can attain. The question is relevant, for scientific knowledge is of its nature bound to be incomplete … Every scientific affirmation gives rise to the further question, Does it really just happen? Is there not a massive obscurantism involved in brushing aside the question that obviously arises whenever any scientific proposition happens to be verified?[4]

We may leave the matter with that question, aware that for Lonergan the question is the important thing, confident that the serious searcher will come to the only answer that makes sense, trusting too in the help of God. As Lonergan said in *Insight* at the end of Chapter 20, on one who seeks the truth: 'Nor will he labor alone ... for the realization of the solution and its development in each of us is principally the work of God.'

I conclude this first phase of fundamental theology with Lonergan's brief account of the way it both differs from the old and resembles the old.

> It differs from the old *theologia naturalis* both in its starting point and in its procedure. Where the old *theologia naturalis* begins from the material universe, the new begins from the self-appropriation of the existential subject. Where the old proceeds from the material universe to God by invoking the principles of a metaphysics, the new advances from the existential subject to God by the claims of a full rejection of obscurantism. The old and the new are analogous for they proceed from knowledge of the finite to a conclusion about the infinite. The old and the new differ, for the old thinks of objects and objective principles while the new adverts to the subject and the exigencies of his intelligence and reasonableness.[5]

2. Belief in Christ: The New Fundamental Christology

I use 'Belief in Christ' as my heading but inevitably I introduce more general considerations. There is a good survey of Lonergan's own position on the whole question in a paper he read at the 1967 Toronto congress on The Theology of the Renewal of the Church, where he moves from renewal more generally to renewal of theology, and continues: '... a renewed theology needs a renewed foundation.' He then critiques the old foundations, and offers 'some indication of the nature or character of the new.'[6] It is that last point that we have to examine.

Lonergan first adduces his work in *Verbum* and *Insight* as already laying foundations, the first 'to assure historical continuity' with Aquinas on cognitional theory, the second 'to take into account the fact of modern science and the problems of modern philosophy' (64). Against that background he offers some approximations on the new foundation.

'As a first approximation, to be corrected and complemented shortly by further approximations,' he considers the foundation of a modern

science. This he places in method, which 'lies not in a set of verbal propositions named first principles but in a particular, concrete, dynamic reality
generating knowledge of particular, concrete, dynamic realities' (64–65).
The foundations, then, are the reality of one's religious conversion.

But the real and close analogy for religious foundations is one person's
love for another. Love is a gift. There is no foundation for it that lies
deeper, that provides a more solid basis, that grounds an argument concluding to love as a consequence. The mother, I believe Lonergan would
say, does not argue herself into love for her child. As the child itself is a
gift, so is her love for the child. It is self-justifying.[7] In the religious
person, this gift is from God, and it is a twofold reality: God's love for us,
and our love for God.[8] Both are sheer gift. Both lack any foundation in
reason, though reason accepts and approves them.

This is not some far-fetched theory. It starts with a well-established
truth: God wishes all peoples to be saved and come to the knowledge of
truth (1 Timothy 2:4). This the church interprets generously but literally
to mean God's universal salvific will. Further, if God wants us all to be
saved, then God will give us the means: namely, sufficient grace to that
end. What form does that sufficient grace take? It does not seem unrea-
sonable to think of it as including love of God: 'it is difficult to suppose
that grace would be sufficient if it fell short of the gift of loving God
above all and loving one's neighbor as oneself.'[9] That, therefore, is the
foundation, the first principle, the starting point.

But this seems a long way from the legitimate aims of 1 Peter and the
old apologetics. Why am I a Catholic (or Protestant, or Jewish, or Muslim)?
Why do I believe that Christ is the Son of God and our Redeemer?
Why do I recognize the authority of the Pope? These matters seem
remote from the foundation in the love of God and religious conversion.
For that matter, how do I know that God and I are united in a bond of
love? I will consider questions on such concrete matters in the concluding
paragraphs of this chapter, but for the present I continue with more
abstract generalities.

There are basic answers and there are secondary answers. Lonergan's
basic answer was given above: love is self-justifying. The secondary answer
is found in Peter's being ready to give an account of the hope we have
and the love we enjoy. There is therefore a foundation *tout court*, and there
is a relative and secondary foundation, with its relative and secondary

answers to our list of questions. To seek such answers, to look for signs of our love of God, and to look for them in reasoned discourse seems quite legitimate to me, and not at all opposed to love's self-justifying character. The case is rather that the two are complementary: to love God is followed by the desire to know God, and so by the defence of our faith that Peter enjoins. '… there exists an unrestricted being in love, a mystery of love and awe, a being grasped by ultimate concern, a happiness that has a determinate content but no intellectually apprehended object.' Those who have this experience will ask, 'With whom are we in love?'[10] and with that question they are on their way with Peter to a reasoned account of their faith.

The basic foundation we appeal to is interior. But on that interior foundation the peoples of the world, Christians and non-Christians, have built their superstructures; they have objectified their faith in various beliefs; they have expressed their adoration of their God in many diverse rites and liturgies; they have related their religion to their daily life in many disparate ways. And those who are deeply concerned with the question whether there is a God and how God may be found are clearly struggling to objectify an interior transcendent reality and so are at one with the world religions in this most basic question of foundations.

Like a magnetic needle in search of the North Pole, my argument continues to veer back to the search for and the discovery of God. It is time to concentrate on the specific theme of Lonergan's Christology, and his search for and discovery of Christ. Now, just as the academic and the plain person find God in different ways, so also they differ in their discovery of Christ; the academics talk endlessly, but it is doubtful whether anyone is convinced, whereas plain men and women find Christ with few words and much conviction. I must consider both, starting with the academics.

For this I turn back to Lonergan's 'Christology Today,' in particular to section 4 of that paper: 'Christology: A Religious Question.'[11] To treat it as a religious question is to presuppose the theme of conversion and foundation, and in fact neither conversion nor foundation is mentioned in section 4; they are presupposed. The focus is on the New Testament and the way modern historical methods affect our search for Christ. Lonergan takes us through five steps till we see that book as not only a religious document calling for religious living, but also as a personal invitation to which the appropriate response is a personal commitment. 'So ineluctably there arises the question, Who is this Jesus?'[12]

The religious question is naturally followed by the theological question (see Chapter 11 above). Now theology tends to become an octopus, reaching out to embrace anything and everything. So Lonergan, at the end of this section, lists a half dozen of the many Christologies that have claimed attention since the New Testament and concludes with an anticipation of the future: 'But in our time of hermeneutics and history, of psychology and critical philosophy, there is an exigence for further development. There are windows to be opened and fresh air to be let in.'[13]

3. Fresh Air and Windows

3.1. What Windows? What Fresh Air?

Let us keep our bearings. We are not examining the basic grounds of our Christian faith, but rather the panoply of history and argument that enables us to give an account of it on a secondary level. I believe that some light on the question comes from study of similar challenges in the past, and that we can use history to overturn a greedy historicism.

To limit my presentation I will take only the three basic questions indicated by the terms: Nicea, the New Testament, and the historical Jesus. There is a general strategy that can be applied in all three cases. This strategy inverts the ordinary procedures of the theology manuals, for they would start with our beginnings in history and move forward through the centuries to the present; our way is the opposite: to start with the present and move back to our beginnings.

Though this does invert the order the manuals use, it finds some support in a high authority, for it is a variation and an application of Newman's 'true way of learning,' namely, not to start with Descartes's universal doubt and try to find an unshakeable beginning on which to build, but rather to begin by accepting all in globo, and then with the exercise of one's critical faculty to slough off and discard what one finds to be false.[14] Thus in my first subdivision, focused on Nicea, I do not follow the route from New Testament to Nicea, but rather start with Nicea and go back from it to the New Testament.

The strategy has its rationale: we are dealing with the emergence of a new formulation of doctrine, but the emergence is the term of a process, and the being of a being-in-process is clarified only in the term of the process. The embryo in the mother's womb is something on the way; but what is on the way? You know what was on the way when it arrives, a human being. There is something analogous in the state of the New Testament writings and the slow emergence after three centuries of the dogma of Nicea, a point we now take up.

3.2. Nicea Emerges from the New Testament

Nicea defined the basic doctrine of the Catholic church: the Son is God in the same sense as the Father is God. This is the Christian doctrine, on which Christianity will stand or fall, the doctrine from which all other Christology derives. Lonergan once remarked in regard to the definition of a circle, 'Search Euclid for a property of the circle that is not demonstrated through the definition of the circle.'[15] In a somewhat similar way, we might search Constantinople, Ephesus, and Chalcedon for a definition on the Son that is not based on Nicea.

There is nothing wrong with the standard approach, which has been to start with the New Testament, or even with the Jewish scriptures and their prophecies, and to follow development forward to Nicea. That is part of the history of Christian doctrine: indeed, a very important part. But it is a search for the later clarity in the earlier obscurity. Let us on the contrary start with the later clarity and ask for its credentials. Here, for example, is some doubting Thomas of a bishop right after Nicea. Three hundred and eighteen of his fellow bishops voted yesterday and declared their faith that the Son is God in the same sense as the Father is God. He wonders, this hypothetical bishop, where that declaration came from.

It came from a reaction against Arius. In Arius's doctrine, however much you dress it up with fine words, the Son is not God in the same sense as the Father is God; the Son, in fact, is a creature. And this, the 318 bishops declared, is clearly opposed to what our church believes and what we believe.[16] The role of Arius in the history of dogma was to make the options clear and thus enable the 318 bishops to see what they had less clearly believed up to that point.

But where did Arius come from? Well, a century earlier, that great scholar and theologian Origen taught a doctrine of the Son which made the Son God in some sense, but not God in the sense in which the Father is God. The Father is divinity itself; the Son is divinity by participation. It was what is called a subordinationist doctrine: the Son is subordinate to the Father. Arius had brought out the full implications of Origenist doctrine.

Now, if Arius is wrong, so was Origen wrong. But Origen was a great biblical scholar, so we are driven back to scripture, coming at it, however, from an angle the opposite to that of the theology manuals.

The key to the difference is in what you look for. If you follow the manuals, starting with the New Testament and knowing in advance what is there, you will look for the wrong thing: namely, for a text in Paul or John that says the Son is God in the same sense as the Father is God. But that is to have the question clear before it was clarified. So don't start there; start rather in 325 where the question is finally clear: is the Son a creature like us or not? Then you will not look for a text that says the Son is God in the same sense as the Father is God, but you will look for that doctrine on the way. Perhaps then our 'sceptic' bishop will find Nicea there, not 'in facto esse' (already established) but 'in fieri' (on the way, coming into being, becoming).

3.3. The New Testament Emerges from the Historical Jesus

This Nicea 'in fieri' that you find in the New Testament is the Christ of faith, or what the early church believed about the Lord Jesus. And that calls now for a second application of our approach, this time to the emergence of the New Testament. Our strategy will be the same: to start where we are in the year 90 (or 80, or 70) and move backwards to the Jesus of the year 30, the historical Jesus. The older apologetics started with Jesus himself and what he said, and moved forward from the year 30 to the New Testament of forty or more years later. For centuries there was no problem with that: what Jesus said was there in black and white in the scriptures. But along came a sense of history, and we discovered that very often we don't know what Jesus himself said, but only what Matthew or John says Jesus said. They attribute to the Lord Jesus words that express the faith of the church in their time, sixty or ninety years later.

Using our new strategy, then, we will not start with the historical Jesus, and go forward to the New Testament writings; rather, we will take those writings as our point of departure and go backwards to what we can learn or surmise from them about the year 30. Once again, perhaps, if our sceptical bishop does not find his faith there 'in facto esse,' he may find it 'in fieri.' And once again, the key to discovery is in asking the right question, which now is not what Jesus said about himself, but the praxis which reveals what and who he is.

Here is the place to remark that we have in our attitude to Nicea and the New Testament an outstanding application of the principle of trust: that is, trust in their witness to their own time and its beliefs. For the New Testament the point is familiar: we trust the authors of the various books to give faithful witness to what their church believed in the year 50, or 70, or 90. But let us not forget that the same principle of trust was operative in our acceptance of Nicea: we trust the 318 bishops when they declare their faith and the faith of their church as it was in the year 325. Much closer to home, we remember that our acceptance of the Second Vatican Council is based on trust in the 2200 bishops who were there as witnesses to their faith and the faith of their church.[17] But trust in Vatican II, and to some extent trust in Nicea as well, is a trust that is subject to verification. Our trust in the New Testament writers is a trust in men and women who stand alone, who are our sole witnesses to what the church of their time and generation believed.

3.4. The Historical Jesus

With that in mind, and keeping the same strategy, we will not look in scripture for a witness 'in facto esse' to Nicea and the divinity of Christ; we will look for it only 'in fieri,' in praxis rather than a proposition, the praxis of Christ and the attitude of those who knew him,[18] instead of doctrine preached by him. Then we find the uncompromising precept, 'Come, follow me,' and the unquestioning response, 'They left all things, and followed him.' We see the exercise of an authority that does not need to search the prophecies, but has its own inner resources: 'It was said in ancient times … But I say to you …' We find the extraordinary demands he made on people: 'He who loves father and mother more than me is not worthy of me.' The high opinion of Christ that made people comply with those demands is the New Testament faith on-the-way.

The older apologetic included such considerations, but more in confirmation of a position that was directly based on truth. In the new fundamental theology, the supreme exigence we see with regard to orthopraxy would receive first and fundamental emphasis. And you would understand the later development as the term of what the New Testament shows as doctrine on-the-way, doctrine discernible in praxis before it became explicit.

The way this worked itself out in regard to the resurrection is worth noting. The turmoil at the death of Jesus illustrates the faith shown in their praxis while Jesus was with them: they could not understand the things that happened to God's favourite Son; hence the recourse to prophecies to show it was all fore-ordained by God. The utterly confused and extremely agitated state of the disciples after the crucifixion are witness to that high view they had had of his person and mission. Then came the resurrection, when the power and glory of Jesus at the right hand of the Father enabled them to give expression to the faith that their praxis had already manifested. The early 'layers' of belief that scholars discern in the preaching of the Acts of the Apostles show the first Christians thinking of Jesus as 'pais theou,' 'thy holy servant Jesus' (Acts 4:27), as one who was made Lord and Messiah: 'Let all Israel then accept as certain that God has made this Jesus, whom you crucified, both Lord and Messiah' (Acts 2:36).

These texts can be seen as 'on the way' to such passages as we find in Paul's letter to the Romans, about the 'gospel God announced ... through his prophets. ... It is about his Son: on the human level he was born of David's stock, but on the level of the spirit – the Holy Spirit – he was declared Son of God by a mighty act in that he rose from the dead' (Romans 1:2-4). Or, '... great beyond all question is the mystery of our religion: "He who was manifested in the body, vindicated in the spirit, seen by angels; who was proclaimed among the nations, believed in throughout the world, glorified in high heaven"' (1 Timothy 3:16). Paul and 1 Timothy give us a kind of overview of the process, from the viewpoint of the term or the approach to the term.

The case is similar with the reading back into the gospel narratives of what is called post-resurrection faith, as when after the storm at sea the disciples fell on their knees, confessing his divinity, and when Peter could add 'the Son of the living God' to his confession of the Messiah (Matthew 16:16). But what the exegetes call post-resurrection faith we may also call post-resurrection interpretation of the pre-resurrection praxis. The first disciples could not articulate their faith in Jesus till after the resurrection and the manifestation of the power of Jesus at the right hand of God. John tells us they did not understand, but after he rose from the dead they remembered that he had said these things (John 2:9, 13, 22).

Whatever our strategy in the area of Christology, we may surmise in early Christian development the play of dialectic. 'By dialectic ... is understood a generalized apologetic conducted in an ecumenical spirit, aiming ultimately at a comprehensive viewpoint, and proceeding towards that goal by acknowledging differences, seeking their grounds real and apparent, and eliminating superfluous oppositions.'[19] Acknowledging differences in the scriptural accounts while aiming at a comprehensive viewpoint, I return to Lonergan's 'Christology Today' for some basic considerations of faith and history with which to round out this chapter, in particular to section 4 on Christology as a religious question.[20]

Apologizing, then, for the repetition, I adduce my earlier remarks: the focus in 'Christology Today' is on the New Testament and the way modern historical methods affect our search for Christ. Lonergan takes us through five steps till we see that book as not only 'a religious document calling for religious living but also as a personal invitation, the appropriate response to which is a personal commitment.'So ineluctably there arises the question,Who is this Jesus?' I have now to add from section 5 the church's criteria for judging new Christologies:'It is in the progressive clarification of Christian experience and in the continuous exercise of spiritual discernment in the Christian community that Christological doctrine developed.'[21]

This long excursus has discussed the way one academic seeks foundations for his faith in Christ and perhaps has done so with no more success than a hundred attempts by other academics.What is fairly certain is that it will do little for the faith of plain men and women who believe without theological argument but surely not without grounds. So what are their grounds? I find in Lonergan the potentiality for a simple and,it seems to me, satisfactory answer to that question. Let me try to develop that potentiality.

The occasion for the doctrine in question was an interview with Lonergan conducted by two professors and a handful of students from McMaster University.[22] At one point a question, not clear on the tape, elicited a fairly clear answer:'I think I explain in Chapter 4 of *Method* how Christianity differs from religion. Religion in general consists of God's gift of his love … But this interior gift is one thing; having an objective expression of God's love in Christ Jesus [is another].' And Lonergan took the example of the love between a man and a woman; if they never avow their love they are refusing themselves the development that that love could have (6–7).

At this point Lonergan, I believe, comes to the grounds of simple faith.'… the first thing a methodologist does when he goes to a study of the New Testament is to start out from a study of charity as described there.' But there are many who have the same gift of God's love,'and so you move to the Christian community, and the Christian community refers you back to Christ, and you inquire about Christ' (7). The operating agency here is people, not argument.You recognize in yourself the gift of God's love; you recognize the same gift in others; if the community you have discovered is Christian, you are led to Christ. That is the 'argument' of the new fundamental theology.

The one concession to the usual approach is the way the gift is recognized. On that point Lonergan brings in values and the fourth level of consciousness. With charity, the eyes of love, 'the person who loves you can see values in you, or the possibility of values that another person does not.' As Pascal puts it, 'The heart has reasons that reason does not know.' The 'heart' here is a person on the fourth level of intentional consciousness and in love, and the eyes of love recognize the values. And one value the eyes see is a judgment on the value of belief (7). 'If you are going to bridge between Research, Interpretation, and History over to Doctrines, Systematics, and Communications, you have to work on that fourth level and acknowledge its validity and in what sense it is objective' (McMaster interview, 8).

I quote the unedited transcription as I found it, but its message is clear enough. It centres on the person who loves God with a self-justifying love, who finds others who love God in the same way, who finds Christians among those others; and Christians lead us to Christ, who is supremely in love with God. Here, I believe, we have a sketch for plain people of a grounded answer to the problems of faith and history. With such a grounding one has no need of 'proof texts,' and one understands Lonergan's dictum: 'I would not want to write the kind of theology that justifies one's faith' (4). Here, too, we have the potentiality for grounding my particular tradition with all its concrete beliefs: why I am a Catholic, and so on.

4. Summary and Reflections

I have been concerned with reasons why. Why are we religious people, religious in the sense that we love a God who loves us? To this fundamental why there is no answer, for it is a first, and to give it a why would make it a second. But there is a secondary why that does have answers: Why do I hold the Catholic faith? The complex answer might include 'Because it was taught me by my parents.' Those, then, who doubt their religion, or think they do, have to determine whether the why they seek is fundamental or secondary. If the former we can only pray; but if the latter, we can help them discern the signs of their religion, beginning with that very search of theirs that to them is so agonizing and to us is so evident a sign of their basic faith.

And why do we believe that Christ is the Son of God? It is clear with a minimum of reflection that we cradle Christians believe this doctrine because it was taught us by others, and clear as we backtrack that those others were taught this doctrine because of an event at Nicea nearly seventeen centuries ago. And why did Nicea declare its faith in this doctrine? And so on, in what I call the Newman pattern for discovering the truth. In other words we receive our faith from the community and its traditions, and the community remains when scholarship falters, for faltering scholarship is powerless to destroy what it was powerless to give: faith in the Son of God. Nevertheless, we gratefully accept what it has to give: namely, a rational accompaniment and counterpart to what is divinely given.

And what if the believing community and historical scholarship find themselves in utter contradiction? 'Jesus is the Son of God.' 'Jesus is not the Son of God.' That, of course, is too easy, for scholarship could not affirm either of these two propositions. So what of the following assertions? 'John says Jesus is the Son of God.' 'John does not say Jesus is the Son of God.' Both are assertions of scholarship, so let the scholars decide. And what if historical scholarship overturns our journey backwards into historical causes? If we turn out to be wrong on some point of history, we have lost a useful ally, but not our faith in the Son of God.

As readers have no doubt caught on, the dispute is more between procedures than between findings. The historians rest their case on a document or a discernible pattern or something else that qualifies as historical evidence. Traditionalists rest their case on community discernment; I repeat that important quotation from Lonergan: 'It is in the progressive clarification of Christian experience and in the continuous exercise of spiritual discernment in the Christian community that Christological doctrine developed.' As for our relation to history, the issue once again is joined at a deeper level: namely, 'that recondite department of hermeneutics that involves one in cognitional theory, epistemology, and metaphysics.'[23] For example, at the level of truth, on the 'detachable' quality of truth that enables it to be transmitted from one person to another, and from one century to another.

With this reading of change and continuity in New Testament times it is easy to accept a similar reading of change and continuity in the Christian centuries.

I have spoken of many changes but in closing I should recall their general nature. They are of a kind that has already occurred more than once. They are changes, not in God's self-disclosure or our faith, but in our culture. They are changes such as occurred when the first Christians moved from Palestine into the Roman Empire, changes such as occurred when the Empire succumbed to the Dark Ages, changes such as occurred when the medieval Church built its cathedrals with their schools and founded its universities, changes such as occurred when Scholasticism yielded to Humanism, the Renaissance, the Reformation and the Counter-Reformation. Ours is a new age, and enormous tasks lie ahead. But we shall be all the more likely to surmount them, if we take the trouble to understand what is going forward and why.[24]

As complement to this we have explicit endorsement of the sources of our Christian faith. 'There has been no new revelation from on high to replace the revelation given through Christ Jesus. There has been written no new Bible, and there has been founded no new church, to link us with him.'[25]

16

Christianity and World Religions

An essay on 'Christ and History' cannot avoid the topic of Christianity and world religions. Lonergan has a broad view of the universality of religion, but what does he mean by 'religion' in that phrase? It is not any of the institutional religions, with their expressed beliefs and codes of conduct, their rituals and customs. All that is not universal at all, but the opposite: a superstructure that differs with different religions. Lonergan would go behind the superstructure to an infrastructure that is to be understood in reference to his sharply defined use of 'experience,' and in particular of 'religious experience.'[1] The pure religious experience that is God's gift of his love, the experience that lies beneath all superstructure – that is 'religion' in the present sense.[2]

Of course the very fact of talking about it, the very fact of giving it the name 'religion,' is already superstructure. By definition it is impossible for talk to get behind talk and reach pure religious experience. As soon as we cease to reflect on the experience and try to approach the purity of the infrastructure, the experience becomes wordless, and mystics have to be commanded by their directors to speak of their experience. It is, however, the business of theology to talk ('theou-logos'), so theologians talk of dialogue among the religions.

1. Vatican II and New Interests

This is a relatively new area for Lonergan. Up to the Second Vatican Council, his interest was focused on theology within the Roman Catholic church. It was almost certainly the Second Vatican Council that widened the range of his interests, for he speaks, as stemming from that council, of the church's 'concern with ecumenism, with non-Christian religions, and with the atheist negation of religion';[3] one surmises that his own concern had the same origin as the church's in regard to these three.

Then, from 1967 on, there is recurring mention of religious studies in their relation to the human enterprise and to theology in particular.[4] The universalist theme and the doctrine of salvation offered to all begins to be considered not just in relation to Catholic doctrines, but in relation to empirical studies of religion.[5]

2. Universal Salvific Will

There is a deep significance in that last point. In a paper that Lonergan wrote but never delivered he describes two approaches to the universalist position.[6] First, it is Roman Catholic doctrine (gradually made clear and explicit in the 1800s and accepted without question in the 1900s) that since God wills everyone to be saved (1 Timothy 2:4), then everyone is given sufficient grace to be saved. Lonergan's second approach, however, is my present interest; in this he borrows from empirical studies of the many religions, to which he will add his own observations from time to time. With some caution he would appeal to Friedrich Heiler, who had 'listed seven features common to all the high religions … I feel that he would recognize at least a rough equivalence between his seven features and what I have said of being in love with God.'[7]

The caution is emphasized and the attitude made more specific a year later: 'For present purposes it will be best to regard Prof. Heiler's position not as an exhaustive empirical statement on the world religions but as an ideal type or model, that is, neither a description nor an hypothesis but a heuristic and expository device open to all the additions and modifications that empirical investigation may dictate.'[8] Heiler continues to be quoted on the seven common areas,[9] but in 'Prolegomena to the Study of the Emerging Religious Consciousness of Our Time' Lonergan turns for support on the empirical side to the arguments of Panikkar and Whitson;[10] then, in 'Philosophy and the Religious Phenomenon,' he simply appeals to them and others without developing their arguments.[11]

In what does that grace, needed and sufficient for salvation, consist? That is the question. Lonergan argues that it includes love, and in this way he ties it to his anthropology (intentional dynamism, self-transcendence realized in love). But his argument is brief in the extreme. At first he simply said, 'it is difficult to suppose that grace would be sufficient if it fell short of the gift of loving God above all and loving one's neighbor as oneself.'[12] Two years later he expands the argument slightly, appealing to Chapter 13 of 1 Corinthians on the necessity of charity for salvation, and to the common consent that charity is sufficient for salvation. If God wills all to be saved, then God wills to give them the necessary and sufficient condition for salvation. 'It follows that he gives all men the gift of his love, and so it further follows that there can be an element in all the religions of mankind that is at once profound and holy.'[13]

On the latter point of salvation offered to all and empirically discernible in the religions, 'Theology and Man's Future' is explicit: 'Finally, there is the theological doctrine that God grants all men sufficient grace for their salvation. This doctrine is relevant to religious studies; it makes them studies of the manifold ways God's grace comes to men ...'[14] It is in this period too that more attention is paid to Christianity in relation to 'the other world religions.'[15] A very useful work in which the several features of this new direction are set forth is the already mentioned paper 'Faith and Beliefs.'[16]

The appeal to the divine universal salvific will supplies the real ground for Lonergan's personal adherence to the universalist position. Further, he extended it beyond the world religions; as he said in 'Faith and Beliefs,' after asking whether 'universalist' should not be so extended, 'As a theologian ... I must expect an affirmative answer; but as a mere theologian, I must leave the factual answer to students of the history of religions.'[17] We have, then, to take 'universal' as meaning for Lonergan just what it says, understanding always that we are talking of what is inmost and vital in the 'religion' of the religions, and in the 'religion' of the non-religious: that is, of what lies below superstructure, namely, religious experience in its purest state as the gift of God.

3. Recent Opinions

Up to recent times, the singular claims of Christianity had gone unchallenged. Scripture teaches that Jesus is the one mediator between God and the human race (1 Timothy 2:5); there is no other name under heaven given to us by which we may be saved (Acts 4:12); we are to go out to the whole world and preach the good news to every creature (Mark 16:15). In former times God spoke through prophets and in varied ways; now, at the end time God has spoken through the Son (Hebrews 1:1-2). What is one to make of these claims if the universal salvific will of God is fulfilled through the gift of divine love to everyone, Christian and non-Christian, in world religions and in primitive religions, in reference to institutional religions or independently of institutions?

There is question here of what is called, in the terms commonly used, the absoluteness or the uniqueness of Christianity, or again, its finality as something not to be surpassed, or its normativity as criterion for judging other religions. Recently, in terms like these, new opinions on the relation of Christianity and world religions have been proposed and vigorously debated. Lonergan's active career was at an end before that happened, and as far as I know, he never treated the question expressly. Nevertheless, his views on related topics impinge on our question.

4. What Is Specifically Christian?

One such topic is the question on what is specifically Christian. He was definite on this.

> To come now to what is distinctive of Christianity, let me quote C.F.D. Moule ... 'At no point within the New Testament is there any evidence that the Christians stood for an original philosophy of life or an original ethic. Their sole function is to bear witness to what they claim as an event – the raising of Jesus from among the dead.' What distinguishes the Christian, then, is not God's grace, which he shares with others, but the mediation of God's grace through Jesus Christ our Lord ... In the Christian ... God's gift of his love is a love that is in Christ Jesus. From this fact flow the social, historical, doctrinal aspects of Christianity.[18]

On the face of it, this passage seems to make Christ the mediator of grace for Christians only. But that was certainly not the position of Lonergan's Christology as he taught it in Toronto and Rome.[19] Has he changed his position in the five years that intervened since he published *De Verbo incarnato*? Possibly. But I think an explanation in terms of contexts more likely. Always it is the Father who has primacy; in the context of the divine missions, the sending of the Son by the Father means that all grace is to be given through the Son, the trinitarian mediator of creation; in the context of world religions Christ, the human founder of Christianity, is in a special way the mediator of that religion. I do not say this solves the problem, but it may remove open contradiction.

In any case the theme of the specifically Christian element requires fuller documentation.

> A classic formulation of Christian religious experience may be found in St. Paul's statement that God's love has flooded our inmost heart through the Holy Spirit he has given us ...

As infrastructure it is the dynamic state of being in love in an unrestricted fashion ...

Its suprastructure, however, is already extant in the account of Christian origins: God sending his only Son ... and the sending of the Spirit.

The distinctiveness of Christianity lies in this suprastructure.[20]

On the question of revelation outside Christianity, Lonergan takes a similar position: 'It isn't complete revelation. It isn't Christian revelation which ... introduces a specific difference. There is an intersubjective element to love that is present in Christianity, inasmuch as God is expressing his love in Christ as well as giving you the grace in your heart, and this element is missing when the Incarnate Lord is missing.'[21] Again,

If I have concluded that there is a common element to all the religions of mankind, I must now add that there is a specific element proper to Christianity. Christianity involves not only the inward gift of being in love with God but also the outward expression of God's love in Christ Jesus dying and rising again. In the paschal mystery the love that is given inwardly is focused and inflamed, and that focusing unites Christians not only with Christ but also with one another.[22]

5. Ultimate Differentiating Factor

The ultimate expression of the differentiating factor of Christianity, I believe, is provided in Lonergan's 1977 address to The Catholic Theological Society of America. The context was his familiar defence of the role of dogma, and his advice on what to do when old dogmatic formulas seem to have lost their meaning.

Personally I should urge that in each case one inquire whether the old issue still has a real import and, if it has, a suitable expression for that import be found. For example, at Nicea the real import was whether Christ, the mediator of our salvation, was a creature. Today many perhaps will be little moved by the question whether we have been saved by a creature or by God himself. But the issue may be put differently. One can ask whether God revealed his love for us by having a man die the death of scourging and crucifixion? Or was it his own Son, a divine person, who became flesh to suffer and die and thereby touch our hard hearts and lead us to eternal life?[23]

This use of Nicea differs notably from its more common use in proof of the divinity of Christ. Instead of focusing on Christ, our mediator with God, we focus on God showing in the sending of the Son the extent of the divine love God has for us, and showing it in the most heart-rending way by delivering up the only Son to death. Christ is seen as God's Isaac, with God's love the analogue for Abraham's sacrifice. But where a higher voice from heaven intervened to spare Abraham's Isaac, there is no higher voice to overrule God's love and save the divine Isaac. So God 'did not spare his own Son, but surrendered him for us all' (Romans 8:32). And 'that is God's own proof of his love towards us' (Romans 4:8; see 1 John 4:8-9). It is in regard to this ultimate act of God that Lonergan comes to full clarity on what is distinctive of Christianity: namely, the primary act of the Father in handing the Son over for crucifixion, and the consequent act of the Son in obedient acceptance of the Father's will.

With this doctrine of what is specific in Christianity we have the entry of the obedient Christ into human history, exercising historical causality through the medium of his life and death and resurrection. So Christ entered our human history, not mainly to receive from it but, of greater importance, to contribute to it. What he contributed was seen in the Scholasticism and *Tertia pars* of Aquinas as the means for our human race to reach our end. It is a supremely important end, one so important to God that as means to it the Only-begotten was sent into the world to be our mediator.

Equally clear, and in no need of proof-texts, is Lonergan's own personal adherence to Christ, and indeed to his Roman Catholic faith (see also Chapter 1 above). Clear, too, is his position on the loyalty Christians and Catholics owe to their tradition; some of his sharpest critiques are reserved for fellow Catholics who seem to hedge their bets on the Council of Nicea and the divinity of Christ.[24]

6. Universal Import of Christianity

There is no doubt, either, about his position on the universal import of Christianity. A good index is his position to the end of his life on the church's mission to preach the gospel. The last chapter of *Method in Theology* dealt with the church's mission to all peoples. A decade later his position was unchanged. In a paper of 1981, he wrote on the church's call 'to leap forward in its apostolic mission by preaching to mankind the living Christ.'[25] A year later, he wrote on the diversity of apostles needed 'to preach the gospel to all nations.'[26]

This raises a number of questions. The immediate practical question regards our *modus operandi* in carrying out the church's mission. We are not to ride roughshod over the beliefs of others; we are to dialogue with the other religions, and not necessarily in our own terms or on our own terms. Speaking of the lack of a common style of religious thinking, and of the long-term approach to such a common style, Lonergan has this to say:

> … at the present time specific discussion of emerging religious consciousness has to proceed on the basis of some convention. If it is not to be merely generic, it has to adopt the formulation of some particular tradition at least as a temporary or momentary convention. Commonly this could be the formulation of the group that is carrying on the discussion or the one most relevant to the material being discussed.[27]

When Christianity is to provide the terms of discussion, we will speak of God's love flooding our hearts. But presumably Judaism, Islam, Hinduism, Buddhism, and other religions could be asked on parallel occasions to provide the terms of the discussion, and then we must hold ours in abeyance.

There are scattered remarks in Lonergan on the way interdisciplinary and ecumenical and interreligious discussions should be carried on. The remarks need to be brought together and studied in relation to his sequence of dialectic, encounter, and dialogue. The move from conflict of statements to encounter of persons would be of particular importance for the present question, but not to overload this chapter with detail, I suggest simply that what Lonergan has to say of the encounter of person with person might be adapted to the encounter of religion with religion. 'Encounter … is meeting persons, appreciating the values they represent, criticizing their defects, and allowing one's living to be challenged at its very roots by their words and by their deeds.'[28]

7. Ultimate Divine Purpose

As yet we have not tackled the real question of the ultimate divine purpose. To be open to dialogue is not to say it's all one with God whether we are Christian or Hindu; rather, it is to try to discover the divine purpose in Christian and Hindu in its widest compass. This is especially urgent when we define what is distinctive of Christianity as an act of God for the people of God. What people? Who are the people of God? To deal with that question I need to go back to still more general considerations, for it is not primarily a question of religions and their relationship, still less of their competing claims, but one of God's direction of universal history.

To begin, then, at the beginning, the matter is more in God's hands than in ours. I return to the end of Chapter 20 of *Insight*, where Lonergan offered this ray of hope to anyone labouring in the search for religious truth: 'Nor will he labor alone ... for the realization of the solution and its development in each of us is principally the work of God who illuminates our intellects ... who breaks the bonds of our habitual unwillingness to be utterly genuine ...'[29] This remark is not a bit of piety dragged in irrelevantly; those who were privileged to attend Lonergan's courses on divine providence and grace will recognize it as intrinsic to and deeply representative of his thinking. Now such an orientation affects our question in a fundamental way. For knowing that the matter is mainly in God's hands, we are led to ask what the divine economy is for the running of the universe, and that question both checks any hubris in regard to responsibility that is not ours, and at the same time opens an avenue to the real, though more humble, exercise of the responsibility proper to our secondary role.

There is, first, the divine economy of the gift of the Spirit, inseparably linked with the gift of God's love. There is a huge and inexplicable gap here in the work of a great many theologians, who can discourse at length on religion and the religions without so much as a single mention of the Spirit, thus effectively ignoring a large part of the divine input and ruling out of court a large part of the available data.

The matter cries out for attention; for the Spirit is real, is really sent into the world, is really present among us, has a real mission on earth that is really related to Christ and history, a mission that is as really distinct as the person of the Spirit is really distinct in the Godhead. But the potentiality of this divine fact for a theology of religion is widely disregarded.

Complementary to God's initiative in giving the Spirit, a fully awakened Christian sensitivity refuses to believe that billions of people, separated by thousands of miles and thousands of years from a gospel preacher, are to be condemned for not believing in Christ; in line with Lonergan's view I would maintain that through the Spirit given them they belong already to God's family.[30]

217

This does not eliminate the need of preaching the gospel. If God, in giving the Holy Spirit to the human race, nevertheless judged it necessary also to send the Only-begotten to be one of us, then we have the strongest possible ground for continuing to preach the gospel, the ground namely of the very example of God. But equally if God can give the Spirit of Love, and yet with infinite patience keep the 'divine secret … in silence for long ages' (Romans 16:25), leaving millions of us without the gospel, then we seem to have in that sequence two excellent clues to the working of divine providence, and two excellent directives on our manner of cooperating with the divine purpose in the exercise of our limited responsibility.

Our reflections have taken a fairly definite direction. The first two aspects of the divine economy, the mission of the Spirit as inner gift and of the Son as outer word, call now for a third aspect: the working out of the divine economy in human history; that is, in the whole of human history. We have not only to try to understand this economy in the long ages of the past; we have also to ask how much we can conjecture about its working out in the long ages that possibly still await us in a future that is marked by contingency. To attempt a view of history in its universal scope and sweep, and within the rationale of a divine economy for the universe, sounds to the non-theologian like hubris. Theologians, however, recognize this kind of thinking as their calling, and here, I believe, is where Lonergan has a profound contribution to make, though he has left us only scattered elements of a theory, not a comprehensive and elaborated view.

The focus is no longer the possibility of salvation for all; that is now taken for granted and as a question is relegated to the margins (as part of our religious living, of course, it is in no way marginal). Neither is the universalist claim of Christianity, nor the claims of any other religion, the focus of discussion. From the perspective that I consider Lonerganian, the relevant questions are these: What is God doing in the divine economy of the twofold mission, an economy that extends over all ages? What was God doing in past ages? What is God doing now? What can we discern of the possibilities the future holds and of the actualities God's intentions may have already determined for us? Some total view of history seems called for: what does Lonergan contribute under that heading?

Here I can bring forward and expand what was settled in our position on the 'essential Lonergan' (Chapter 12). In a first approach to his thought we can discern two ways of attempting an overall view of history. The first is the familiar trio of progress, decline, and redemption. This he calls the structure of history, but the history has progress as its ultimate goal. There is another history that ends in permanent decline, and this too has a kind of structure that I will come to in a moment. So I would modify that term and suggest that we speak of synchronic and diachronic structures. The structure of progress, decline, and redemption is synchronic, not sequential; though emphases may vary in different sequences, we are always progressing in some way, always in some degree declining, and equally always being redeemed.[31] That synchronic view is paralleled in the field of religions by the simultaneous presence among us of the many religions, each with its fidelity to the Spirit present in them (progress), each with its infidelity to the promptings of the Spirit (decline), each being led to the ultimate end of all creation (redemption).

The other way to attempt an overall view is to study sequences in history: sequences in meaning and expression, in social institutions and culture, in all that pertains to human living; sequences also whether it be a question of progress or a question of decline. For the human race, or some part of it, can advance when the emphasis is on progress, from level to level of meaning; and equally the human race, or some part of it, can decline from bias to bias when the emphasis is evil, until a rich heritage has been squandered.[32] There is a structure here, too, even in the disintegrating sequence of decline, but in that case the irrational sequence of a surd in history. Including both the positive and the negative, I have proposed that we call this the diachronic structure of history.

In the context of this diachronic structure the question of Christianity and world religions arises in a new way. God has seen fit to allow – and promote through the gift of the Spirit – the simultaneous existence of many religions; has God a 'plan' also for sequences in the various roles of the various religions? Are some transient, and others meant to endure to the end, if there is to be an end? What is the rationale of the appearance at a particular time in the Judaic religion, when Augustus was Roman Emperor, of the birth of Jesus of Nazareth? Was the appearance of Jesus 'timed' not only in relation to Augustus but also in relation to the stage of development reached by the world religions?

In the wide context of such questions one could attempt to insert and interpret the scattered remarks and essays Lonergan has given us on the economy of salvation history and on the mission of Christianity: what he wrote in his student days on restoring all things in Christ;[33]

what he wrote of the fullness of time in which Christ came;[34] what he wrote 'on the concrete universal that is mankind in the concrete and cumulative consequences of the acceptance or rejection of the message of the Gospel';[35] what he was preparing in his unfinished work on the historical causality of Christ;[36] his views on the diversity of Eastern, Semitic, and Western religion;[37] his attempt, in 'Philosophy and the Religious Phenomenon,' to give 'some account and ordering of the various contexts in which ... religious living occurs and ... investigations of religious living are undertaken.'[38] And so on.

Besides collecting data on these and other particular questions, we would inevitably be led to questions of great generality in the background. For example, the question of the order of the universe: this was a key concept for Lonergan's Latin theology of the 'convenientia' of the incarnation.[39] It would have to be rethought now to relate the role of the Holy Spirit to the order of universal history: we have studied the 'convenientia' of the incarnation, but what is the 'convenientia' of the interior gift of the Spirit to God's people? How should we conceive the overarching order of a universe when we give equal attention to the presence of Son and to the presence of Spirit? Theologians argue whether theology should be Christocentric or theocentric; but their neglect of the Spirit's role leads to the omission of a prior question: is a view that makes the Son the centre of theology to be modified by a view in which Son and Spirit are equally central, as are the foci of an ellipse? Only then should we take up the question of relating this to a theocentric theology.

For another example, there is the question of contingency; for Lonergan there is no contingent decision of God without a counterpart in creation. Only if the created universe exists is it true to say God creates. To put it starkly, as of now there is no tomorrow; if at midnight God so wills, tomorrow will come into existence as another today.[40] That is no great problem. The problem arises when we realize the implication: that as of now, God has no will for tomorrow, or for anything else that still does not exist or is not determined by its existing causes. The problem arises more acutely in the Christian religion with the question of what was really contingent on Mary's 'Fiat mihi' (Luke 1:38) to Gabriel, of what was really contingent on the 'Non quod ego volo, sed quod tu' (Mark 14:36) of Jesus in the garden, with the question of what alternatives were available to God had the responses been other than they were.

The problem arises personally and contemporaneously, in the context of our own limited secondary responsibility, with the question of what is really contingent on my decisions from day to day, and what is really contingent for the human race on the aggregate of our decisions. If God's 'plan' is already in place for us, that is, in the 'already' of our 'now,' then to that extent we are no longer free, to the extent namely that the 'plan' has already determined it. And if God has a determinate 'plan' in place for Christianity and the world religions, then we will let be what must be. But suppose God has no such plan; suppose that God loves a slow-learning people enough to allow them long ages to learn what they have to learn; suppose that the destiny of the world religions is contingent on what we all learn and do – let us say, on Christians being authentically Christian, Hindus being authentically Hindu, and so on. Then responsibility returns to us with a vengeance, and the answer to the question of the final relationship of Christianity and the world religions is that there is no answer – yet.

To elaborate a Lonerganian theology of the divine economy working in human history would therefore be a long and difficult task,[41] and I do not know whether in the end enough data would be found for a comprehensive view; what I feel is the fascination of the question, the possibility that such a study would shake up very thoroughly the relation of Christianity to world religions, the hope that someone may yet be able to undertake the study. In any case it is a task for another occasion.

Epilogue

Beyond History to the
Secret Counsels of God

To keep the promise of my prologue it seems I have only to refer again to Ephesians 4:13, which speaks of our attaining 'to the unity inherent in our faith and our knowledge of the Son of God – to mature manhood, measured by nothing less than the full stature of Christ.' One might say that my whole essay has been heading toward that conclusion. Lonergan voiced a similar view when he wrote that 'It was at the fulness of time that there came into the world the light of the world.'[1]

But perhaps I am in danger of overreaching myself. I have written an essay on Christ and history only to arrive at a point beyond history. For surely in 'attaining to the unity inherent in our faith … measured by nothing less than the full stature of Christ' we are beyond history. Similarly, the fullness of time is beyond the succession of events that we associate with history. History deals with what is going forward, but surely in attaining the full stature of Christ and the fullness of time we are no longer going forward; we have arrived; we are beyond history and should yield the floor to eschatology.

That seems a valid argument, but it supposes a transition from a term *from* which, *terminus a quo*, to a term *toward* which, *terminus ad quem*. Perhaps something may be said from the side of the former to link the historical process of the essay with the point beyond history where the process concludes. The transition is from our world to what is beyond it, but what do we mean by 'our world'? It could be the physical world of space and time with its uncountable members from our solar system to the most distant star. It could be the 'human' world of 'family and mores, community and education, state and law, economics and technology' in the areas of 'art, religion, science, philosophy, history.'[2] It could be, for Christians, this world as created by God and on some 'natural' level put

222

at our disposal, the divine-human world to which God sent the only-begotten Son to save. We have to decide which of these worlds, and various others we could list, are the present concern.

Besides, linked with our various concepts of 'world,' there are as well different ways of conceiving the phrase 'beyond history.' The Christian belief in the resurrection is belief in another world that is linked to a previous world by merits or demerits and their reward, but has no empirical communication with our present world. It is a world beyond our history. Another conception of 'world' is based on our zeal to build a better world in our future. This too is in a way belief in a world beyond history, for the only history we know is history of our past.

But the most fertile way to conceive our world is the one mentioned a moment ago, in which we consider the present world as subject to divine governance, as obedient to the secret counsels of God; this world is beyond history in a special way. It is beyond history in the sense that there exists a force mysteriously at work that we cannot understand or control. But it operates within history, for the divine activity has empirical effects. Can we study that activity and pierce through our darkness to the divine counsels? Only if God has left clues to the divine purpose. And since I am not writing an encyclopedia but describing the Christology of Bernard Lonergan, the question is whether Lonergan has found any such clues and pinpointed them for us. Vatican II has taught us to read the signs of the times; what signs, if any, has God given us on a world beyond history? Lonergan had little use for idle speculation on unverifiable hypotheses,[3] but there is such a thing as sober speculation on the signs of the times.

As boundaries for our thinking we might take on one side the incarnation, and on the other the prophets of doom. The incarnation is forever. Does that not suppose the continuing existence of our world? Christ is 'always living' to plead on behalf of those who approach God through him (Hebrews 7:25). Yes, of course, but that is our world transformed, a 'new creation' (Galatians 6:15), a 'new world' (2 Corinthians 5:17). Of course, we also presume reasonably enough that God is free to start an altogether different world, even one that has the eternal Word entering it as Alpha and Omega, but a world that would have no more relation to ours than the angelic worlds have now. But the question is not about other possible worlds, and it is not about our transformed world as the Blessed experience it.

On the opposite side from the eternal world of the incarnation is the boundary of apocalyptic disaster. When the year that we arbitrarily number 2000 was approaching, the prophets of doom had a field day, predicting the dire events we might expect with the final tick of the 1999 clock. It was a laughable worry, a completely irrational attitude based on the irrational mystique attached to a figure with three noughts, and this in turn based on the irrational and arbitrary choice of ten as the unit to use for quicker counting. Some such choice to aid our counting was quite rational, but why ten? The fact that our species has normally ten fingers and ten toes? Twelve would have been more convenient as a unit in arithmetic. Or why not choose a unit already operative, the four-year Olympiad with its honourable pedigree? But ten became the arbitrary choice and we seem to be stuck with it.

Far more realistic is the sombre prospect of a world destroyed by our own senseless cultivation of weapons of mass destruction. It is perhaps just happenstance that this prospect emerged with the approach of the year we call 2000. To be precise, the sombre prospect became a real possibility on August 6, 1945, and became a real threat soon after when a second world power entered the scene. With two powers ready to destroy the world to save themselves, the rest of us could do little but pray. Or, did anyone seriously doubt what Stalin would choose to do if he had the option of saving the world but at the cost of allowing the Soviet Union to go under? Let us not dismiss this question as a useless hypothesis; it has the very useful purpose of forcing us to be clear and honest in our thinking.

From boundaries to our thinking, we move back to what is central: our actual world and its future beyond history. The question regards each of our various worlds, and first the physical world. It is, but it came to be quite contingently; it could have not been, and by the same token it could cease to be. There is a double contingency here: one from the intrinsic fragility of the world itself, another from the divine freedom to intervene in it. So the key notion to focus our thinking is contingency, to be considered from the side of our world and from the side of God.

Our human world is equally contingent, intrinsically so. Over long ages we have learned to talk, to sing, to converse, to play, to govern our material environment, to think and discourse and argue, to worship and pray. But our world was seated in contingency. If an apple fell on Newton's head it was a contingent event leading to a contingent scientific law. Further, many of such achievements are accidentally acquired and all are precariously maintained; we are always apt to squander our cultural riches and pollute our material environment. Our world, then, has to accept its limited dominion and responsibility, deriving from an outside authority (Genesis 1:28, 'fill the earth and subdue it') and it has to cope with a Master should the Master decide to destroy life and start a new course of light-years of evolution to regain it. In the pursuit of destiny, manifest or not, there is the collective responsibility of our race and the individual responsibility of those in power.[4]

Our divine-human world is likewise contingent. We have mentioned the world of the risen Christ and the transformed world of the Blessed. But let us go back further and consider the original divine decision to enter our human world through the incarnation. God could have saved the world in a different way from the one chosen; the incarnation was a free choice.[5] There is a difference, however, in the contingency of the divine-human world: it is the contingency that belongs to the infinite mystery, the secret counsels of God. What has God in mind for our planet? Could God call it off, write *finis* to what began long ago with Adam and Eve? If so, our question would vanish; we would be left with the transformed world of the Blessed. Is the apocalyptic literature to be taken literally, as the prophets of doom believe? Or, is God standing by to save us, to save us from ourselves as well as from our enemies? Or, is God's secret counsel not yet determinate, as real contingency requires? That answer supposes the ongoing existence of our world and asks what views we can hazard about its future. It is a world with a component beyond history, a world contingent on the secret counsels of God and a decree hidden in the depth of the riches of the wisdom and knowledge in God.

So we are dealing with contingency from the side of creation and contingency from the side of the Creator. On the former there is no mystery, except the mystery of iniquity, but simply ignorance. On the latter, however, there is mystery indeed but also intelligibility of the highest order; it offers a compelling challenge to theologians.

I just now asked this question: Is God's secret counsel not yet determinate? Notice the word 'yet'; it locates the discussion in our human time. The will of Mary was not determined, was not yet at the point of decision when Gabriel came to her with his message. The will of Jesus in the garden of Gethsemane was not yet at the point of acceptance when he prayed to be excused from what the Father wished. To the same extent and in the same sense of 'yet' the divine will in its infinite freedom was not yet determinate. God could still have chosen another way; the divine will was not yet committed to a decision. By the same token divine knowledge of an event does not exist except in simultaneity with the event; God does not 'know' the event unless the event exists.

The matter, despite the gallons of ink spilled on it, is quite simple. St Thomas Aquinas was adamant on the point. If some future event or occurrence is known today as a truth, then that event, still future to us, must necessarily occur. The case is the same for our tomorrow. Does tomorrow exist at this point in our time? Of course not. Well, by the same token God's will to create tomorrow or not create tomorrow remains supremely free. The objection is likely to be more warmly put when there is question of knowledge as well as of will. Let us grant that God has not yet *willed* the existence of tomorrow. But, the objector will maintain, knowledge is not time-bound, God *knows* today if tomorrow will exist, and so tomorrow must necessarily come to be. To which we must answer the same 'no.' God does not know yet, in the 'yet' of our time frame, does not yet know tomorrow as existing, if it is truly contingent. The answer is always the same: does the morrow exist already? Of course not. Well then, neither does God know its existence yet.[6]

So, unavoidably, the question comes back to what God wills and, more fundamentally in our thinking, to what God has in mind, what the divine 'plan' for creation is. And how do we discover God's mind and the divine decision? Theology tells us that any contingent truth about God requires, for it to be truth, some corresponding element in created reality. That God made the world is true but its truth, to be truth, requires the existence of the created world; before creation it was not true that God made the world. Similarly, if it is true that God has decreed the end of the world, there exists somewhere in creation that created entity required for all contingent statements about God. Such an 'entity' might be a word in scripture announcing God's decree.

Lonergan's thinking is on the edges of such questions. He spoke of the fullness of time in which Christ came.[7] Likewise of the concrete universal that is mankind in the concrete and cumulative consequences of the acceptance or rejection of the message of the gospel.[8] His sober style did not admit of unverifiable hypotheses, much less of wild speculation on the end of the world. Still, as I maintained earlier, there is such a thing as sober speculation, there are the signs of the times, and we have the theologian's duty to raise questions even when we cannot answer them. Among such questions, for an essay on Christ and history, is that of the secret counsel of God in regard to what is beyond history.

At this point I have to acknowledge a glaring omission in my argument. I have conducted it from the viewpoint of a Christian world. But early on I took the position that a Christology should be thought out in conjunction with a Pneumatology, the place of the Spirit in creation, and in conjunction with a Patrology, the place of the Father in creation. In both cases we are beyond history. That is where Christology brings us. It seems a good place to conclude this study of Lonergan's Christology.

Endnotes

Prologue

1   LETTER–1. This letter is the only documentation we have on the discussions that preceded this choice. Lack of classroom space for eight hundred students dictated the division of second and third year into two classes, but there was real difficulty in finding a Trinity professor when Lonergan relinquished that post and kept his Christology chair. Lonergan does not say so explicitly but it is certain that as senior professor, with a new Trinity professor coming up from the ranks, he would be given the choice between Trinity and Christology.

2   METHOD. Lonergan had struggled through six years (1965–71) of poor health and a precarious hold on life to complete the work.

3   MAC-DYN and FOR-NEW.

4   INSIGHT: see the Index under Heuristic Method, scissors-action of.

5   Herbert Butterfield, *Christianity and History* (London: Collins Fontana Books, 1957), 91.

6   INSIGHT 210 (186 = page in 1958 edition; I will regularly give this figure in brackets).

7   Arnold J. Toynbee, *A Study of History* (Abridgement of Volumes I–VI by D.C. Somervell; New York and London: Oxford University Press, 1947): see the Index under Withdrawal. But Lonergan had read the first six volumes unabridged; see CARING 88 (in the interview of February 16, 1981).

8   LETTER–2 (for this letter the Lonergan Archives are indebted to Emerine Glowienka). For a lengthy quotation see METH–JLS, 18 (2000) 81.

9   INSIGHT 9 (xv). The code letters for the three editions of *verbum* are respectively VERBUM–1, VERBUM–2, and VERBUM–3, but when the reference is general or obvious, I simply use *Verbum*. I have a similar usage for *Insight* and *Method*.

10 LETTER–3.

11 COLL–2, 268 (in '*Insight* Revisited).

12 DIM 55; the context was Lonergan's remark on the need to know the subject if you would write its history.

13   On the eight functional specialties see METHOD, Chapter 5. The first four are research, interpretation, history, and dialectic. I do not carry my essay to the level of dialectic.

14   It is important to keep in mind the distinction of the history that happens and the history that is written (or spoken): METHOD 175. The incarnation 'happened' in the divine sense of the word; what Paul wrote on the incarnation is, first, history that is written, becoming also history that happens on being accepted as the word of God.

Chapter 1

1   CARING 59 (in the interview of February 16, 1981).

2   See the question put in *pantôn* (METH–JLS, 9:2 [October 1991] 150): 'Why are there economic forces, making it impossible for industrialists to pay workmen a living wage and for workmen to raise a family?' – An obvious link with our quotations from the Montreal papers.

3   See F. Crowe, 'Bernard Lonergan as Pastoral Theologian,' *Gregorianum* 67 (1986) 451–70, at 452–53, a passage I quote freely in the present essay.

4   The *Messenger* articles are: 'The Mass and Man,' 57 (1947) 345–50. 'A New Dogma' (originally a radio address) 61 (1951) 11–15. 'Devotion to the Sacred Heart of Jesus and the Immaculate Heart of Mary,' ibid. 345–48. There intervenes here the unpublished 'domestic exhortation' on 'The Mystical Body of Christ,' November 1951. Returning to the *Messenger*: 'Humble Acknowledgment of the Church's Teaching Authority,' 62 (1952) 5–9. 'Respect for Human Dignity,' 63 (1953) 413–18. Add from the Montreal period 'The Mystical Body and the Sacraments,' *The Canadian League* (The Catholic Women's League of Canada) March 1941, 8–10, 32.

5   MYST–1, p. 2 of MS.

6   COLL–2, 156 (in 'The Future of Christianity'). In like manner the Trinity is 'the Most Blessed Trinity' (passim).

7   See METHOD, Chapter 5. The first phase of theology with its four specialties (research, interpretation, history, and dialectic) can be the work of uncommitted theologians; the second phase with its four specialties (foundations, doctrines, systematics, and communications) belongs to committed theologians.

8   The phrase 'our Lady' occurs three times in the first paragraph of Lonergan's article 'The Assumption and Theology' (ASSUMP). Contrast *The Encyclopedia of the Bible* (Englewood Cliffs, NJ: Prentice-Hall, 1965) 158, where Mary is the 'wife of Joseph.' We shall find the spirit of the committed theologian pervading the *de bono* (DBM, Chapter 9 below), where text after text after text reveals to the sympathetic reader the commitment of Lonergan to the Lord Jesus, Son of God and consubstantial with the Father, and to the scriptures that mediate the Lord Jesus to us.

9   COLL–1, 27–28. The two aspects, truth and affection, are combined also in the link Lonergan establishes between Mary and her Son (ASSUMP 72–73).

10   GRACE–5. The Archives have two files (Doran catalog, A164 and A161) of autograph notes with the heading 'Grace and the Spiritual Exercises of St. Ignatius'; one of two pages (the reference in my text is to page 2 of this file), one of four pages. They are probably to be dated 1947–53, the period of Lonergan's first teaching at Regis College. They are written partly in the cryptic style he often used on such occasions – just a set of headings to guide him in his lecture; nevertheless one could turn them into a running essay, and do so with great profit.

11   Ibid., p. 2 of the longer file.

12   Ibid. See also COLL–1, 231: 'one longs for the priesthood and later lives by it' (in '*Existenz* and *Aggiornamento*').

Chapter 2

1   DVI–3, 416.

2   For the date, title, and content of *de bono* (*sic* hereafter in the text, but often DBM in the notes) see Chapter 9 below. In the Boston College Workshop of 1974 Lonergan returns to the need for a work on historical causality, still without mention of *de bono* (see Chapter 11 below).

3   '*Pantôn Anakephalaiôsis.*' METH–JLS, 9:2 (October 1991) 139–72, with an Editors' Preface by F. Crowe and R. Doran, 134–38. References hereafter: *pantôn* in the text, PANTON in the notes.

4   LETTER–4.

5   PANTON 140–42.

6   Editorial endnote 39, p. 168 of the published PANTON (referring to page 155 of the text) adds these details: that the insert is not attached to any point in the text, being written along the length of the margin, that it probably belongs to the phrase 'through dogma,' and that twice in the insert 'through dogma' is substituted by hand for 'of dogma.'

7   *Quas Primas* (1925). DS 3675–79; DB (in Lonergan's time) 2194–97.

8   *Ubi arcano* (1922). DB 2190.

9   *Quadragesimo Anno* (1931). DS 3725–44. DB 2251–70.

10   On Lonergan's death there was found among his papers a file he had entitled '713–History.' Among the contents is a group of eight documents, some very short and some (like the PANTON paper we have just examined) rather longer, that deal very clearly with history and seem to form a unit going back to his student days, 1935–38. The file was kept alive on his return to Canada, for it has extensive notes on Toynbee, whom Lonergan read while in Montreal in the 1940s (see note 13 below).

11 In 1973 Lonergan gave a lecture he entitled '*Insight* Revisited' and later published (COLL–2, 263–78). We read in it (271): 'It was about 1937–38 that I became interested in a theoretical analysis of history'; then he gives us his current analysis, and it accords perfectly with his position forty-five years earlier in the student papers of File 713. There is no doubt that the work of 1937–38 has been preserved in that File.

12 The *de bono* has been cropping up repeatedly in my research, and with good reason, for it is a hinge work in this complex history. As such it is too important to be dispatched in a short footnote. A full account of it will be given in Chapter 9; for now it is enough to say that letters from Lonergan in 1956, 1957, and 1958 establish it as largely finished by 1958.

13 CARING 88 (in the interview of February 18, 1981): 'When I was teaching at L'Immaculée-Conception I read the first six volumes of Toynbee's *A Study of History* in the long winter evenings. (Jim Shaw used to procure them from the McGill library for me.)' The mention of his teaching would date this in the period of 1940–46, but Jim Shaw's role would probably narrow it to 1940–42, when Shaw and Lonergan were in the same community.

14 See COLL–3, Index, under Toynbee.

15 Ibid., 178 (in 'Natural Right ...'); see also 214 (in 'A Post-Hegelian Philosophy ...').

16 Ibid., 109, note 8 (in 'Healing and Creating ...').

17 On INSIGHT see note 4 to the Prologue, above; on METHOD, see note 2, ibid. On my reason for calling METHOD and INSIGHT an organon, see F. Crowe, *The Lonergan Enterprise* (Boston: Cowley Press, 1980).

18 COLL–2, 277 (in INSIGHT–R): 'The new challenge came from the *Geisteswissenschaften* ... It was a long struggle that can be documented from my Latin and English writing during this period and from the doctoral courses I conducted.'

Chapter 3

1 'Finality, Love, Marriage,' COLL–1, 17–52; first published as an article in *Theological Studies* 1943. Note that in the present work *Collection* (COLL–1) refers to the Collected Works edition of this volume, published in 1988. The original edition was published in 1967 under the title *Collection: Papers by Bernard Lonergan, S.J.* I shall refer to this edition as COLL–X when I quote from it editorial material not included in the Collected Works edition.

2 Review of Dietrich von Hildebrand, *The Canadian Register* (Quebec edition), May 23, 1942, p. 5. Lonergan wrote two letters in the ensuing correspondence: ibid., June 6, 1942, p. 9, and June 20, 1942, p. 9. I do not include them in my series of references.

3 COLL–1, 259.

[4]   COLL–X, xxi.

[5]   'On God and Secondary Causes.' COLL–X, 54–67; COLL–1, 53–65.

[6]   COLL–X, xxi–xxii.

[7]   COLL–1, 267.

[8]   DVI–3, 416.

[9]   The standard pattern for class notes at L'Immaculée was formed from a foolscap sheet which doubled and printed front and back became four octavo pages. There are two sets headed 'De sacramentis in genere,' one of twelve pages – let us call it DSG–12, and the other of fourteen – let us call it DSG–14; and there are four pages 'De materia confirmationis.' As it happens, all my references will be to DSG–12.

[10]   GRACE–2. He would refer to this publication as his 'abbreviated dissertation.'

[11]   DSG–12, 8–9: 'Fundamentum primumque principium est [Christum] Dominum qua hominem ita exstitisse causam efficientem instrumentalem divinitati coniunctam ut omnia ad finem incarnationis consequendum facere posset … unde passio [Christi] *efficienter* nostram redemptionem operata est … quae redemptio atque iustificatio hominibus per sacramenta communicatur …'

[12]   Ibid., 9: '… entia spiritualia agere non caeca spontaneitate sed imperando.'

[13]   Ibid.: 'ita ipsa sacramenta agunt … Ergo sacramenta significando causant.'

[14]   Ibid., 10–12.

[15]   Ibid., 10–11: 'agens per intellectum quod se habet ad opposita et imperando effectus exseret; et agens per naturam quod caeca spontaneitate conditionibus impletis effectus producit. Iam vero cum esse sacramenti sit esse signi, cumque agere esse sequatur, statim habetur sacramenta significando agere; at solus qui imperat effectum significando agit; ergo sacramenta sunt instrumenta Dei gratiam imperantis.'

[16]   Ibid., 11: 'Causa causae est causa causati.'

[17]   There is a typo in the mimeo copy; the typist had written, 'Causa causae est causa Dei; ergo …,' missing a whole line and introducing the heresy of a God who is caused. The correct text is 'Deus non possit esse causa intermedia. Causa causae est causa causati; sed sacramentum non potest esse causa causati quin sit causa Dei; ergo sacramentum est nullo modo causa gratiae…' Though the passage is the doctrine of adversaries whom Lonergan is critiquing, the key assertion itself, 'Causa causae est causa causati,' is Lonergan through and through. The assertion does not occur in his dissertation where he discusses God as causing causation (see GRACE–4, 86–90), and he does not seem to have got it from Thomas; if he got it from others he certainly made it his own.

[18]   'Reportatio' by F. Crowe of a course on the sacraments taught by John Hochban, 1947–48, at Christ the King Seminary in Toronto. My references to the pages of the 'Reportatio' will be given in round brackets in the text.

[19]   On the 'virtus artis' see the several headings under 'Virtus' in the index to GRACE–4.

20   'The Notion of Sacrifice' (Translation by Michael Shields of *De notione sacrificii*), published METH–JLS 19 (2001) 3–34. My references will be to the published version of the translation, with page numbers given in brackets in the text.

Chapter 4

1   Adhémar d'Alès, *De Verbo incarnato* (Paris: Beauchesne, 1930).

2   GRACE–4, 10.

3   Once he slyly told of a famous radio comedian who would hold up a sign to the studio audience: 'Laugh.' When a guest on the program, another famous comedian, said, 'On my show we don't use signs telling the audience to laugh,' the host retorted, 'Ah! But my audience can read.' As it came to us in Latin, 'Nostri auditores possunt legere.'

4   F. Crowe, 'Reportatio' of Lonergan's Christology course of 1948, Lonergan Archives, Toronto. 73 pages, 8-1/2 x 11. Reference to the MS page numbers will be given in my text.

5   DB 2073–91; DS 3476–92; my 'reportatio,' 15–20.

6   DB 54; DS 125.

7   Other points of interest may be indicated for those who wish to pursue Lonergan's thought. On the 'subordinationists' he takes a benign view – they were writing before the clarifications that time would bring (37, re thesis 6). On person, nature, substance (38, re thesis 8). On the 'communicatio idiomatum' (41, re thesis 10: take it concretely: the divinity is not born of Mary, but God is). On Chalcedon (43, re thesis 12) Lonergan follows the tradition, with notes on Lutheran 'ubiquismus' and on the 'kenosis' (45). There are useful notes on 'operatio' as either 'actus' or 'actio'; on 'actus' in the sense of perceiving, understanding, and so on; on 'actio' as the exercise of efficient causality; on 'actus' as second act; and on 'voluntas' (46, re thesis 13).

8   COLL–2, 237 (in 'Revolution in Catholic Theology').

9   Lonergan's references to metaphysics and other branches of knowledge are recurrent. Researchers might begin with VERBUM–1, which deals with the order of psychology and metaphysics (see the index under Psychology); they might continue with 'Metaphysics as Horizon' (COLL–1, 188–204), and might turn to the three linked questions, 'What am I doing when I am knowing? Why is doing that knowing? What do I know when I do it?' (COLL–2, 37; the answers to these questions are cognitional theory, epistemology, and metaphysics). From that point on, one might consult the indices of the published volumes, but it will be useful to add at once the fourth level of science from Lonergan's 'Response to Questionnaire': '... the basic and total science is ... the compound of (1) cognitional theory, (2) epistemology, (3) the metaphysics of proportionate being, and (4) existential ethics' (METH–JLS 2:2 [October 1984] 5).

10 DCC, 8 pages, with 22 subdivisions, as numbered by Lonergan. (Note that editors later introduced further subdivisions to make 32 in all, but my references will be to the autograph numbers.) There is a reference at the bottom of page 6, 'BL/wan'; this must refer to the late Walter Niesluchowski, then a student at Christ the King Seminary, and it means that he typed that page from the autograph for mimeographing. Batch 2, file 5, in the Archives has copies of the mimeo sheaf, part of the papers he gave the Lonergan Center in 1972, but there is no trace of the autograph, nor is it listed in Lonergan's own catalogue of his papers.

11 VERBUM–1, at TS 10, 366, note 28; VERBUM–3, 198, note 28.

12 INSIGHT, Chapter 11, section 1, 'The Notion of Consciousness,' 344–46 (320–21) and see the subsequent sections. For the order in which Lonergan wrote the chapters see INSIGHT xxi.

13 The notes were taken by the late Thomas Hanley; pages 68–70 in the Hanley notebook deal with what would become Chapter 11 in the book.

14 Paul Galtier, *L'unité du Christ. être ... personne ... conscience*, 2nd ed., Paris: Beauchesne, 1939, to which the mimeo notes of 1952 refer. In an article published in 1967 Lonergan wrote, 'For the past thirty years ... attention has increasingly turned to the consciousness of Christ' (COLL–2, 25, in 'The Dehellenization of Dogma,' 11–32); possibly Galtier's work thirty years earlier marks the turn for Lonergan.

15 'Quae operationum praesentia est duplex: si enim operatio consideratur inquantum dicit subiecti mutationem, passionem, operationis receptionem, operationis praesentia dicitur experientia; si vero operatio consideratur inquantum dicit subiecti attentionem, intentionem, nisum, actionem, operationis praesentia dicitur conscientia' (DCC, page 4, # 10; translation by M.G. Shields).

16 Bernard Lonergan, DCCOP 157. But two years later, seven years after DCC, the lectures on *Topics in Education* use the language of 1952: 'Consciousness means that one is *doing* the thinking' (TOPICS 81).

17 'Unde ille qui est Deus ita est conscius propriae visionis Dei ut certo possit affirmare et certo affirmat se ipsum cognoscentem esse eundem ac Verbum visione cognitum' (DCC, p. 8, # 21).

18 COLL–X, xxii–xxiii. This 'Introduction' did not appear in the 1988 edition of *Collection*.

19 COLL–1, 71.

20 Ibid., 72.

21 Ibid., 72–73.

22 Ibid., 69, note 15.

23 METHOD 320.

24 Ibid., 353.

25 See F. Crowe, 'Dogma versus the Self-Correcting Process of Learning,' in Philip McShane, ed. *Foundations of Theology: Papers from the International Lonergan Congress* (Dublin: Gill and Macmillan, 1972), 22–40. See Lonergan's reply, ibid., 223–34, at 224 (in 'Bernard Lonergan Responds'). Note especially his remark (224) that behind his change 'there is a greatly enlarged notion of theology.'

Chapter 5

1 COLL–2, 266.

2 Carolus Boyer, *De Verbo incarnato* (Ad usum auditorum) (Rome: Gregorian University Press, 1948). Lonergan probably used this edition or an unchanged reprint of it.

3 *Supplementum schematicum: De ratione convenientiae eiusque radice, de excellentia ordinis, de signis rationis systematice et universaliter ordinatis, denique de convenientia, contingentia, et fine incarnationis.* There are twelve pages, single-spaced, legal size, numbered 1 to 12. Attached also are two pages called 'A Possible Solution' ('Aliqua solutio possibilis') and numbered 65 bis and 66; they answer a difficulty on the liberty of Christ. In the 'reportatio' of the whole course found years later by John Brezovec (see above, in the text), pages 1 to 64 turn out to be student work; then come those pages 65 bis and 66; and the set continues with page 67 and on. There is an autograph work, File 519 (Lonergan's catalogue) in the archival papers, titled 'De fine incarnationis': twenty pages with seven numbered divisions (each with numerous subdivisions marked by Roman letters, and one of the latter with further subdivisions marked by Greek letters – a typical Lonergan ordering). This is evidently the original, as far as it goes, for DRC, but it is not complete.

4 At one point in the composition of *Insight* Lonergan gave the title 'The Structure of History' to the material that finally became Chapter 20 of that book. See INSIGHT (the CWL edition of 1992) 805, note *a*; also *'Insight* Revisited' which links Chapter 20 with the work of 1937–38 (COLL–2, 271–72).

5 DRC, p. 8, # 5 *e*. (The relation of the theological virtues to Christ and history is studied in Chapter 14 below.)

6 GRACE–4, 107: 'If Socrates is running, then necessarily he is running' ('necesse … est Socratem currere dum currit' – quoting Thomas: Super I Sententiarum, d. 38, q. 1, a. 5 ad 4m.); also INSIGHT 685 (662): 'Socrates, dum sedet, necessario sedet.' ('Socrates, while he is seated, necessarily is seated.')

7 The title as translated by Michael G. Shields of a work Lonergan wrote in Latin: DCCOP. Our references, given in round brackets in the text, will be to the English translation, but due to the alternating pages of Latin will not be continuous (see section 2.1 for some samples).

8 Ibid., 5, 7.

9 VERBUM–3, 59, 60 (VERBUM–2, 45–46, 47).

10 DCCOP 191 and alternate pages to 285.

11   COLL–1, 162–63.

12   DCCOP 157 and alternate pages to 189. Add COLL–1, 293, note *m*: 'conscious-ness … is not an inner sense.'

13   TOPICS 149; here he even creates a new and awkward term: 'the presentness of the data of consciousness.'

14   An article which he published under the title 'Christ as Subject: A Reply,' *Gregorianum* 40 (1959) 242–70; reprinted in COLL–1, 153–84. My references will be to the latter; here (182) we have the useful definition 'A subject is a conscious person.'

Chapter 6

1   Bernard Lonergan, *De Verbo incarnato* (ad usum auditorum) (3rd edition, Rome: Gregorian University Press, 1964). This differs significantly on certain questions from the 741-page 1st edition of 1960; the 2nd edition of 1961, as repeating the first, may be omitted from my study. All three belong to what Lonergan would later call the antiquated system of the time (see 'Critique of Scholasticism,' Chapter 7 below). My references (given in brackets in the text) will regularly be to the 1964 edition.

2   DVI–3, 313. First edition: *De Verbo incarnato dicta scriptis auxit B. Lonergan, S.I.* Ad usum privatum (Romae 1960: Gregorian University). The 1960 edition made it quite clear that theses 1 to10 were on the hypostatic union, listing them as follows (735–37): 'De unione hypostatica: Doctrina NT … De unione hypostatica: Concilia Oecumenica … De unione hypostatica: Scholastici … De unione hypostatica: De subiecto.'

To speak of scripture on the hypostatic union may offend New Testament scholars, but there is a precedent for it in the fourth century, with its bitter debate over the introduction of the unscriptural 'homoousios' into the creed. When the turmoil subsided, the church was able to see and accept the 'homoousios' as meaning what Athanasius meant in asserting that the same things are said of the Son as are said of the Father (Lonergan, WAY-NIC. 91), and as meaning what in our time George Prestige meant in saying the Son is God in the same sense as the Father is God (*God in Patristic Thought* [London: SPCK, 1952], 213). The parallel would be to understand the unscriptural 'hypostatic union' as meaning that it is the same one who is God from eternity and was born man of the Virgin Mary in time, and this is not so far from scripture.

3   LETTER–5. The letter is interesting, not only for Lonergan's mind on scripture, but also as a window into his work at the Gregorian. Here is a paragraph from the letter.

> I teach De Verbo Incarnato this year from October to Xmas and Easter to the End. Spent the first two months and a half on SScr proof, the role of metaphysics in theology, and the consciousness of Xt. Re the SScr I solved what had been a main difficulty for me, at least in prin-

ciple: set up proof from documents as they stand, ie what was meant by authors of Mark, Matthew, Luke, John, Epistles, instead of procedure of Boyer and Galtier &c who try to argue about what Our Lord meant; in the latter case one is engaged in a historical extrapolation in which one has to take isolated statements and recreate for them an earlier Sitz-am-Leben [*sic*]; that draws one into the abyss of endless hypotheses with practically no possibility of verifying any of them; it is the playground of the Liberals and Modernists who recreate the earlier context in the light of what they think must be understood; at least a dogma prof is under no need to go into that and, if he doesn't, he can have a fairly easy time pointing out that the totality of extrapolations are just speculative hypotheses that admit endless revision. This is approximately just.

This is surely a remarkable instance of the jagged line of trench warfare, for the doctrine of the letter is ahead of the practice of the manual.

4   For a quick view on this see the references to the German Historical School in CARING: 25, 113, 120, 121 (in the interviews of February 16 and February 18, 1981); also INSIGHT–R, 276–77.

5   This appears in the care he exercised in the choice of an author to guide his class through the New Testament at Harvard in 1971–72 (personal communication) and in his Laval lecture of 1975 (CHR-TODAY) to be examined in Chapter 11 below. For earlier use of the term 'historicity,' see the example of DVI–3, 27, and previous editions.

6   DVI–3, 5–16 on modern adversaries ('Adversarii recentiores').

7   VERBUM–3, 61 (VERBUM–2, 47). That term 'schema' keeps recurring; if we leap ahead fifteen years to 'Christology Today' we find there (p. 90) the same three schemata he set forth here in 1960. The notion needs study.

8   INSIGHT 116, and see the index under Recurrence, Schemes of. See also DCCOP 151, where, speaking of the more difficult acts of apprehension, Lonergan writes that for them we need a certain artifice; we cannot understand anything without a phantasm, but in more difficult questions the imagination needs the help of a suitable diagram where the elements of the question are symbolically represented.

9   DAT–SS ('De argumento theologico ex sacra scriptura'). The document was distributed in advance to ten professors from the Gregorian and seven from the Biblical: 'It was the materia praelegenda for a discussion I led' (LETTER–6). My references will be given in brackets in the text.

10 DCCOP 255: consciousness is that 'through which the operating subject is rendered present to itself' ('per quam subiectum … sibi praesens efficitur'). DAT–SS (p. 2) had spoken of the presence of the divine Word to the man Jesus, but without mention of presence to self.

11   DPCA 230–31.

12   DVI–3, 267: 'id quo subiectum est sibi praesens et actus subiecti subiecto sunt praesentes' (the same in DVI–1, 366).

13   DVI–3, 272–73. Lonergan's whole development on conscious presence, leading up to DVI–3, may be traced through a series of loci: the DCCOP of 1956; the early trinitarian lectures of 1957 (DPCA); the existentialism lectures of 1957 (PHEN–LOG); the *Insight* lectures of 1958 (UND–BEING, 401, note *g*); and the article 'Christ as Subject: A Reply' of 1959 (on which see COLL–1, 293, notes *m* & *n*; and ibid., 302, note *i* and 305, note *d*). There is a simpler exposition of presence addressed to a group mainly of teachers in the lectures on education of 1959: TOPICS 81–82, also 149 and 225–26 with note 44. The development found an interesting expression in the list of theses he drew up for year-end examinations on his course at the Gregorian: in 1958 the thesis on the consciousness of Christ does not mention presence; in 1960 the same thesis states that the person of the Word is present to himself both in a divine manner and a human (Lonergan Archives, Toronto). A late and authoritative exposition of presence is that of 'Christology Today', COLL–3, 91–92 (see Chapter 11 below); the occasion is polemical, but the doctrine is important.

14   See his formulation with his brief exposition, DVI–1 (1960) 446–50, and DVI–2 (1961) 333–37.

15   DVI–3 (1964); see Terms, 332–49; Evolution of the doctrine, 353–54; Index of opinions, 354–58; Documents showing the early tradition, 359–82.

16   Ibid., 332: 'Praeter scientiam divinam Christus his in terris degens humanam habuit scientiam, eamque tum ineffabilem tum effabilem; comprehensor enim scientia ineffabili, quae etiam beata dicitur, tum Deum immediate cognovit tum eodem actu sed mediate alia omnia quae ad munus suum pertinerent; viator autem scientia effabili eos elicuit actus cognoscitivos naturales et supernaturales qui vitam suam constituerunt humanam et historicam.'

17   Ibid., 337: 'in quo nobis est quodammodo omnis scientia originaliter indita' (with a reference to Acquina's *De veritate*, q. 10, a. 6 c. ad finem).

18   DVI–3, 338: 'Quod lumen non aliud est quam intentio entis intendens … Quod ergo nos naturali intellectus lumine intendimus et desideramus et adhuc nescimus, illud Christus homo immediate perspexit. Quod autem in nobis facit intentio, illud in Christo homine fecit immediata cognitio. Sicut enim ex intentione entis ad effabilem nostram scientiam acquirendam procedimus, ita et Christus homo ex ineffabili eius cognitione ad effabilem suam scientiam efformandam processit.'

19   In Lonergan's view, Paul's experience as recorded in 1 Corinthians 13:12 (and see 1 John 3:2) was immediate knowledge of God (DVI–3, 336, 337), and thus related to the vision Christ had.

20   COLL–3, 242.

21   DVI–3, 429, 431

22 GRACE–4, 109.

23 'Attamen in eodem signo veritatis sunt et tale praeceptum et [ipsius] Christi actus, ut non prius verum sit Patrem ita praecipere quam verum sit Christum hominem praeceptis Patris obedire' (438). 'We deny ... that it pertains to the essence of obedience that the precept be prior *in time* to the obedience' ('Negamus ... ad essentiam obedientiae pertinere ut praeceptum *tempore* prius sit quam obedientia') (441).

24 'Pater non prius praecipit quam scit et vult. Sed scientia et volitio Patris sunt in signo simultaneo veritatis cum ipsa Christi electione. Ergo etiam praeceptum Patris est *in signo simultaneo veritatis* cum eadem electione' (p. 66 of Brezovec report, in notes due directly to Lonergan: 'confectae sunt ab ipso P. Lonergan.'

25 DVI–3, 548: 'Satisfactio Christi vicariae passioni et morti addit expressionem summae detestationis omnium peccatorum et summi doloris de omni offensa Dei.' Note that at this time there was a public lecture on the redemption, delivered in Montreal and dated 1958; in strict chronology I should consider that next, but for reasons I will explain in Chapter 9, I judge it to fit better after *de bono*.

26 DVI–3, 551: 'Quam autem peccati detestationem Christus per acceptam passionem et mortem expressit, eandem etiam Deus expressit.'

27 There is an interesting application of this doctrine to the Nicene decree on the *homoousios*. That decree is not just a statement on the Son's divinity but equally a statement on the Father's primary role in the event of the cross: see COLL–3, 198.

28 DVI–3, 552: 'Dei Filius ideo homo factus, passus, mortuus, et resuscitatus est, quia divina sapientia ordinavit et divina bonitas voluit, non per potentiam mala generis humani auferre, sed secundum iustam atque mysteriosam crucis legem eadem mala in summum quoddam bonum convertere.'

Chapter 7

1 For Cano 'Theology was to consist in a set of medieval doctrines to be proved by an appeal to the [sources]' (PGT 31). Again, theology 'owed its mode of proof to Melchior Cano' (COLL–2, 57, in 'Theology in Its New Context') and was 'classicist in its assumptions' (ibid. ,109, in 'Absence of God').

2 'The Future of Thomism,' COLL–2, 43–53, at 50–52.

3 Quoted from page 3 of a sheaf in Batch IX ('Various Papers') of the Archives; the sheaf is headed 'Method in Theology,' and page 3 is headed 'Historical consciousness' (see also a passage under the same heading, p. 9, # 5). The whole sheaf appears to be Lonergan's notes for the Georgetown University lectures of summer 1964 and so could be given that precise date. The earliest occurrence I can document of 'historical consciousness' is in TOPICS 76–78 and note 77, dated 1959.

Also from Batch IX, in a file headed 'History' (Doran catalog A686) # 7, f, pp. 4–5: 'historical consciousness is concerned with man, not as nature and substance, but as subject, knower, chooser, agent.'

'Historicity' begins to appear in the indices with the 1960 lecture on The Philosophy of History (COLL–4, Index). It is identified in METHOD (1972; MS submitted 1971) as follows.

> ... the theoretical premises from which there follows the historicity of human thought and action are (1) that human concepts, theories, affirmations, courses of action are expressions of human understanding, (2) that human understanding develops over time and, as it develops, human concepts, theories, affirmations, courses of action change, (3) that such change is cumulative, and (4) that the cumulative changes in one place or time are not to be expected to coincide with those in another (METHOD 325).

So important to Lonergan was the concept of historicity that later in life (1976) he made acknowledgment of it as a fifth transcendental precept: 'Acknowledge your historicity' ('Questionnaire,' # 4.23).

[4]   'An Interview with Fr Bernard Lonergan, S.J.,' COLL–2, 209–30, at 220. Add CARING 25 (in the interview of February 16, 1981): 'It was the German Historical School which introduced historical thinking.' And COLL–4, 95 (date of lecture: 1962): 'German contribution to thought, the contribution worked out in the nineteenth century ... has been the main influence on my own thinking on this issue' (in 'Time and Meaning'). But we should beware of oversimplification in dealing with influences on Lonergan. He says of his reading in the early 1930s: 'Dawson's *The Age of the Gods* introduced me to the anthropological notion of culture and so began the correction of my hitherto normative or classical notion' (COLL–2, 264, in INSIGHT–R); on Dawson see also the 1973 interview with McMaster University professors and students, p. 9 of the transcript of the tape-recording (Lonergan Archives).

[5]   COLL–2, 277 (in '*Insight* Revisited').

[6]   The Hünermann book was *Die Durchbruch geschichtlichen Denkens im 19. Jahrhundert*. See the references to it in CARING 25, 26 (in the interview of February 16, 1981 – quoted in note 7, below). Lonergan's first reference to it, as far as I can determine, was in 1969; see COLL–2, 136 (the date '1957' there for the Hünermann book seems to be simply a typo). Note that for my comments on *Die Durchbruch* I rely on Lonergan's testimony, not on my acquaintance with the book.

[7]   CARING 26 (in the interview of February 16, 1981): 'I had to go into history and interpretation, and into *Verstehen*.' Ibid., 59 (in the interview of February 17, 1981): 'I had to master interpretation and history and dialectic and get them in perspective.' Ibid., 26: 'I had to get Hünermann's book.'

[8]   CARING 59 (in the interview of February 17, 1981).

[9]   COLL–2 (interview of 1970) 212.

[10]   Ibid., 197 (in 'Philosophy and Theology,' a lecture of 1970).

[11]   CURIOSITY 408.

12   COLL–2, 231–32 (in 'Revolution in Catholic Theology,' a lecture of 1972).

13   PGT 15 (lecture of 1972). Add from the interview with the McMaster group (note 4 above, p. 10 of the transcript): 'I taught theology for 25 yrs under impossible conditions and the solutions to those problems are in the book *Method*.'

14   'Theology and Understanding,' COLL–1, 114–32 (first published, *Gregorianum* 1954).

15   He pinpoints it at 1680: COLL–2, 55.

16   His campaign in the 1950s was to replace conceptualism by intellectualism as the source for understanding essences; in the 1970s it was to replace essences by history. Two personal reminiscences illustrate this: one day in the late 1940s after the reading at table in his religious community, conversation opened in the dining room, and Lonergan started it at his table by asking, 'What is the essence of food?' But in the 1970s when in conversation someone referred to essences, Lonergan said, 'Forget about essences; study the history of the idea.'

17   COLL–1, 245; Lonergan on that point is worth repeating: 'Classical culture cannot be jettisoned without being replaced; and what replaces it cannot but run counter to classical expectations. There is bound to be formed a solid right that is determined to live in a world that no longer exists. There is bound to be formed a scattered left, captivated by now this, now that new development … But what will count is a perhaps not numerous center …' (in 'Dimensions of Meaning,' 1965).

18   COLL–1, 244. See COLL–2, 196: 'The new methods and conclusions do not imply a new revelation or a new faith, but certainly they are not compatible with previous conceptions of theology' (in 'Philosophy and Theology,' 193–208). Also ibid., 163:

> I have spoken of many changes but in closing I should recall their general nature. They are of a kind that has already occurred more than once. They are changes, not in God's self-disclosure or our faith, but in our culture. They are changes such as occurred when the first Christians moved from Palestine into the Roman Empire, changes such as occurred when the Empire succumbed to the Dark Ages, changes such as occurred when the medieval Church built its cathedrals with their schools and founded its universities, changes such as occurred when Scholasticism yielded to Humanism, the Renaissance, the Reformation and the Counter-Reformation. Ours is a new age, and enormous tasks lie ahead. But we shall be all the more likely to surmount them, if we take the trouble to understand what is going forward and why.

(in 'The Future of Christianity,' 1969). Also COLL–2, 237–38 (in 'Revolution in Catholic Theology'), comparing changes today with those in the Middle Ages.

See METH–JLS, 2:2 (October 1984) 13–14 (in 'Response to Questionnaire'): 'Today Scholasticism is barely mentioned and Neoscholasticism a lost cause. It remains that something must be devised to put in their place. For what they achieved in their day was to give the mysteries of faith that limited and analogous understanding (DB 1796, DS 3016) that helped people find them meaningful.

Today that help is not forthcoming.' Also COLL–3, 75, on issues the more grave 'now that we have set Scholasticism aside without as yet putting in its place any commonly accepted doctrine' (in 'Christology Today,' 1975). Ibid., 239: 'For centuries ... schools differed from one another ... But all shared a common origin in medieval Scholasticism, and so they were able to understand one another ... But with the breakdown of Scholasticism, that common ancestry is no longer a bond' (in 'Unity and Plurality,' 1982).

[19]   COLL–3, 239–50, at 245–46 (in 'Unity and Plurality, 1982).

[20]   Speaking of acceptance of the modern: 'It is an acceptance that, at least for me, was prepared by years of teaching theology and by two detailed studies of Aquinas' – p. 22 of the MS for a lecture on 'A New Pastoral Theology,' New Haven 1974.

[21]   VERBUM–3, 110–16 (VERBUM–2, 101–11).

Chapter 8

[1]   DS 3475–3500; in the edition Lonergan would have used: DB 2071–2109.

[2]   COLL–2, 94 (in 'Belief: Today's Issue,' 1968). See also ibid., 112: 'When they [the churchmen] were confronted with a heresy, which they considered to be the sum and substance of all heresy, they named it modernism. So far were they from seeking to enrich modern culture with a religious interpretation that they had only mistrust for a Pierre Teilhard de Chardin' (in 'Absence of God,' 1969). For my three headings on modernity (modern science, modern scholarship, modern philosophy) see the index to *A Second Collection*, under Modern, modernity.

[3]   See COLL–1, 245, for the passage already quoted: 'Classical culture cannot be jettisoned without being replaced; and what replaces it cannot but run counter to classical expectations.'

[4]   WAY–NIC.

[5]   'The Origins of Christian Realism,' (OCR–1). This was an informal talk of 1961, eventually published in volume 6 (COLL–4) of the Collected Works. The other lecture with that title (OCR–2) was more formally delivered in 1972 as The Annual Robert Cardinal Bellarmine Lecture, Saint Louis University School of Divinity, and published first in *Theology Digest*, then in *A Second Collection* (COLL–2, 239–61).

[6]   DIM. A lecture, 'Method in Catholic Theology,' given at Nottingham University, 1979, and published METH–JLS, 10 (1992) 3–23, coincides in part with the course DIM.

[7]   A number of references are given in COLL–4, 129, note 13 (in 'Consciousness and the Trinity,' 122–41). For the Prestige reference see George L. Prestige, *God in Patristic Thought* (London: SPCK, 1952) 213.

[8]   Significantly, the chapter is entitled 'Communications.'

[9]   'Dimensions of Meaning,' May 12, 1965; see COLL–1, 232–45, at 240–41.

¹⁰ METHOD 362.

¹¹ Ibid.: Chapter 12, on Doctrines, Section 9, on The Permanence of Doctrines (320–24); my references will be given in round brackets in the text. Note that the booklet, *Doctrinal Pluralism* (Milwaukee: Marquette University Press, 1971) covers the same ground as this chapter, often in the same words (see METHOD ix – p. x in the reprints). Note also that in this chapter Lonergan departs from his purpose of writing on method and not on theology, and gives us a short theological treatise on the 'permanence of the meaning of dogmas [as] taught in … the first Vatican council' (320).

Chapter 9

¹ An untitled and unpublished book-length work in the Lonergan Archives, Toronto. It is sometimes known by the title of its first chapter, *De bono et malo*; see my discussion of the title in the text below.

² DVI–3, 344–46.

³ Article 21 (DBM 142–45), *De virtute resurectionis*; in the manuals it is simply part 7 of a lengthy thesis.

⁴ Compare, on the sacramental analogy for satisfaction, DBM article 26 in Chapter 5, and DVI–3, 544–48. My own references to both *de bono* and *De Verbo incarnato* on that analogy are given in the text rather than a footnote.

⁵ One must admit that the Latin of *de bono* appears rather flat compared to the English of *Topics* a year or so later (TOPICS 257):

> The death and resurrection of Christ express the victory of truth and goodness in spite of every kind of suffering: physical, in reputation, and in every other way. The example of Christ and the grace of God that comes to us through Christ constitute a historical force that, in Christ's own words, amounts really to this: Fear not, I have overcome the world (John 16:33). Christ himself overcame the world by resisting the powers of evil in suffering everything they would inflict upon him. And he rose again the third day. It is this Christian hope that is a supreme force in history.

⁶ 'The Redemption,' COLL–4, 3–28; Chapter 1 in *Philosophical and Theological Papers 1958–1964* (Toronto: University of Toronto Press, 2002); my references, given in brackets in my text, will be to this edition. The lecture was delivered September 25, 1958, at the Thomas More Institute, Montreal, in the TMI course 'The God of Christian Teaching.' It was recorded and a transcription was published some years later in a booklet *Bernard Lonergan: 3 Lectures* (Montreal: Thomas More Institute, 1975).

⁷ LETTER–12. In this letter, dated December 22, 1959, Lonergan says that Boyer's manual is running out of print and there is need of finding a new solution to that problem.

8   I have lost the reference for this remark.

Chapter 10

1   LETTER–7 (September 24, 1954); see also the letters of October 16 (LET-TER–8) and November 9, 1954 (LETTER–9), and of January 25, 1955 (LETTER–10) – the context shows he is speaking of the book.

2   LETTER–10, of January 25, 1955.

3   DIM. My references, given in the text, will accord this document the status of a book.

4   In a document of which the last page is numbered 129, but some pages are missing. The Lonergan Archives in Toronto owe the photocopy of this to the kindness of the late Fr Ted Zuydwijk.

5   'De systemate et historia': autograph, 18 pages; my references, given in the text, will be to this document. The 1960 lecture at Thomas More Institute on 'The Philosophy of History' (COLL–4, 54–79) is contemporaneous, and may be consulted with profit for the present question.

6   'De methodo theologiae' (DMT) is again a student 'reportatio,' consisting of 60 pages, legal size, single-spaced. It was used first in Rome for the Lonergan's graduate course in the spring semester and immediately afterward made available for the 1962 summer institute in Toronto.

7   There is an extremely interesting reference to Husserl in this connection. On February 6, 1973, a group of professors and students from McMaster University interviewed Lonergan over a range of subjects. From the transcript of the recording, I quote two passages. Page 9: 'Bill Ryan did a thesis on Husserl and myself and according to him, epoche is "Let's forget about the objects and let's attend to our acts." Which is very close to me.' The other passage is from page 14 of the same document; in the context of the history of his thinking Lonergan says: 'Unfortunately phenomenology was not accessible to me [Lonergan seems to refer to the time of the *verbum* articles]. The business of the epoche, "Let's forget about objects and think of operations," was a revelation to me. But doing phenomenology in terms of Insight saves one from going into the endless descriptions that you have in Husserl.' I am unable to pinpoint the date of the 'revelation' Lonergan received – was it early enough to influence the 1962 DMT? For more documentation add the following two remarks: (1) phenomenology 'brackets reality to study acts in their intentionality' (COLL–3, 28 (in 'Mission and the Spirit'); and (2) 'if we hold back from the world of objects, if our whole attention is not absorbed by them, then along with the spectacle we can advert to the spectator' (METH–JLS, 15 [1998] 13).

8   Page 6 of notes made by Sr Rose Wilker; data is the field of natural science, data with a meaning the field of human studies, and meaning that is true the field of theology. I first noticed this tableau in a letter of March 31, 1963 (LETTER–11). There is in Batch IX of the Lonergan papers a sheaf of thirty-some pages, single-spaced,

called 'Various Papers,' discovered by Ivo Coelho and believed by him to be Lonergan's autograph notes for the Georgetown lectures; for the history of Lonergan's thought this file could be very important. (Note that in Lonergan's running head for his notes method *of* theology has now become method *in* theology.)

9 COLL–3, 82 (in 'Christology Today').

10 DVI–3, thesis 12, pp. 332, 344–47. The 1960 edition lacks this study, and above I suggested the possibility that its appearance in 1964 is due to new work on chapters 5 and 6 in *de bono.*

11 See, in Chapter 11 below, the way this theme was treated at the Boston College workshop in 1974.

12 'Ulterius desideratur consideratio de causalitate historica quam Christus homo manifeste exercet': DVI–1, 485; DVI–3, 416 (already quoted more than once in my text above).

13 'Eiusdem mortis causalitatem historicam exhibet S. Ioannes, qui non solum continuam Iudaeorum oppositionem narrat … sed etiam ea altiora principia proponit quae hanc oppositionem communi rerum humanarum cursu fere necessariam fuisse suadent' (DVI–1, 531–32; DVI–3, 453).

14 These two elements are related to the role of God in the statement (DVI–1, 532–33; DVI–3, 453–54) that, while we grant the role of secondary causes and grant the role of historical causality, nevertheless the omnipotent God rules and governs all things through those secondary causes and according to historical laws ('agnitis causis secundis, agnita causalitate historica, nihilominus Deus omnipotens per causas secundas et secundum leges historicas omnia regit atque gubernat').

15 *Lonergan Workshop* 10 (1994) 160. Fr Komonchak in conversation added Lonergan's remark that the resurrection was coming in strong in current theology – a hint perhaps that Lonergan himself meant to give it closer study; he had in fact begun to incorporate it passim into his work on redemption; see DVI–3, 479–84, and add 446, 447, 449, 459, 460, 461, 462, 463, 473, 474, 478, 485.

16 See the indices to VERBUM–3 and INSIGHT. For a little history of Lonergan's thought on meaning see COLL–1, 308–9, note *a* (the first editorial note to Chapter 16, 'Dimensions of Meaning').

17 See COLL–1, 306, note *m*. Eric O'Connor once pointed out to me the sequence of three lectures Lonergan gave at this time: 'Time and Meaning' in 1962, 'The Analogy of Meaning' in 1963, and 'Dimensions of Meaning' in 1965.

18 COLL–4, 96–104 (in Chapter 5, 'Time and Meaning').

19 Ibid., 101.

20 Chapter 9, 'The Analogy of Meaning,' COLL–4, 183–213, at 188–89. Note that the Gonzaga University summer lectures of 1963 dealt extensively with meaning – further evidence of the importance of the years 1962–63 for Lonergan's thought on that topic.

21   COLL–4, 205. This recalls the trio of the Georgetown lectures of 1964 (see note 8 above): data, data with a meaning, data with a meaning that is true.

22   COLL–4, 206. The theme of incarnate meaning returns for a short non-Christological mention in METHOD 73, but the phrase is also used with reference to Christ in the papers of that period, notably though briefly in COLL–2, 175 (in 'Response of the Jesuit').

23   COLL–4, 160–82, at 176 (in Chapter 8, 'The Mediation of Christ in Prayer').

24   Ibid., 177–78.

25   Ibid., 178–82. Further references will be given in the text.

26   COLL–1, 222–31; see 229. Further references will be given in the text. Note: the whole talk is found in the sheaf we believe to be Lonergan's lecture notes for the Georgetown lectures in the summer of 1964 (Lonergan Archives).

27   CARING 59 (in the interview of February 17, 1981). One tends to think of the eight functional specialties as the great achievement of this breakthrough, but equally and perhaps even more important is the contrast of the first and second phases of theology; see METHOD 133: 'theological operations occur in two basic phases. If one is to hearken to the word, one must also bear witness to it.' So in the first phase we have the specialties of research, interpretation, history, and dialectic, and in the second phase the specialties of foundations, doctrines, systematics, and communications.

28   Peter Hünermann, *Die Durchbruch geschichtlichen Denkens im 19. Jahrhundert*. The book was published in Germany in 1967, though a typo in *A Second Collection* (136, note 2) makes the date 1957 (see note 6 to Chapter 7 above). The papers of *A Second Collection* cover the years 1966 to 1974 but there is no clear mention of Hünermann in the first nine papers; the earliest indication of Lonergan's reading him is in the tenth, dated 1969 ('Theology and Man's Future,' at 136, note 2). I say 'no clear mention' because the date of the reference in paper number 10 is ambiguous. For the importance the book had for Lonergan see CARING 25, 26 (in the interview of February 16, 1981).

29   A rough comparison might make *A Second Collection* the record of Lonergan's coming to terms with historicity and *A Third Collection* as more concerned with exploiting the newly gained position. (My later references in this chapter to *A Second Collection* will be given, for the most part, in the text.)

30   On this *Begrifflichkeit* and Lonergan's struggle with it, see the paper '*Insight* Revisited,' COLL–2, 263–78, especially at 277; also CARING 25, 26 (in the interview of February 16, 1981), 113, 120, 121 (in the interview of February 17, 1981).

31   COLL–2, 1–9, at 8–9.

32   I may mention other themes in *A Second Collection* that are somewhat to our purpose. One of them has to do with dogma and its relation to Hellenism ('The Dehellenization of Dogma,' on Leslie Dewart's work of that title; see 22–27 in

Chapter 2). The Florida interview of 1970 (209–30) touches on a variety of topics; for example, pages 211–13 deal with the 'hopelessly antiquated' situation in which Lonergan had taught theology, and they have some remarks on his teaching, on what is still valid in it, and on the way his method relates to that period. The 1972 lecture, 'The Origins of Christian Realism' (239–61) deals once more with a topic Lonergan had often treated: the history of Nicea and Chalcedon (251–53), and the 'one person' in Christ (253–60).

[33] METHOD (1972) xii. 2nd edition, with correction of misprints, 1973. Reprinted Toronto: University of Toronto Press, 1990, 1994, 1996, 1999 (A note on the new page ix explains the two minor changes found in the reprint). My further references will be given in the text.

[34] Ibid. And see 367–68, 'The Church and the Churches.' Lonergan even anticipates the wider ecumenism of his later lectures, as when (109–10) he lists the areas common to the world religions.

[35] Contrast this with the section on incarnate meaning above in this chapter; see especially 'The Analogy of Meaning,' COLL–4, 183–213, at 188–89 (and consult the index to that volume, under Incarnate).

Chapter 11

[1] Reginald H. Fuller's *The Foundations of New Testament Christology* (New York: Charles Scribner's Sons, 1965) functions somewhat like a manual for this part of the course (he was Lonergan's careful choice after much consultation).

[2] I reproduce a transcript of the tape-recording as faithfully as I can, with minimal editing.

[3] COLL–3, 81 (in 'Christology Today').

[4] Robert Doran was at the question session when Lonergan made these remarks, and remembers him suggesting in this particular remark a possible analogy for the human and divine in Christ: 'As the ego is to the self, so perhaps the human consciousness in Christ is to the divine' (personal communication). This, too, is explained a little in 'Christology Today' (92): 'More radically, educators and moralists have ever urged people to become their true selves, and their contention finds more than an echo in Jungian thought. It can depict a genesis of the ego under the guidance of the archetypes; it views complexes on the analogy of the ego and so has an explanation of multiple personality; it describes an individuation process from a life centered on the ego to a life centered on the self.'

[5] COLL–3, 92.

[6] CHR-TODAY, published first in the proceedings of the colloquium *Le Christ, Hier, Aujourd'hui et Demain* (Quebec: Laval University Press, 1976), 45–65, and then in COLL–3, 74–99.

7   The seven parts of the paper are not numbered in the autograph, but the Laval volume introduced the numbers 1 to 7, and added 8 for the conclusion; COLL–3 followed Laval's usage.

8   COLL–3, 75. Further references to this paper will be given in brackets in the text.

9   It would be an interesting piece of research to trace anticipations of this theme of the two ways of human development. *Method* itself with its two phases of theology would be an implicit case, but the theme appears nominatim in several essays of *A Third Collection*: 'Mission and the Spirit,' 32; 'Christology Today,' 76–77, 79–80, 82; 'Healing and Creating in History,' 106, 107–8; 'Lectures on Religious Studies and Theology,' passim; 'Natural Right and Historical Mindedness,' 180–81; 'Theology and Praxis,' 196–97. There are occurrences also in the two papers contemporary with CHR–TODAY: 'Response to Questionnaire' (for a conference of Jesuit philosophers in 1976) and 'The Human Good' (paper at a conference on human values, Saint Mary's University, Halifax, in the same year). It is a remarkable number of occurrences within a short space of time as if Lonergan were exploiting a new and fascinating discovery.

10 CURIOSITY 426.

11 The same remark was made some years earlier, in the 1958 lecture on 'The Redemption'; see COLL–4, 26; 'The New Testament above all is a document of salvation.'

12 *A Third Collection*, fifteen essays from 'Dialectic of Authority' in 1974 to 'Unity and Plurality' in 1982, published posthumously (New York/Mahwah: Paulist; and London: Chapman, 1985). A good number of lectures, interviews, and writings continued to appear elsewhere in journals and collective works: 'The Human Good' in *Humanitas* (1979); 'Reality, Myth, Symbol' in the collection *Myth, Symbol, and Reality* (1979); 'Response to Questionnaire on Philosophy,' METH–JLS (1984); 'The Origins of Christian Realism,' ibid. (1987); the *Pantôn* essay, ibid. (1991); 'Analytic Concept of History,' ibid. (1993); 'Philosophy and the Religious Phenomenon,' ibid. (1994); 'Moral Theology and the Human Sciences,' ibid. (1997); 'The Scope of Renewal,' ibid. (1998); 'Variations in Fundamental Theology,' ibid. (1998); 'The Notion of Sacrifice,' ibid. (2001). These in turn are being republished in the Collected Works of Bernard Lonergan, volume by volume.

Chapter 12

1   '… any reflection on modern history and its consequent "Crisis in the West" reveals unmistakably the necessity of a *Summa Sociologica*': PANTON, in *Method: Journal of Lonergan Studies* 9:2 (October 1991) 134–72, at 156. See also 156–57 on the command of Pius XI that candidates for the priesthood study social matters: 'This command has not yet been put into effect, nor can it be till there is a *summa sociologica*.'

2   COLL–2, 114 (in 'Absence of God'). See also, ibid., 183 (in 'Response of the Jesuit') another list, somewhat shorter but adding further topics.

3   METHOD 31.

4   COLL–2, 276–77 (in '*Insight* Revisited'); and see CARING 25, 26 (in the interview of February 16, 1981), 113, 120, 121 (in the interview of February 18, 1981).

5   FUTURE. *Lonergan Workshop* 17, 1–21.

6   COLL–3, 65.

7   INSIGHT 559 (536).

8   METHOD 305.

9   TOPICS 38.

10   PGT 2–3.

11   TOPICS 55.

12   QUEST.

13   Aquinas, *Summa theologiae*, 1–2, q. 109, a. 8: '… in repentinis homo operatur … secundum habitum praeexistentem' (with a reference to Aristotle, *Ethica* 3, c. 8, 1117a 18–22); see Thomas, *In 3 Ethicam*, lect. 17, # 579: '… in repentinis homo non potest deliberare. Unde videtur operari ex interiori inclinatione, quae est secundum habitum.' Also *Summa theologiae*, 2–2, q. 123, a. 9: '… in repentinis periculis maxime manifestatur fortitudinis habitus.'

14   LETTER–4. I would note also the significance of the motto from Thomas Aquinas that he prefixed to his student essay of 1935, PANTON 139–62, at 139; it is not Thomas on insight into phantasm; it is Thomas on the development of human thinking (*Summa theologiae*, 1, q. 85, a. 3).

15   COLL–3, 239–50, at 247 (in 'Unity and Plurality'). And see the analyses of history here and there in that chapter: p. 244 on 'the issue … transported from the fifth century to the thirteenth … and to the twentieth'; p. 245 on the five steps in the great medieval task: Abelard, Gilbert of Porreta, the books of *Sentences*, commentaries on those books, and fifth, a conceptual system adequate to the theologian's needs.

16   TOPICS 233–34.

17   COLL–3, 169–83, at 171 (in 'Natural Right and Historical Mindedness'). He speaks (ibid.) of the German Historical School and 'its massive, ongoing effort to reveal, not man in the abstract, but mankind in its concrete self-realization.' Elsewhere, urging us to live and operate on the level of the times, he says: 'To put it bluntly, until we move onto the level of historical dynamics, we shall face our secularist and atheist opponents, as the Red Indians, armed with bows and arrows, faced European muskets' (QUEST 15).

18   DIALOGUES 305.

19   METHOD 319.

20 COLL–2, 263–78, at 271–72 (in '*Insight* Revisited'); here he tells of his work in 1937–38 and declares: 'The whole idea was presented in chapter twenty of *Insight*' (272).

Chapter 13

1 F. Crowe. *Three Thomist Studies*, ed. Michael Vertin. (Supplementary Issue of *Lonergan Workshop*, vol. 16, 2000.) See '*duplex via*,' 81–91.

2 COLL–3, 26 (in 'Mission and the Spirit'). See ibid., 31: on the self-communication of divinity in love: 'It resides in the sending of the Son, in the gift of the Spirit, in the hope of being united with the Father.' And ibid., 53 (in 'Aquinas Today'): 'the threefold giving that is the gift of the Holy Spirit … the gift of the divine Word … the final gift of union with the Father.' And yet again, COLL–2, 174 (in 'Response of the Jesuit): 'The Father is not only the light in which there is no darkness but also love … The Son is his Word … sent into the world to manifest the Father's love … The gift of the Spirit is what floods Christian hearts with God's love.'

3 Aquinas, *Summa theologiae, Prima pars*, questions 42–43.

4 Ibid. Prologue to question 2.

5 PANTON 145, as published in METH–JLS, 9:2; see Chapter 2 above. References to this publication will be given in my text.

6 COLL–2, 272 (in '*Insight* Revisited').

7 COLL–2, 55 (in 'Theology in Its New Context').

8 COLL–2, 45–46 (in 'The Future of Thomism').

9 Ibid., 50–51.

10 Ibid., 51.

11 'Theology and Understanding,' COLL–1, 114–32; see Chapter 7 above. For the new interests emerging see COLL–1, 127: 'If Aristotelian and scholastic notions of science seem to me to be adequate for a formulation of the nature of speculative theology … I should acknowledge the existence of contemporary methodologiocal issues that cannot be dispatched in so expeditious a fashion.' Nevertheless, the old theology still serves the preacher well; see ibid., 125: '… the Catholic priest … spontaneously expounds the epistle or gospel of the Sunday in the light of an understanding that is common to the ages' (quoted in Chapter 7 above).

12 INSIGHT 253 (228). For Lonergan on chance, fate, destiny, see 'The Mediation of Christ in Prayer,' COLL–4, 173–74; also TOPICS 231–32, 257.

13 INSIGHT 802 (editorial note *r* to Chapter 17).

14 Bernard Lonergan, 'Philosophy and the Religious Phenomenon' (code hereafter: PRP, with references given in the text), METH–JLS, 12 (1994) 125–43, at 138.

Chapter 14

1   COLL–4, 24; and see TOPICS 257: 'It is this Christian hope that is a supreme force in history,' Let us keep in mind the complementary truth, that for its healthy survival Christianity needs a domicile and a tradition and history just as history needs Christianity. 'While a historical tradition can retain its identity though it passes from one culture to another, still it can live and function in those several cultures only if ... it effects its shift to the idea, in harmony with the style, the modes of forming concepts, the mentality, the horizon proper to each culture.' What is true of a historical tradition in general is verified in the Catholic tradition (COLL–2, 159 [in 'The Future of Christianity']).

2   COLL–2, 159–60. There is the inverse of this influence on history in the church's appeal to history (note that these two are the two 'viae' of reception and motion): 'Christianity has always been a historical religion. The Fathers appealed to the Scriptures, the medieval theologians both to the Scriptures and to the Fathers, later theologians to all their predecessors.' But they lacked modern scholarship. 'So they assumed ... unchanging modes of apprehension and conception' (COLL–2, 136 [in 'Theology and Man's Future']).

3   COLL–2, 113 (in 'Absence of God').

4   COLL–2, 93–94 (in 'Belief: Today's Issue'). Another passage adds variables to the constants in the tradition: 'There are the constants of Christianity and the variables. The constants are man's capacity and need for self-transcendence, the Spirit of God flooding men's hearts with God's love, the efficacy of those who mediate the word of God ... But there also are the variables. Early Christianity had to transpose from its Palestinian origins to the Greco-Roman world. The thirteenth century had to meet the invasion of Greek and Arabic philosophy and science' (COLL–2, 181 [in 'Response of the Jesuit']).

5   COLL–4, 76–77 (in 'Philosophy of History').

6   COLL–3, 107–8 (in 'Healing and Creating').

7   TOPICS 257.

8   'Leeming's course on the Incarnate Word ... convinced me that there could not be a hypostatic union without a real distinction between essence and existence' (COLL–2, 265 [in *Insight* Revisited']).

9   COLL–1, 162 (in 'Christ as Subject').

10   COLL–2, 67 (in 'Theology in Its New Context').

11   COLL–2, 161 (in 'Future of Christianity').

12   METHOD xi.

13   Ibid., 361.

14   COLL–2, 175–81 (in 'Response of the Jesuit'). My further references will be to 'Response of the Jesuit' and will be given in our text.

15 There is no attention to this problem in 'Theology and Understanding' of 1954; in words already quoted from that essay, the Catholic priest preaches 'in the light of an understanding that is common to the ages' (COLL–1, 125).

16 METHOD 355; further references to this chapter will be given in the text.

17 Ibid., 140.

18 Ibid., 114.

19 See Herbert Butterfield in his *Christianity and History*, Chapter 4, 'Cataclysm and Tragic Conflict in History.'

20 METH–JLS, 11:1 (Spring 1993) 25 (in 'Analytic Concept of History,' 5–29, File 713 in the Archives). See also 'Analytic Concept of History, in Blurred Outline' (also in File 713) which makes the same point, listing seven factors opposing decline: penance, faith, authority, higher reason, hope, charity, evangelical counsels.

21 COLL–1, 112. Other loci: INSIGHT, 763 (741), and see 720–25 (698–703); also DRC 6, 8–9.

22 COLL–2, 8 (in 'The Transition').

23 METHOD 117. Add to this 'last' quotation the very important paper 'Moral Theology and the Human Sciences,' METH–JLS, 15 (1997), 5–18, at 14; its special significance derives from its location here in a wide range of Lonergan's thinking. And see Boston College Question Sessions, 1974, on the possibility of reversing the counter-positions (session 4, page 6 of transcript). Also the Question Sessions of June 1976 (session 3, pages 21–22): 'But how do you deal with … all these determinisms. Well, it is hope beyond hope … that will break them. Distributive justice will just duplicate the evils. If it's an eye for an eye well there won't be many eyes left.'

    For Augustine on this question see Fred Lawrence, 'Athens and Jerusalem …,' *Gregorianum* 80 (1999) 227: against the charge that Christianity caused the downfall of Rome, Augustine appealed (book 19 of *The City of God*) to the transformative effects on the *civitas terrena* of the theological virtues of faith, hope, and charity.

    See likewise Lonergan, 'Response to Questionnaire' (1976), METH–JLS, 2:2 (October 1984) 16, 19.

24 COLL–3, 158.

25 Ibid., 84.

26 The *International Lonergan Congress 1970*. On this congress see 'Bernard Lonergan Responds,' *Foundations of Theology* and 'Bernard Lonergan Responds,' *Language Truth Meaning* in the Bibliography. Two volumes of the papers have been edited and published by Philip McShane: *Foundations of Theology* and *Language Truth and Meaning* (Dublin: Gill and Macmillan, 1972). Some of the other papers have been published singly by their authors. Most or all of the unpublished papers are available in the Lonergan Archives.

27 Dan Berrigan's paper is a 5-page typescript, untitled and undated, in the Lonergan Archives.

28   What *would* he reply? The question is hypothetical, for there is no record of an actual reply; indeed we are not even sure he had seen Berrigan's paper.

29   UND–BEING 184.

30   Typical phrases of his are 'horror of mere destructiveness' (COLL–2, 99); 'destructive power' (ibid., 113); the need to 'banish all tendencies to hatred, reviling, destroying' (ibid., 187). In periods of decline 'Human activity settles down to a decadent routine, and initiative becomes the privilege of violence' (INSIGHT 8 [xiv]). Inauthenticity 'is the root of division, opposition, controversy, denunciation, bitterness, hatred, violence' (METHOD 291).

31   COLL–1, 245.

Chapter 15

1   METH–JLS, 16 (1998) 98 (in 'Scope of Renewal').

2   METH–JLS, 16 (1998) 7–8 (in 'Variations in Fundamental Theology').

3   Ibid., 98–99 (in 'Scope of Renewal').

4   Ibid., 99–100.

5   Ibid., 100.

6   'Theology in Its New Context,' COLL–2, 55–67, at 63–67. Further references to this paper will be given in my text.

7   The theme of the 'self-justifying' has deep roots in Lonergan's thought. We might start with INSIGHT (356 [332]): 'if rational consciousness can criticize the achievement of science, it cannot criticize itself. The critical spirit can weigh all else in the balance, only on condition that it does not criticize itself. It is a self-assertive spontaneity that demands sufficient reason for all else but offers no justification for its demanding.'

     From there we might go to METHOD on love of God (283–84): 'it provides the real criterion by which all else is to be judged; and consequently one has only to experience it in oneself or witness it in others, to find in it its own justification … there is no need to justify critically the charity described by St Paul' in 1 Corinthians 13.

8   METH–JLS, 16 (1998) 14 (in 'Variations').

9   COLL–2, 174 (in 'Response of the Jesuit').

10   PGT 54. See page 51: 'Religious experience at its root is experience of an unconditioned and unrestricted being in love. But what we are in love with, remains something we have to find out.' Philosophers find it out in one way, theologians in another.

11   COLL–3, 82–85 (in 'Christology Today').

12   Ibid., 84.

13   Ibid., 85–89.

[14]   J.H. Newman, *An Essay in Aid of a Grammar of Assent* (London: Longmans, Green and Co., 1930), 377.

[15]   VERBUM–3, 49, note 168 (VERBUM–2, 35, note 164).

[16]   Henry Chadwick, *The Early Church* (Harmondsworth, Middlesex: Penguin Books, 1967), 130: out of the 220 bishops attending the Council an astonishing 218 signed the creed proposed to them.

[17]   The document on the church passed by a vote of 2,151 to 5; thus Avery Dulles, *The Documents of Vatican II*, eds. Walter M. Abbot and Joseph Gallagher (New York: The America Press, 1966), 11.

[18]   The following sentences in my text simply try to expand the hint given by Lonergan, responding to a question at the Boston College workshop of 1974; see our Chapter 11 above.

[19]   METHOD 130.

[20]   COLL–3, 82–85.

[21]   Ibid., 88.

[22]   The interview was held at Regis College, Toronto, on February 6, 1973. The two professors attending from McMaster were John Robertson and Ben Meyer. The proceedings were tape-recorded with partial success and an unedited transcription was made. Our sources are therefore not the best, but sufficiently reliable, I believe, for the present purpose. Page references (in brackets in the text) are to the transcription.

[23]   COLL–3, 87.

[24]   COLL–2, 163 (in 'Future of Christianity'); see also 237–38 (in 'Revolution in Catholic Theology').

[25]   COLL–1, 244 (in 'Dimensions of Meaning')

Chapter 16

[1]   For a sketch of the meanings of 'experience' see COLL–3, 55–73, at 57.

[2]   F. Crowe, 'Lonergan's Universalist View of Religion,' METH–JLS, 12 (1994) 147–79, at 148–49); further references will be given in my text. This chapter will be almost entirely a rewrite of that article.

[3]   COLL–2, 138 (in 'Theology and Man's Future'). This was a paper of 1968; the same trio of new interests was listed the previous year, COLL–2, 55–67, at 62 (in 'Theology in Its New Context'). A curious result of this rather sudden new interest was that Lonergan did not say much on ecumenism of the churches but leaped at once to the wider ecumenism of the religions.

[4]   COLL–2, 55–67, at 62–63 (in 'Theology in Its New Context'). See also ibid., 101–16, at 107 (in 'Absence of God'); and ibid., 135–48, at 138 (in 'Theology and Man's Future').

5   COLL–2, 146 (in 'Theology and Man's Future'); also 'Future of Christianity,' ibid., 149–51, 156.

6   'Philosophy and the Religious Phenomenon,' METH–JLS 12 (1994) 125–43, at 135.

7   COLL–2, 146 (in 'Theology and Man's Future'). See also note 9 below.

8   'Faith and Beliefs,' (unpublished paper for the American Academy of Religion, October 1969, Lonergan Archives) 22, note 7, in the autograph; see also note 16 below. This attitude on Heiler parallels very exactly Lonergan's use of Toynbee on history: caution in accepting Toynbee's empirical side, with esteem for his 'ideal types' as tools of thought; see Lonergan's 'Dialectic of Authority,' COLL–3, 5–12, at 10.

9   METHOD 109; also COLL–3, 202–23, at 217 (in 'A Post-Hegelian Philosophy'). See also COLL–2, 149–63, at 149–51 and 155–56 (in 'Future of Christianity').

10   COLL–3, 55–73; see especially 65–70. But Lonergan's acceptance of Panikkar was qualified; see F. Crowe, 'Lonergan's Universalist View of Religion,' METH–JLS, 12 (1994) 147–79, at 161, note 45.

11   Philosophy and the Religious Phenomenon,' METH–JLS, 12 (1994) 125–43, at 135 (see also F. Crowe, 'Lonergan's Universalist View,' ibid., 159–61).

12   COLL–2, 165–87, at 174 (in 'Response of the Jesuit').

13   PGT 10. See METHOD 282: 'if this gift [God's gift of his love] is offered to all men, if it is manifested more or less authentically in the many and diverse religions of mankind ...' – where it is clear that for Lonergan the hypotheses are verified.

14   COLL–2, 135–48, at 139 (in 'Theology and Man's Future').

15   Ibid., 155–63 (in 'Future of Christianity').

16   See note 8 above; also F. Crowe, 'Lonergan's Universalist View,' note 18.

17   'Faith and Beliefs' 14.

18   COLL–2, 156 (in 'Future of Christianity'). Note that while Lonergan seems here to deny a special Christian ethic, he does speak of an ethic in a quite different sense that is specifically Christian, namely, the law of the cross, ibid., 9 (in 'The Transition').

On what is distinctive of Christianity see also 'Bernard Lonergan Responds' (*Foundations of Theology*, ed. Philip McShane [Dublin: Gill and Macmillan, 1971; Notre Dame: University of Notre Dame Press, 1972] 223–34, at 233); 'religious conversion ... becomes specifically a Christian conversion when the gift of the Spirit within us is intersubjective with the revelation of the Father in Christ Jesus.' Likewise PGT 10: 'there is a specific element proper to Christianity. Christianity involves not only the inward gift of being in love with God but also the outward expression of God's love in Christ Jesus dying and rising again.' And ibid., 67: 'The religious experience of the Christian is specifically distinct from religious experience in general. It's intersubjective. It's not only this gift of God's love, but it has an objective manifestation of God's love in Christ Jesus.'

19 DVI 325: 'Gratia capitis est gratia Christi qua caput corporis sui mystici; ideoque est gratia secundum quam Christus est mediator, fons omnis gratiae … Christus est mediator omnis gratiae quia dilectio Patris erga Filium aeternum extenditur (1) in Filium qua hominem, unde gratia Christi sanctificans, et (2) mediante Filio in filios adoptionis.' The same mediation is found in Lonergan's Trinitarian theology; see his *De Deo trino* (2 vols., Rome: Gregorian University Press, 1964) vol. 2, 239.

What Lonergan's view takes for granted is that mediation starts with God the Father, whose infinite love is the primary mediating agent. The pattern here corresponds to that of 'Theology and Praxis' (to be quoted at once in my text) where it is in the Father that we find the meaning of the question whether we were saved by a creature or by a divine Son.

20 COLL–3, 71 (in 'Prolegomena to the Study,' a paper first presented in 1975). See also 'The Ongoing Genesis of Methods,' ibid., 161, on God's love flooding our hearts, and the focus of the Christian message in the sending of Son and Spirit.

21 PGT 20. In his unpublished paper (New Haven, 1974) 'Sacralization and Secularization,' Lonergan quotes (from INSIGHT 237 [212]) his own position that 'primitive community is intersubjective.'

22 PGT 10.

23 COLL–3, 184–201, at 198 (in 'Theology and Praxis')

24 One may note the curiosity that in *A Third Collection,* one of Lonergan's most outspoken papers on universalist religion (Chapter 5) happens to be followed by a paper with his equally outspoken critique of fellow Catholics on their Christology (Chapter 6).

25 COLL–3, 224–38, at 237 (in 'Pope John's Intention').

26 Ibid., 239–50, at 243 (in 'Unity and Plurality').

27 COLL–3, 55–73, at 70 (in 'Prolegomena to the Study').

28 METHOD 247.

29 INSIGHT 751 (730). A similar point is made in the homely context of one's personal spiritual life: 'When you learn about divine grace you stop worrying about your motives; somebody else is running the ship' (CARING 145 [in the interview of February 19, 1981]).

30 Some years ago I expressed my concern at the way theologians of religion neglect the role of the Spirit: *Son of God, Holy Spirit, and World Religions: The Contribution of Bernard Lonergan to the Wider Ecumenism* (Toronto: Regis College Press, 1984). This lecture was reprinted as Chapter 19 in Michael Vertin's edition of my papers and articles, *Appropriating the Lonergan Idea* (Washington, D.C.: The Catholic University of America Press, 1989) 324–43. My suggestion (ibid., 339, note 26, and see 335–36) that 'anonymous Spiritans' is preferable in Christian conversation to 'anonymous Christians' (both may be found offensive by non-Christians) has a

basis in Lonergan: 'there is a notable anonymity to this gift of the Spirit. ... What removes this obscurity and anonymity is the fact that the Father has spoken to us of old through the prophets and in this final age through the Son' (COLL–2, 165–87, at 174–75, in 'Response of the Jesuit'). But only when we know as we are known (1 Corinthians 13:12) will all obscurity and anonymity vanish; meanwhile we are anonymous members of the family of the Father from whom every family takes its name (Ephesians 3:15) – maybe 'anonymous children in God's family' would come nearer the truth than either anonymous Spiritans or anonymous Christians.

[31] For Lonergan's very early work on the history that happened (as distinguished from the history that is written) see his 'Analytic Concept of History,' METH–JLS, 11 (1993) 5–35. This essay certainly belongs to the period 1937–38, for some thirty-five years later he mentions it in '*Insight* Revisited' as the time of his early interest in the topic (COLL–2, 263–78, at 271–72). In the same paper he speaks (272) of Chapter 20 of *Insight* as presenting the whole idea, and it seems that at one point in writing the book he planned to call Chapter 20 'The Structure of History' (INSIGHT 802, editorial note *r*). The three-membered structure runs through his work; it returns in METHOD 52–55, in 'Response to Questionnaire' (METH–JLS, 2:2 [October 1984]) 33, and elsewhere; but the creative work goes back to his student days.

On progress, decline, and redemption as concurrent see TOPICS 69: 'in the concrete all three function together. They are intertwined. They do not exist in isolation.'

[32] The data on the diachronic structure of history, like those on the synchronic, begin in the unpublished papers Lonergan wrote as a student and kept in a file numbered 713 and called 'History' (now in the Lonergan Archives); for example, in the paper entitled 'Philosophy of History' (not to be confused with a 1960 paper that has a similar title). More data are found in Chapter 17 of *Insight*, in 'Levels and Sequences of Expression' (592–95 [568–73]). Likewise in *Method in Theology*, in 'Stages of Meaning' (85–99). But these are only high points in a long list of references, among which this very paper 'Philosophy and the Religious Phenomenon' (see pp. 19–23) is not least in importance.

For the sequences in the disintegrating order of decline see 'Role of a Catholic University': 'besides the succession of higher syntheses characteristic of intellectual advance, there is also a succession of lower syntheses characteristic of sociocultural decline' (COLL–1, 110–13, at 110). Also INSIGHT 256 (231), on 'the successive lower viewpoints of the longer cycle' of decline; and METHOD (55) on the steps by which a 'civilization in decline digs its own grave with a relentless consistency.' But again the references are legion.

[33] See Chapter 2 above.

[34] INSIGHT 764 (742) – one should read the whole long paragraph: 'It was at the fulness of time that there came into the world the Light of the world.' See also COLL–1, 117–52, at 22 (in 'Finality, Love, Marriage'): '... only when and where

the higher rational culture emerged did God acknowledge the fulness of time permitting the Word to become flesh and the mystical body to begin its intussusception of human personalities and its leavening of human history.'

35 INSIGHT 764 (743).

36 See Chapter 9 above.

37 METHOD 114:

Eastern religion stressed religious experience. Semitic religion stressed prophetic monotheism. Western religion cultivated the realm of transcendence through its churches and liturgies, its celibate clergy, its religious orders, congregations, confraternities. It moved into the realm of theory by its dogmas, its theology, its juridical structures and enactments. It has to construct the common basis of theory and of common sense that is to be found in interiority and it has to use that basis to link the experience of the transcendent with the world mediated by meaning.

38 METH–JLS, 12 (1994) 138.

39 Both ideas, 'ordo' and 'convenientia,' may be studied in the little work DRC (see Chapter 5 above).

40 The regular context for Lonergan's doctrine on God's contingent acts and the corresponding created entity is his Trinitarian theology of the divine missions; see DDT, volume 2, assertum XVII, 226: 'Divinae personae missio ita per divinam relationem originis constituitur ut tamen per modum condicionis consequentis terminum ad extra exigat.'

41 The task would be complicated by genetic and dialectical factors in the history of Lonergan's thinking and personal development: we cannot simply juxtapose what he wrote in his student days and what he wrote as a seminary professor, or what he wrote as a seminary professor and what he wrote in his *Method* period.

Epilogue

1 INSIGHT 764 [742]; relevant also is Lonergan's thought on the Mystical Body and total history.

2 The categories are from Lonergan's 'Philosophy and the Religious Phenomenon' (METH–JLS, 12 [1994] 121–43, at 138).

3 INSIGHT 102–7 (78–83).

4 COLL–3, 169–83, at 169 (in 'Natural Right And Historical Mindedness'); also ibid., 5–12 ('Dialectic of Authority').

5 See our Chapter 9 above, in reference to *de bono*, Chapter 45, 'cur Deus homo.'

6 The basic discussion in Thomas Aquinas is *In Peri Hermeneias*, Book 1, lectio 14.

7 COLL–1, 17–52, at 22).

8 INSIGHT 764 (742).

Bibliography of Works of Lonergan

Articles

'A Note on Geometrical Possibility.' *Collection*, 92–107.

'A Post-Hegelian Philosophy of Religion' (A paper delivered to the International Association for the History of Religions, Winnipeg, 1980). *A Third Collection*, 202–23.

'An Interview with Fr. Bernard Lonergan, S.J.' *A Second Collection*, 209–30.

'Analysis of Faith.' *METHOD: Journal of Lonergan Studies* 20 (2002) 125–54.

'Analytic Concept of History.' *METHOD: Journal of Lonergan Studies* 11 (1993) 5–35.

'Appendix: Three Drafts on the Idea of Sacrifice.' *METHOD: Journal of Lonergan Studies*, 29–34.

'Aquinas Today: Tradition and Innovation.' *A Third Collection*, 35–54.

'Belief: Today's Issue.' *A Second Collection*, 87–99.

'Bernard Lonergan Responds,' *Foundations of Theology*. Papers from the International Lonergan Congress 1970, ed. Philip McShane. (Dublin: Gill and Macmillan; and Notre Dame: University of Notre Dame Press, 1972), 233–34, 257.

'Bernard Lonergan Responds,' *Language Truth Meaning*. Papers from the International Lonergan Congress 1970, ed. Philip McShane. (Dublin: Gill and Macmillan; and Notre Dame: University of Notre Dame Press, 1972), 306–12, 343.

'Christ as Subject: A Reply.' *Collection*, 153–84.

'Christology Today: Methodological Reflections.' *A Third Collection*, 74–99.

'Consciousness and the Trinity.' *Philosophical and Theological Papers 1958–1964*, 122–41.

'Dimensions of Meaning.' *Collection*, 232–45.

'Exegesis and Dogma.' *Philosophical and Theological Papers 1958–1964*, 142–59.

'*Existenz* and *Aggiornamento*.' *Collection*, 222–31.

'Faith and Beliefs' (A lecture at a plenary session of the American Academy of Religion, October 1969, with Wilfred Cantwell Smith and Herbert Richardson as respondents). Extant in the Archives are Lonergan's autograph MS of 23 pages, and what seems to be a retyping by William Shea (13 pages, single-spaced), the latter with a transcription from the tape-recording of the discussion between Lonergan and Smith (pp. 13–15). There is an inaccuracy in the program listing of the title.

'Finality, Love, Marriage.' *Collection,* 17–52.

'Healing and Creating in History.' *A Third Collection,* 100–9.

'Humble Acknowledgement of the Church's Teaching Authority.' *Messenger* 62 (1952) 5–9.

'*Insight* Revisited.' *A Second Collection,* 263–78.

'*Insight*: Preface to a Discussion.' *Collection,* 142–52.

'Isomorphism of Thomist and Scientific Thought.' *Collection,* 133–41.

'Method in Catholic Theology.' *Philosophical and Theological Papers 1958–1964,* 29–53.

'Mission and the Spirit.' *A Third Collection,* 23–34.

'Moral Theology and the Human Sciences.' METH-JLS 15 (1999), 5–18.

'Natural Knowledge of God.' *A Second Collection,* 117–33.

'Natural Right and Historical Mindedness.' *A Third Collection,* 169–83.

'Openness and Religious Experience.' *Collection,* 185–87.

'*Pantôn Anakephalaiôsis: A Theory of Human Solidarity ...*' (the full title is much longer). *METHOD: Journal of Lonergan Studies* 9:2 (October 1991) 139–72.

'Philosophical Positions in Regard to Knowing.' *Philosophical and Theological Papers 1958–1964,* 214–43.

'Philosophy and the Religious Phenomenon.' *METHOD: Journal of Lonergan Studies* 12 (1994) 121–43.

'Pope John's Intention.' *A Third Collection,* 224–38.

'Prolegomena to the Study of the Emerging Religious Consciousness of Our Time.' *A Third Collection,* 55–73.

'Questionnaire on Philosophy.' See 'Response to Questionnaire.'

'Reality, Myth, Symbol.' *Myth, Symbol, and Reality,* ed. Alan M. Olson (Notre Dame & London: University of Notre Dame Press, 1980) 31–37.

'Religious Commitment.' *The Pilgrim People,* ed. Joseph Papin (Villanova: Villanova University Press, c.1970) 45–69. (The congress was held in 1971.)

'Religious Experience.' *A Third Collection,* 115–28.

'Religious Knowledge.' *Lonergan Workshop* 1 (1978) 1–26.

'Respect for Human Dignity.' *Messenger* 63 (1953) 413–18.

'Response to Questionnaire on Philosophy.' *METHOD: Journal of Lonergan Studies* 2:2 (October 1984) 1–35.

'Revolution in Catholic Theology.' *A Second Collection*, 231–38.

'Sacralization and Secularization.' (An unpublished paper, Regis College, Toronto, 1973; repeated elsewhere with slight changes, 1974.)

'The Absence of God in Modern Culture.' *A Second Collection*, 101–16.

'The Analogy of Meaning.' *Philosophical and Theological Papers 1958–1964*, 183–213.

'The Assumption and Theology.' *Collection*, 66–80.

'The Concept of *Verbum* in the Writings of St. Thomas Aquinas.' *Theological Studies* 7 (1946) 349–92; 8 (1947) 35–79, 404–44; 10 (1949) 3–40, 359–93.

'The Future of Christianity.' *A Second Collection*, 149–63.

'The Future of Thomism.' *A Second Collection*, 43–53.

'The Mass and Man.' *Messenger* 57 (1947) 345–50.

'The Mediation of Christ in Prayer.' *Philosophical and Theological Papers 1958–1964*, 160–82.

'The Mystical Body of Christ.' (Unpublished 'Domestic Exhortation,' a talk Lonergan gave to his religious community.) Toronto, November 1951.

'The Notion of Sacrifice.' *METHOD:: Journal of Lonergan Studies* 19 (2001) 3–28.

'The Notion of Structure.' *METHOD: Journal of Lonergan Studies* 14 (1996) 117–31.

'The Original Preface of *Insight*.' *METHOD:: Journal of Lonergan Studies* 3:1 (March 1985) 3–7.

'The Origins of Christian Realism.' *A Second Collection*, 239–61.

'The Philosophy of History.' *Philosophical and Theological Papers 1958–1964*, 54–79.

'The Redemption. *Philosophical and Theological Papers 1958–1964*, 3–28.

'The Response of the Jesuit as Priest and Apostle in the Modern World.' *A Second Collection*, 165–87.

'The Role of a Catholic University in the Modern World.' *Collection*, 108–113.

'The Scope of Renewal.' *METHOD: Journal of Lonergan Studies* 16 (1998) 83–101.

'The Subject.' *A Second Collection*, 43–53.

'The Transition from a Classicist World-view to Historical-mindedness.' *A Second Collection*, 1–9.

'Theology and Man's Future.' *A Second Collection*, 135–48.

'Theology and Praxis.' *A Third Collection*, 184–201.

'Theology and Understanding.' *Collection*, 114–32.

'Theology as Christian Phenomenon.' *Philosophical and Theological Papers 1958–1964*, 244–72.

'Theology in Its New Context.' *A Second Collection*, 55–67.

'Time and Meaning.' *Philosophical and Theological Papers 1958–1964*, 94–121.

'Unity and Plurality: The Coherence of Christian Truth.' *A Third Collection,* 239–50.

'Variations in Fundamental Theology.' *METHOD: Journal of Lonergan Studies* 16 (1998) 3–24.

Books, Lectures, Interviews

'A New Pastoral Theology.' Unpublished lecture. Toronto, 1973; New Haven, 1974.

A Second Collection: Papers by Bernard J.F. Lonergan, S.J., ed. William F.J. Ryan and Bernard J. Tyrrell. London: Darton, Longman & Todd, 1974, and Philadelphia: Westminster, 1975; reprinted Toronto: University of Toronto Press, 1996.

A Third Collection: Papers by Bernard J.F. Lonergan, S.J., ed. Frederick E. Crowe. New York: Paulist Press, and London: Geoffrey Chapman, 1985.

Bernard Lonergan: Three Lectures. Montreal: Thomas More Institute Papers, 1975.

Caring about Meaning: Patterns in the Life of Bernard Lonergan, ed. Pierrot Lambert, Charlotte Tansey, Cathleen Going. Montreal: Thomas More Institute, 1982.

Collection: Papers by Bernard Lonergan, S.J., ed. F. Crowe. New York: Herder and Herder, 1967.

Collection. 2nd ed., ed. Frederick E. Crowe and Robert M. Doran. Toronto: University of Toronto Press, 1988. Original work published 1967.

Curiosity at the Center of One's Life: Statements and Questions of R. Eric O'Connor, ed. J. Martin O'Hara, Gerald MacGuigan, Charlotte Tansey. Montreal: Thomas More Institute, 1984. (Includes interviews with Lonergan.)

De constitutione Christi ontologica et psychologica. Rome: Gregorian University Press, 1956.

De Deo trino. 2 vols. Rome: Gregorian University Press, 1964.

De ente supernaturali: Supplementum schematicum, ed. Frederick E. Crowe, Conn O'Donovan, Giovanni Sala. Toronto: Regis College edition available in photocopy, 1973. Originally notes for students, Montreal: College of the Immaculate Conception, 1946.

De intellectu et methodo. Notes taken by students of lectures in theology course. Rome: Gregorian University, 1959.

De ratione convenientiae eiusque radice, de excellentia ordinis … Rome: 1953–54. This *Supplementum schematicum* was provided for his students the first year Lonergan taught Christology at the Gregorian University.

De scientia atque voluntate Dei: Supplementum schematicum. Unpublished notes for students of the course *De praedestinatione.* Toronto: Christ the King Seminary (now Regis College), March 1950.

De systemate et historia. Notes probably for a course with that title at the Gregorian University, 1959–60.

De Verbo incarnato. 3rd ed. Rome: Gregorian University Press, 1964.

Dialogues in Celebration, ed. Cathleen M. Going. Montreal: Thomas More Institute, 1980. (Has an interview with Lonergan: 'Questions with Regard to Method: History and Economics.')

Discussions, Toronto Congress on the Theology of Renewal of the Church, 1967. Toronto: Institute of Mediaeval Studies, 1968. Discussions with Lonergan, # 3, 5–8. Mimeograph report transcribed from tapes.

Doctrinal Pluralism. Milwaukee: Marquette University Press, 1971.

Enchiridion Symbolorum Definitionum et Declarationum de Rebus Fidei et Morum. The Denzinger-Bannwart-Umberg editions, DB, nos 10–27, were probably the ones Lonergan used as a student. The Denzinger-Schoenmetzer editions, DS, nos 32–, would have been used by him as a professor.

For a New Political Economy, ed. Philip McShane. Toronto: University of Toronto Press, 1998.

Grace and Freedom: Operative Grace in the Thought of St Thomas Aquinas, ed. J. Patout Burns. London: Darton, Longman & Todd; New York: Herder and Herder, 1971.

Grace and Freedom: Operative Grace in the Thought of St Thomas Aquinas, ed. Frederick E. Crowe and Robert M. Doran. Toronto: University of Toronto Press, 2000.

Gratia Operans: A Study of Speculative Development in the Writings of St. Thomas Aquinas. Doctoral dissertation. Rome: Gregorian University, 1940.

'Hermeneutics.' Unpublished lecture. Toronto: Regis College, 1962.

Insight: A Study of Human Understanding. 5th ed., ed. Frederick E. Crowe and Robert M. Doran. Toronto: University of Toronto Press, 1992.

Macroeconomic Dynamics: An Essay in Circulation Analysis, ed. Frederick Lawrence, Patrick Byrne, and Charles Hefling. Toronto: University of Toronto Press, 1999.

Method in Theology. London: Darton, Longman & Todd, Ltd; New York: Herder and Herder, 1972; 2nd ed., 1973.

Phenomenology and Logic: The Boston College Lectures of 1957, ed. Philip J. McShane. Toronto: University of Toronto Press, 2000.

Philosophical and Theological Papers 1958–1964, ed. Robert C. Croken, Frederick E. Crowe, and Robert M. Doran. Toronto: University of Toronto Press, 1996.

Philosophical and Theological Papers, 1965–1980, ed. Robert C. Croken and Robert M. Doran. Toronto: University of Toronto Press, 2004.

Philosophy of God, and Theology: The Relationship Between Philosophy of God and the Functional Specialty, Systematics. With a Foreword by Patrick B. O'Leary. London: Darton, Longman and Todd, 1973.

The Ontological and Psychological Constitution of Christ. Translated by Michael G. Shields from the 4th edition of De constitutione Christi ontologica et psychologica. Toronto: University of Toronto Press, 2002.

The Way to Nicea: The Dialectical Development of Trinitarian Theology, trans. Conn O'Donovan. London: Darton, Longman & Todd; Philadelphia: Westminster Press, 1976. (Trans. of first part of *De Deo trino.*)

Theological Studies. Volumes 7, 8, and 10; respectively September 1946, March 1947, September 1947, March 1949, September 1949. See 'The Concept of *Verbum …*'

Topics in Education: The Cincinnati Lectures of 1959 on the Philosophy of Education, ed. Robert M. Doran and Frederick E. Crowe. Revising and augmenting the unpublished text prepared by James Quinn and John Quinn. Toronto: University of Toronto Press, 1993.

Understanding and Being: The Halifax Lectures on INSIGHT, ed. Elizabeth A. Morelli and Mark D. Morelli. Toronto: University of Toronto Press, 1990.

Verbum: Word and Idea in Aquinas, ed. David B. Burrell. Notre Dame: University of Notre Dame Press, 1967. 2nd ed., ed. Frederick E. Crowe and Robert M. Doran. Toronto: University of Toronto Press, 1998.

Code Letters for References

ABSENCE. 'The Absence of God in Modern Culture.' COLL–2, 101–16.

ANALOGY. 'The Analogy of Meaning.' COLL–4, 183–213.

AQUINAS. 'Aquinas Today: Tradition and Innovation.' COLL–3, 35–54.

ASSUMP. 'The Assumption and Theology.' COLL–1, 66–80.

BELIEF. 'Belief: Today's Issue.' COLL–2, 87–99.

BERNARD. *Bernard Lonergan: Three Lectures.* Montreal: Thomas More Institute Papers, 1975.

CARING. *Caring about Meaning: Patterns in the Life of Bernard Lonergan,* ed. Pierrot Lambert, Charlotte Tansey, Cathleen Going. Montreal: Thomas More Institute Papers 1982. An edited transcript of conversations with Lonergan, February 1981 and May 1982.

CHR–SUBJ. 'Christ as Subject: A Reply.' COLL–1, 153–84.

CHR–TODAY. 'Christology Today: Methodological Reflections.' COLL–3, 75–99.

COLL–1. *Collection,* ed. Frederick E. Crowe and Robert M. Doran. Toronto: University of Toronto Press, 1988.

COLL–2. *A Second Collection: Papers by Bernard J.F. Lonergan, S.J.,* ed. William F.J. Ryan and Bernard J. Tyrrell. London: Darton, Longman & Todd, 1974; Philadelphia: Westminster, 1975. Reprinted Toronto: University of Toronto Press, 1996.

COLL–3. *A Third Collection: Papers by Bernard J.F. Lonergan, S.J.,* ed. Frederick E. Crowe. New York: Paulist Press; London: Geoffrey Chapman, 1985

COLL–4. *Philosophical and Theological Papers 1958–1964,* ed. Robert C. Croken, Frederick E. Crowe, and Robert M. Doran. Toronto: University of Toronto Press, 1996.

COLL-X. *Collection: Papers by Bernard Lonergan, S.J.,* ed. F. Crowe. New York: Herder and Herder, 1967.

Concept of *Verbum* ... (1946–49). See below VERBUM–1.

CURIOSITY. *Curiosity at the Center of One's Life: Statements and Questions of R. Eric O'Connor,* ed. J. Martin O'Hara, Gerald MacGuigan, Charlotte Tansey. Montreal: Thomas More Institute, 1984. (Includes interviews with Lonergan.)

DAT–SS. *De argumento theologico ex sacra scriptura.* Notes for lecture at seminar of professors from the Gregorian University and the Biblical Institute. Rome: Gregorian University, 1962.

DB. Denzinger-Bannwart-Umberg editions of *Enchiridion Symbolorum.*

DBM. *De bono et malo.* Title borrowed from title of first chapter. Autograph MS (probably dated 1958) intended as supplement to *De Verbo incarnato.*

DCC. *De conscientia Christi.* Mimeographed notes for course *De Verbo incarnato.* Toronto: College of Christ the King, 1952.

DCCOP. *De constitutione Christi ontologica et psychologica* Rome: Gregorian University Press, 1956.

DDT. *De Deo trino.* 2 vols. Rome: Gregorian University Press, 1964.

DE–SYS. *De systemate et historia.* Notes probably for a course with that title, Gregorian University, 1959–60.

DES. *De ente supernaturali: Supplementum schematicum.* Mimeographed notes for course *De gratia.* Montreal: College of the Immaculate Conception, 1946. Regis College edition, Toronto, 1973.

DIALOG. *Dialogues in Celebration,* ed. Cathleen M. Going. Montreal: Thomas More Institute, 1980. (Has an interview with Lonergan: 'Questions with Regard to Method: History and Economics.')

DIM. *De intellectu et methodo.* Unpublished *reportatio* of a graduate course, Gregorian University, 1958–59.

DMT. *De methodo theologiae.* Notes for graduate course at the Gregorian University, 1961–62. Rome: North American College, 1962.

DNS. *De notione sacrificii.* Autograph notes for course at Regis College, Toronto, 1959–60. Regis edition, Willowdale, Toronto, 1973.

DOCT-PLUR. *Doctrinal Pluralism.* Milwaukee: Marquette University Press, 1971.

DRC. *De ratione convenientiae eiusque radice, de excellentia ordinis* … Mimeographed notes for the course *De Verbo incarnato,* Gregorian University, 1953–54.

DS. Denzinger-Schoenmetzer editions of *Enchiridion Symbolorum.*

DSVD. *De scientia atque voluntate Dei: Supplementum schematicum.* Toronto: College of Christ the King (Regis College), March 1950.

DUBLIN–1. Six lectures on *Insight,* given at Dublin, Easter 1961.

DUBLIN–2. Two-week institute on *Method in Theology,* Dublin, summer 1971.

DVI–1. *De Verbo incarnato dicta scriptis auxit B. Lonergan.* Rome: Gregorian University Press, 1960.

DVI–2. *De Verbo incarnato.* Editio altera. Rome: Gregorian University Press, 1961.

DVI–3. *De Verbo incarnato.* Editio tertia. Rome: Gregorian University Press, 1964.

EX–AGG. '*Existenz* and *Aggiornamento*.' COLL–1, 222–31.

FOR–NEW. *For a New Political Economy*, ed. Philip J. McShane. Toronto: University of Toronto Press, 1998.

FUT–CHR. 'The Future of Christianity.' COLL–2, 149–63.

FUT–THOM. 'The Future of Thomism.' COLL–2, 43–53.

GOD–SEC. 'God and Secondary Causes.' COLL–1, 53–65.

GRACE–1. Publication under various titles of four articles on Grace, *Theological Studies* 1941–42 (see GRACE–2).

GRACE–2. 'St. Thomas' Thought on *Gratia operans*.' *Theological Studies* 1941–42. Abbreviated publication in four articles of GRACE–1. Title of article varies. Fourth article, with additions, submitted as 'Excerpta' from GRACE–1.

GRACE–3. *Grace and Freedom: Operative Grace in the Thought of St Thomas Aquinas*, ed. J. Patout Burns. London: Darton, Longman & Todd; New York: Herder and Herder, 1971. Publication in book form of GRACE–2.

GRACE–4. *Grace and Freedom: Operative Grace in the Thought of St Thomas Aquinas*, ed. Frederick E. Crowe and Robert M. Doran. Toronto: University of Toronto Press, 2000. Part One is new edition of GRACE–3; Part Two is first complete publication of GRACE–1.

GRACE–5. 'Grace and the Spiritual Exercises of St. Ignatius.' (To appear, METH–JLS.)

GRATIA–1. *Gratia Operans: A Study of the Speculative Development in the Writings of St. Thomas Aquinas,* Lonergan's doctoral dissertation as submitted to the Gregorian University, 1940; published as Part Two of GRACE–4.

GRATIA–2. *Gratia Operans: A Study of the Speculative Development in the Writings of St. Thomas of Aquin.* Excerpta from doctoral dissertation, Gregorian University, May 1940. Published as fourth article of GRACE–2, with 2-page Introduction, 1946. Complete dissertation published as Part Two of GRACE–4.

HEALING. 'Healing and Creating in History.' COLL–3, 100–9.

HUMBLE. 'Humble Acknowledgement of the Church's Teaching Authority.' *Messenger* 62 (1952) 5–9.

INSIGHT–P. '*Insight*: Preface to a Discussion.' COLL–1, 143–52.

INSIGHT–R. '*Insight* Revisited.' COLL–2, 263–78.

INSIGHT. *Insight: A Study of Human Understanding*. 5th edition eds Frederick E. Crowe and Robert M. Doran. Toronto: University of Toronto Press, 1992; frequently reprinted.

LETTER–1. A letter of Lonergan to F. Crowe, December 11, 1962.

LETTER–2. A letter of Lonergan to Gerard Smith, July 13, 1958.

LETTER–3. A letter of Lonergan to F. Crowe, March 3, 1980.

LETTER–4. A letter of Lonergan to H. Keane, 1935.

LETTER–5. A letter of Lonergan to F. Crowe, December 27, 1955.

LETTER–6. A letter of Lonergan to F. Crowe, May 21, 1962.

LETTER–7. A letter of Lonergan to F. Crowe, September 24, 1954.

LETTER–8. A letter of Lonergan to F. Crowe, October 16, 1955.

LETTER–9. A letter of Lonergan to F. Crowe, November 9, 1954.

LETTER–10. A letter of Lonergan to F. Crowe, January 25, 1955.

LETTER–11. A letter of Lonergan to F. Crowe, March 31, 1963.

LETTER–12. A letter of Lonergan to F. Crowe, December 22, 1959.

LON-RES1. 'Bernard Lonergan Responds,' *Foundations of Theology.* Papers from the International Lonergan Congress 1970, ed. Philip McShane. (Dublin: Gill and Macmillan; and Notre Dame: University of Notre Dame Press, 1972), 233–34, 257.

LON-RES2. 'Bernard Lonergan Responds,' *Language Truth Meaning.* Papers from the International Lonergan Congress 1970, ed. Philip McShane. (Dublin: Gill and Macmillan; and Notre Dame: University of Notre Dame Press, 1972), 306–12, 343.

MAC–DYN. *Macroeconomic Dynamics: An Essay in Circulation Analysis.* Toronto: University of Toronto Press, 1999.

MASS. 'The Mass and Man.' *Messenger* 57 (1947) 345–50.

MESSENGER. *The Canadian Messenger of the Sacred Heart.*

METH–CT. 'Method in Catholic Theology.' COLL–4, 29–53.

METH–JLS. *METHOD: Journal of Lonergan Studies.*

METH–TV. 'Method: Trend and Variations.' COLL–3, 13–22.

METHOD. *Method in Theology.* London: Darton, Longman & Todd; New York: Herder and Herder; 1972. 2nd ed, 1973; frequently reprinted, Toronto: University of Toronto Press.

MISS–SP. 'Mission and the Spirit.' COLL–3, 23–34.

MORAL-HS. 'Moral Theology and the Human Sciences.' *METHOD: Journal of Lonergan Studies* 15 (1997) 5–20.

MYST–1. 'The Mystical Body of Christ' (Domestic Exhortation, College of Christ the King, Toronto) November 1951.

MYST–2. 'The Mystical Body and the Sacraments.' *The Canadian League*, March 1941, 8–10 & 32.

NAT–D. Natural Desire.

NAT–K. Natural Knowledge.

NAT–R. Natural Right.

NEW–DOG. 'A New Dogma.' *Messenger* 61 (1951) 11–15.

NOT–SAC. 'The Notion of Sacrifice,' trans. Michael Shields. METH–JLS, 19 (2001) 3–28.

OCR–1. 'The Origins of Christian Realism' (1961). COLL–4, 80–93.

OCR–2. 'The Origins of Christian Realism' (1972). COLL–2, 239–61.

OPCC. *The Ontological and Psychological Constitution of Christ*. Translated by Michael G. Shields from the 4th edition of De constitutione Christi ontologica et psychologica. Toronto: University of Toronto Press, 2002.

PH–HIST. 'The Philosophy of History.' COLL–4, 54–79.

PH–TH. Philosophy and Theology.

PHEN–LOG. *Phenomenology and Logic: The Boston College Lectures on Mathematical Logic and Existentialism*, ed. Philip J. McShane. Toronto: University of Toronto Press, 2001.

PJI. 'Pope John's Intention.' COLL–3, 224–38.

POST–HEG. 'A Post-Hegelian Philosophy of Religion.' COLL–3, 202–23.

PROLEGOM. 'Prolegomena to the Study of the Emerging Religious Consciousness of Our Time.' COLL–3, 55–73.

PRP. 'Philosophy and the Religious Phenomenon.' METH–JLS, 12 (1994) 125–43.

QUEST. 'Response to Questionnaire on Philosophy,' METH–JLS, 2:2 (October 1984) 1–35.

REDEMP. 'The Redemption.' COLL–4, 3–28.

RES–JES. 'The Response of the Jesuit as Priest and Apostle in the Modern World.' COLL–2, 165–87.

RESPECT. 'Respect for Human Dignity.' *Messenger* 63 (1953) 413–18.

REV–CATH. 'Revolution in Catholic Theology.' COLL–2, 231–38.

TH–MF. 'Theology and Man's Future.' COLL–2, 135–48.

TH–NEW. 'Theology in Its New Context.' COLL–2, 55–67.

TH–PRAX. 'Theology and Praxis.' COLL–3, 184–201.

TH–UND. 'Theology and Understanding.' COLL–1, 114–32.

TOPICS. *Topics in Education: The Cincinnati Lectures of 1959 on the Philosophy of Education*, ed. Robert M. Doran and Frederick E. Crowe. Toronto: University of Toronto Press, 1993.

TRANSITION. 'The Transition from a Classicist World-View to Historical-Mindedness.' COLL–2, 1–9.

UND–BEING. *Understanding and Being: The Halifax Lectures on INSIGHT*, ed. Elizabeth A. Morelli and Mark D. Morelli. Toronto: University of Toronto Press, 1990.

VERBUM–1. 'The Concept of *Verbum* in the Writings of St. Thomas Aquinas.' *Theological Studies* 1946–49 (five articles).

VERBUM–2. *Verbum: Word and Idea in Aquinas*. Notre Dame: University of Notre Dame Press, 1967; London: Darton, Longman & Todd, 1968, ed. David B. Burrell. Publication in book form of VERBUM–1.

VERBUM–3. *Verbum: Word and Idea in Aquinas*, ed. Frederick E. Crowe and Robert M. Doran; new edition of VERBUM–2. Toronto: University of Toronto Press, 1992.

Index of Names and Concepts

D

Acknowledgments

I thank Kenneth Melchin, Daniel Monsour, and Michael Shields for specific contributions to this volume, all the staff of the Lonergan Research Institute and Michael Vertin for countless acts of kindness that contributed to the production of *Christ and History*.

Some passages in Chapter 8 have appeared in *Lonergan Workshop*, and Chapter 16 was previously published in *METHOD: Journal of Lonergan Studies*.